Bassett's Blades

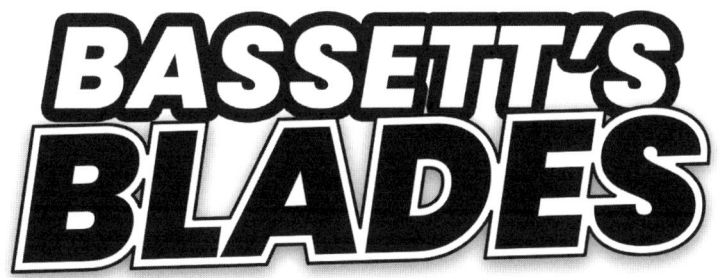

BASSETT'S BLADES

INSIDE THE SHEFFIELD UNITED ERA THAT INSPIRED A GENERATION

DANNY HALL WITH NATHAN HEMMINGHAM

VERTICAL editions

verticaleditions.com

*For my girls: Charlotte, Natalie,
Marie and Kathleen. Thank you
for everything. I love you.*

– Danny Hall

*For my wife and children:
Caroline, Georgie and
Alfred — my world.*

– Nathan Hemmingham

First published in the United Kingdom in 2024 by Vertical
Editions, Unit 41 Regency Court, Sheffield, S35 9ZQ

www.verticaleditions.com

Follow us on Twitter:
@VerticalEds
@dannyhall04
@NathanH79

Cover images courtesy of the *Sheffield Star,*
Allstar/Alamy, PA Images/Alamy

ISBN 978-190-8847-218

First Edition

A CIP catalogue record for this book is available from the British Library

Printed and bound by Jellyfish Print Solutions, Curdridge, Hants

CONTENTS

.

FOREWORD

He has a very unfair reputation from some people in football but having worked under Dave Bassett, I am convinced that he would have been perfect for today's game. Absolutely 100 per cent perfect. He was one of the best man-managers in football and although he'll tell you himself that he isn't the best coach in the world, he had the ability to put teams together, the ability to motivate them and the ability to let characters be characters and then produce on a football pitch, which is not always an easy thing to do. Football has changed a lot over the years but a Dave Bassett figure now would be awesome. He was awesome back in the day.

He was *different*, you know? If you look at all the characters from Wimbledon ... they weren't just characters, but all good footballers as well. So his eye for a footballer was as good as his eye for a character and his forte was finding players who could benefit him and the team, without spending loads and loads of money. That was probably his greatest strength, for me.

I was 35 years old by the time I got to work with Harry, at Sheffield United, but it could have been a lot earlier. He was interested in signing me when he was going to Crystal Palace and we'd agreed a deal, but I came back from holiday and he'd changed his mind and stayed at Wimbledon. He was also keen when I went to Leeds from Stoke, and Middlesbrough wanted me as well. But Howard Wilkinson locked me in his office until I signed. We won the league that season with United just behind us in second place.

Unitedites won't remember Leeds' 4-0 win at Elland Road too fondly but it more or less sealed the league for us, I think. It was a hard-fought battle between two teams who took nothing for granted and two managers, in Howard and Harry, who were really good friends but also knew that their teams would give everything in that situation.

We were under no illusions that was the biggy for us, and that we had to win. I believe we wouldn't have gone up that year if we'd lost that game, but Harry managed to pick up his team and carry them more or less over the line.

After Leeds, I went down to Luton, but I found it difficult. I didn't want to go in the first place. That's nothing to do with Luton as a football club, but I wasn't, in my own mind, fully fit. I'd just come back from injury and Howard threw me straight back into the team that had won the First Division, and I soon realised that he'd stuck me back in to sell me. I was still catching up fitness-wise and stayed in Wakefield, commuting to Luton. I know the M1 is only one road, but it was two hours each way and I left a lot of my legs in the car. So I was desperate to get back up north and one day David Pleat pulled me to one side, to tell me Harry was interested in taking me to United on loan. I was back in the Premier League, and then signed permanently a bit later.

It was a tough school at United. Carl Bradshaw was one of the jokers, that's one thing I remember. I don't think I ever saw Alan Cork go out for a warm-up, in either of my two spells at United. But he'd go out and stick the ball in the back of the net. It was incredible. There were some amazing characters that you probably wouldn't get anywhere in this day and age, because they didn't conform to what football should be like today. People tell you the game's faster and it's this, that or the other. It's a fantastic spectacle, the Premier League. But it was a fantastic spectacle when we played as well.

My United career came to an end after that heartbreaking day at Chelsea, when we were relegated in the last minute. I didn't play that day but I had a clause in my contract which would have given me another year if we stayed in the Premier League, so I lost out on that as well. I'd already agreed to go out to America to do some coaching for the summer while the 1994 World Cup was on, and I was based at a girls' high school in Dallas with my future up in the air. I never thought we'd be relegated and I'd be looking for a new club, but it all worked out in the end. Fate took over and I moved to Bradford, where I moved into coaching and management. If United had stayed up and the course of history had been changed, who knows what would have happened?

In my coaching career, I took bits from all my managers. From Howard, from Lenny Lawrence, and definitely from Harry. You have to be your own man but you can definitely learn from the experiences, especially in terms of dealing with people. Harry was great with that. Howard had the blinkers on a little bit and if you didn't fit into his plan, then you were out. But Harry was different, I think. Even if you weren't in the side, you were still a part of the club and made to feel as if you were involved. The staff were a big part of that too. I still joke that Derek French was the worst physio I'd ever been involved with and maybe that was part of Harry's motivation. He didn't want players in the treatment room and when Frenchy was treating you, you were never 100 per cent sure that the machine was switched on!

When I made the transition to punditry it was nice to work again with another Bassett – Harry's daughter Carly. She worked at *Sky Sports* when I was on *Soccer Saturday* with Jeff Stelling, and was my link with the studio. She's good as gold and a real character, like her dad. It just goes to show what a small world it is. I remember a young girl who was probably in nappies when I was at United and then years later, we ended up working together. She was even the link when I missed that sending off live on air at Portsmouth! It has been a great family to be involved with and to be a part of Harry's history is an honour, really. I hope you enjoy the book.

Chris Kamara, 2024

*"Perhaps the poorest professional
standards within the memory
of anyone at Bramall Lane —
certainly the worst in my 15 years
with the club — brought a defeat
as shameful as it was unforgettable
on Saturday. Oldham Athletic, a
team struggling all season to shake
off the relegation quicksands from
around their ankles, came, saw and
conquered with such ridiculous ease
that it was all scarcely believable."*

– Tony Pritchett

1

"GO AND GET DAVE BASSETT"

I t was a damp and dreary Sheffield afternoon – the wettest January 2 on record, in fact – and 9,000 or so hardy Sheffield United supporters had shuffled into Bramall Lane more in hope than expectation. Their side languished 18th in the old Second Division table, already low on belief after a 4-1 chastening at Blackburn Rovers the day before and with little promise that the new year would bring about any real change.

The dark clouds intensifying over Bramall Lane were not just weather-related. Oldham Athletic were the visitors that day, making the trip over the Pennines just a point and a place above the Blades in the table. Frankie Bunn, their striker whose son Harry had a brief loan spell at United some years later, had a day to remember; United goalkeeper Andy Leaning one he'd probably rather forget. *Sheffield United 0, Oldham 5.*

It wasn't supposed to be this way. United were formed back in 1889 with the vehement aim of becoming a dominant force in English football and, for a time, they made a pretty decent fist of it. They were crowned champions of England within their first decade of existence, finishing runners-up on two further occasions, and won four FA Cups. Their record of being the only club to have fielded 10 England internationals in the same game, dating from the 1903/04 season, is likely to endure, given how football in this country has diversified. For good measure, United regularly paired those 10 with left-back Peter Boyle, who was capped five times by the Irish national team.

United retained their place in the top division for more than 40 years but that four-year spell of one title and two second-place finishes was as good as it got and relegation in 1934 began a yo-yo era that, save for a few brief periods, has largely endeared to this day. Unitedites may have wondered if their luck was beginning to turn when the legendary 1974/75 side – containing the likes of Alan Woodward and Tony Currie, who fans still sing about half a century on – finished sixth in the First Division and finished a point off the Europe qualification places. Those supporters should probably have known better – the following season United were relegated, Currie was sold to Leeds United and within five years, they were in the bottom tier of English professional football.

United's only dalliance with the basement division to date did at least provide fans with some overdue enjoyment as their side stormed to the title at the first attempt, following it with promotion back to the Second Division two years later. Ian Porterfield, a tough and determined Scot who had scored Sunderland's winner in their shock 1973 FA Cup win over the mighty Leeds, was prised from United's neighbours Rotherham United just months after winning the 1980/81 Third Division and repeated the trick in the tier below in his first season at Bramall Lane.

Reg Brealey, the United chairman, recruited Porterfield with the aim of returning the Blades to the top division in five years; he got halfway there before he was sacked in January 1986, to his great shock and surprise. But the football was uninspiring and the average Bramall Lane attendance told its own story, with crowds regularly dipping below the 10,000 mark.

Towards the end of his time, Porterfield had relied – too heavily, some felt – on experienced players such as Peter Withe, Ken McNaught and Phil Thompson. All three men had lifted the European Cup in previous footballing lives, but it was an expensive gamble that did not pay off. After his illustrious time in the luxury of Liverpool, life in the Second Division did not hold the same appeal for Thompson, who retired at 31; McNaught was forced to call it a day through injury problems. All three still outlasted Porterfield at Bramall Lane.

Chairman Brealey was keen for some continuity in Porterfield's succession and so turned to Billy McEwan, who Porterfield had brought to Bramall Lane as youth coach. Initially stepping in as caretaker manager, McEwan accepted the full-time job in the summer of 1986 and was given the brief of uncovering young, hungry (and cheap) players to reprofile the ageing United squad. He did unearth some gems – including Peter Duffield, Peter Beagrie and a certain Chris Wilder – but United also missed out on the signings of Dean Saunders and Mark Bright, who were both available and would, some behind-the-scenes figures believed, have been landed by a more experienced manager.

McEwan was an old-school character, shaped by the tough-as-teak Scottish great Eddie Turnbull at Hibernian, but found it difficult to really impose his authority on an ageing squad well past its best. On the whole it was a largely uninspiring period in the memory of most Blades fans, Porterfield proved a tough act to follow and United, in their 99th year, were in danger of kicking off their 100th back in the Third Division.

The final straw came early in the new year. United were well beaten 4-1 in the pouring rain at Ewood Park, returning to Bramall Lane the following day for a 5-0 pounding at home to Oldham. *The Star's* United correspondent Tony Pritchett described a defeat "as shameful as it was unforgettable," with United "totally devoid of confidence, ragged at the back, flimsy in midfield and with nothing of any quality delivered to their front players." It was a tough introduction to first-team football for young midfielder Mark Todd, who had been brought in from Manchester United and made his league debut at Blackburn before his first start against Oldham, and the memories are still vivid more than three decades on. "The team was shit," was his succinct verdict.

"Billy was like most Scots, quite fierce. The day before Blackburn, he introduced me and Clive Mendonca at 4-0 down. 'Cheers, Gaffer.' We came off the bench and said: 'Let's just run about.' We managed to win our time that we were on the pitch, but my introduction to league football was a 9-1 aggregate defeat in two days. I probably should have given up there and then."

McEwan paid the price, the decision reducing Brealey to tears but providing some festive cheer to United's players who were on their Christmas do in Sheffield when they heard the news. While Todd and Brian Smith propped up the bar at the Montgomery Hotel in Nether Edge, as the last men standing, thoughts turned to the future. United were floundering badly and desperately needed a spark to shock them back into life.

And boy, did they get one.

****

Reg Brealey, a man from humble beginnings who went on to own a helicopter, a chain of hotels and a Rolls Royce, was a man who knew how to make money. A distant descendant of a wealthy cotton trader, Brealey was the middle child of seven who built a successful business empire of his own, at one point acting as the chairman of 24 different companies in a diverse range of fields. A Lincolnshire native, Brealey had previously sat on the board of Lincoln City before being introduced to Sheffield United chairman John Hassall by club secretary Dick Chester.

There was little initial affinity between Brealey and Sheffield but Hassall extended an invitation to join the Blades board in 1980. Watching from the stands as United were dismantled 4-0 at Grimsby Town perhaps ought to have persuaded Brealey to run a mile rather than get involved, but on an otherwise miserable day the fervent support of the Unitedites in the away end struck him. He made up his mind. He was in.

Less than a year later United were in the Fourth Division, Hassall was gone and Brealey was the club's chairman. In a bid to improve United's financial situation Brealey launched a new share issue and ended up owning most of them after a lower-than-anticipated take-up. With United losing £725,000 that year alone, and facing debts of over £1m – which was a sizeable sum in 1980, especially for a club that regularly attracted crowds of less than 10,000 – Brealey overhauled United's operations behind the scenes, effectively introducing the idea of corporate hospitality and the club's first real souvenir shop as additional sources of income. He was the instigator of the redevelopment of the south stand, to include new dressing rooms, offices and the popular social club.

Derek Dooley, the Sheffield football legend who was later invited to the board by Brealey, maintained that no one did more to revive United's fortunes than Brealey in his first spell at Bramall Lane. It is often said that the easiest way to become a millionaire is to be a billionaire already and then buy a football club. Although Brealey did not quite pump cash into United at that sort of level, Brealey did back up his grand ideas – in the early days, at least – with the funds to match. His first managerial appointment, of Ian Porterfield, had been successful. Now, after the departure of his successor Billy McEwan, Brealey had to repeat that trick.

"Billy inherited a dressing room that still contained some of the big names and old boys on big wages," remembered journalist Alan Biggs, who worked with both McEwan and Porterfield during their time at Bramall Lane. "There were some players of stature and it was difficult for him to impose his authority. He also came in at a time when Reg Brealey had largely spent up, a very successful manager had gone and there were too many older players. Porterfield was a very determined character, fiercely focused, and Billy was another character from the old school. He was, for my money, just in the wrong place at the wrong time."

United cast the net far and wide for McEwan's successor and as they sifted through the applicants during a five-hour board meeting at Bramall Lane, were certainly not limited in their ambition. Names on the shortlist included the former Norwich manager Ken Brown and Lawrie McMenemy, whose success at Southampton had seen him become the highest-paid manager in English football at Sunderland before leaving the Stadium of Light in March 1987.

Keith Burkinshaw, then at Sporting Lisbon, and Torquay's young manager Cyril Knowles were also interested, while Brealey's earlier approach for Aberdeen's young Scottish manager is lesser known. Alex Ferguson, who later became the most decorated manager in British football history and *Sir* Alex, knocked back the approach – and who knows how different things could have been, for both parties, if he had been persuaded?

Determined to learn their lessons from the failed McEwan experiment, United's board resolved to target a manager with a proven track record and experience, who could get the best out of a squad of players without requiring huge sums of money to lavish in the transfer market. After taking out a formal advertisement for a "manager-coach" in some national newspapers, United received around 50 applications for the job but in the end the standout candidate was one who had thrown his hat in the ring late on, formally registering his interest in the job via telephone. Brealey had been contemplating a change of manager for a while and contacted Ron Noades, the Crystal Palace owner, for some advice. His reply was short, sweet and to the point.

"Go and get Dave Bassett."

Bassett's miracles at Wimbledon had been achieved on a shoestring budget and backed by crowds of 6,000 or so; United were short of money, low on support and sliding dangerously towards a return to the Third Division. On the surface it seemed a perfect fit. The only fly in the ointment was that Bassett was in work, having accepted the opportunity to succeed Graham Taylor at Watford in 1987.

With United's own form poor under McEwan, Brealey had already covertly sounded out Bassett about potentially replacing him. But Brealey and the rest of his board resolved to hold out until the new year, with managing director Dooley making it clear that he would not support any decision to sack McEwan before Christmas. He had suffered the same fate himself, by United's city rivals Wednesday, on Christmas Eve in 1973 and had never really got over the hurt and humiliation it caused. The delay suited Bassett, too, with the sense that the writing was on the wall at Vicarage Road after struggling to replicate his remarkable success at Wimbledon.

The Dons had risen spectacularly from the Southern League to sixth in the First Division during Bassett's 13-year association as player, assistant manager and manager, with Bassett taking them from the fourth tier to the first in five seasons. But Watford were languishing at the bottom of the top tier when Noades, who had appointed Bassett in one of his last acts as Wimbledon owner before leaving for Palace, picked up the phone. Noades had known Bassett, a school friend of Noades' younger brother Colin, since he was 12 years old and spoke in characteristically blunt terms. "Listen, you're obviously going to get the sack [at Watford] … so why don't you speak to Reg?"

Bassett can smile about it now but Noades was right, and the brief Watford adventure came to an end in January 1988. It was a move he later regretted, failing to do the correct due diligence on just why Taylor, who was a legend at Vicarage Road, had been persuaded to move to Aston Villa. But Bassett's stock was also high when he left Wimbledon, speaking to Manchester City amongst other clubs as he considered his next move. Then things changed quickly. Bassett can still remember vividly pulling onto the drive of his home in Hertfordshire and seeing his wife Christine opening their front door with a flushed look on her face. "You'd better come in," she blurted to her baffled husband. "There's someone here to see you."

A million scenarios raced through Bassett's mind but nothing could quite prepare him for the sight of Elton John in his living room, the pop superstar dressed in typically flamboyant fashion and dancing out to greet him. As well as one of the biggest-selling artists of his generation, John was the chairman of his beloved Watford and had earmarked Bassett to replace the departing Taylor, making a personal pilgrimage to the Bassett family home to make his pitch.

Not ordinarily a man prone to speechlessness, Bassett was in awe. "He was offering me this and that," he remembered. "I thought it would surely be the other way around, me auditioning for the job?"

John was persuasive, and Bassett was keen. "Of course things can look brilliant on the surface and not always be so brilliant underneath," he said. "I didn't do enough due diligence and had people telling me to go, that it was ideal. But it was the wrong decision. I knew John Barnes was going to Liverpool but I didn't know that a few other players were also going and when I looked at the videos, it was Barnes who seemed to create or score all the goals. So it was an uphill battle from the start."

John and his fellow Watford director Muff Winwood, a songwriter and record producer who was in the Spencer Davis Group alongside his older brother Steve in the 1960s, were sold on Bassett – but their fellow board members were told, rather than consulted, about Bassett's appointment, which was sealed with a dance in his living room. "Stupidly, I should have spoken to one or two people," Bassett admitted. "I needed someone to say: 'Harry, fucking leave this alone and tell him you can't make a decision this quick.' I should have sussed out why Graham was leaving because he was a god there."

To this day Bassett maintains that his task was made harder by what he perceived as an agenda in the local media, who dug into his past running of a Sunday League side as a 21-year-old and used Wimbledon's "hooligan" reputation as a stick with which to beat him. The tone, Bassett felt, was along the lines of: "Is this the right type of manager for a club like Watford?" and even victory in his first game – poetically against Wimbledon – didn't completely win supporters over.

His position was hardly strengthened by John's attempts to sell the club, and relations behind the scenes became so strained that Bassett felt he couldn't trust his own secretary. The team's struggles placed strain on his marriage and in his autobiography, Bassett remembered Christine even copping for some flak from other parents on the school run.

"We just didn't win the games," admitted Bassett. "It got to the point where I left a few favourites out and gave a load of young players their debuts, like Timmy Sherwood. We were winning at Portsmouth and they scored a spawny goal to equalise. The next game Tottenham scored an offside goal and we lost.

"We played Manchester United at home and Tony Agana absolutely ran riot. Viv Anderson was chasing him all over and how we lost, I'll never know. When things are going against you, then they go against you."

The call that Bassett was expecting eventually came while his in-laws were round at his house for a late new year's lunch. John had summoned him to the house of his manager John Reid, just up the road in Hertfordshire. Lockwell House was set in 15 acres – Bassett joked that its drive was so long that it had a Little Chef halfway up it – and boasted three separate cottages, a helicopter landing pad and a leisure complex called "The Barn" which featured a gym, a sauna and a billiard room that transformed into a cinema with a screen that lowered from the ceiling. After a glass of champagne and some polite preamble in Reid's magnificent lounge, John clapped his hands and told Bassett they were going to play a game with the die-shaped cushion next to him. "Right, Harry..." John said. "Roll that. "One to five, you get the sack."

The odds aren't very good, are they? Bassett thought to himself. "What happens if I get a six?" he asked.

"It's obvious, Harry," John replied. "You have another throw."

With that, Bassett's Watford time was over. The pair toasted their divorce by getting royally drunk and when Bassett eventually went back home, at four in the morning, he did so as a free man. John was apologetic about Bassett's treatment, buying the club Jaguar for his former manager as a parting gift and sending him and his family on holiday to America. With his salary and pay-off, Bassett calculated that he had earned more in six months at Watford than he had in 13 years at Wimbledon. And the tingle of excitement at the next challenge was already building inside of him.

2

"DIRTY HARRY"

B orn just a couple of miles north of Wembley Stadium, in Stanmore, London, it was somewhat inevitable that David Thomas Bassett would have football in his blood from an early age. Life at Brent Road School in Willesden did not exactly spark any sort of academic passion, with his mild dyslexia hardly helping, but it did at least present an opportunity to chase relentlessly after a ball on the cracked tarmac with the type of commitment that would come to define Bassett's career and life.

Bassett was the only child of mum Joyce and dad Harry, which is where Bassett Jr.'s ubiquitous nickname arose. There have been suggestions over the years that it arose from comparisons with Harry Houdini's famous escape acts while Bassett was Sheffield United manager, but its origins were far earlier and simpler. Growing up there were a lot of other Daves in that part of London and to avoid confusion, his school pal Tony started to call him Harry. The rest, as they say, is history and to this day, the mere mention of the name Harry amongst Wimbledon or United fans of a certain vintage would spark a knowing nod of appreciation.

The gift of a football in his formative life began a love affair with the game that endears to this day but growing up, Bassett didn't follow a team religiously or even pay attention to certain players. In a way he didn't want to limit himself; why watch one team or footballer when any game of football can hold equal appeal? There was particular admiration for the famous Busby Babes of Manchester United, so cruelly decimated by the Munich air disaster in 1958 when Bassett was 13, and a leaning, if pushed, towards West London rivals Chelsea and Fulham. Those who have spent a life watching football, rather than playing it, can only imagine the thrill when both clubs later offered a young Bassett a trial. He turned down Fulham and eventually left Chelsea after becoming disillusioned with a lack of opportunities, preferring to drop into non-league and try his luck with the amateur club Hayes. He was still only 17 years old but even then, Bassett was determined to do things his way.

It was at Hayes that Bassett first encountered his future right-hand man Geoff Taylor and after catching the eye as a quick forward with a knack for scoring goals, he was taken on by Watford as an amateur following a successful trial. Manager Ken Furphy, another future United manager, was impressed enough with Bassett's reserve-team performances to offer a professional deal, but the youngster turned it down. He had joined the Scottish Life insurance company as a teenager and after he had risen steadily up the ranks, the terms on offer from Watford didn't match what he was earning as an insurance salesman and part-time player. Plus, he had a company car.

Confident and with perhaps just a touch of youthful arrogance, the young Bassett was determined to excel, rather than simply exist, in whatever field he tried his hand at. He was realistic enough to appreciate that he was unlikely to become a top-level player, and the idea of life as a middling third-tier professional would have probably frustrated rather than fulfilled him. He would have to wait a while longer for a taste of the top.

His decision proved a wise one as two sliding-doors moments changed the course of Bassett's life. Firstly, a young Miss England and Miss Great Britain beauty finalist by the name of Christine Carpenter joined Scottish Life and was assigned to be Bassett's secretary. Christine's then-boyfriend made the decision to emigrate to Australia, she made the decision not to go with him to the other side of the world and Bassett made the decision to take his chance and invite her out for a drink. He has always been a believer in fate. He and Christine married in 1972, and the pair celebrated 50 years of marriage with a boat ride down the Thames.

Their courtship began during an 18-month injury absence from the game for Bassett. By then playing for Tony Currie's hometown club Hendon, and recovering from a nasty virus, an injury to fellow striker Jimmy Quail left the door wide open for Bassett to nail down his place. To regain a bit of match sharpness, he dosed up on medication in order to turn out for Thames FC in the local Sunday League. "It was thick, really," Bassett later admitted. He broke his leg in the game and as a result missed the chance to play at Wembley in the 1966 Amateur Cup final against Wealdstone, just months before Alf Ramsey's England heroes won the World Cup on the same hallowed turf.

When Bassett returned to action it was as a midfielder who specialised in breaking up play – or, as he remembers, "kicking the shit out of everybody" – and made a move across the Athenian League from Hayes to Walton & Hersham. Bassett thrived under the guidance of Walton's manager Allen Batsford, earning England amateur honours and exercising the demons of missing that Wembley final by lifting the Amateur FA Cup as the Swans' captain at the national stadium in 1973. His time with England saw him work closely with coach Charles Hughes, who Bassett described in his autobiography as one of the best coaches the British game has ever seen. Hughes and his methods were a big influence on Bassett's own coaching career but he was said to be somewhat startled some years later when his former mentor insulted his style of play.

"I have never associated myself with the practice of hoisting the ball up the middle in order to win it back by planting an elbow in the face of the centre-half," Hughes, then the FA's director of coaching, wrote in his 1990 book *The Winning Formula.* "Nor with trading possession solely for distance, nor with the theory that ours will become a game denominated by giants or thugs. Except for their FA Cup final, I have never been to see Wimbledon play. I do not have to look at Watford, Sheffield United, Leeds or anyone else who has come into that category. Liverpool represent the finest example of the way I believe the game should be played." Liverpool won the title that season, but Leeds and the Blades finished level on points in the top two positions in the Second Division to join them in the first. More than one way to skin a cat, you could say.

Bassett flourished under Batsford at Walton & Hersham, their time together including a famous 4-0 victory over Brian Clough's Brighton in the first round of the FA Cup in 1973 which the great Clough described as one of his darkest days in football. Batsford then moved on after being offered the chance to take over a semi-professional team in the Southern League called Wimbledon, but the switch could hardly be described as money-orientated. Wimbledon's financial situation was so bleak that Batsford had to take a pay-cut from the amateur side to join, but it proved inspired and after returning to sign Bassett, Wimbledon won three successive league titles before finally being elected into the Football League for the 1977/78 season.

By the time Wimbledon took their first steps on the English professional ladder Bassett had been promoted into a de-facto player/coaching role, with Dario Gradi brought in as Batsford's assistant. Batsford understandably felt a little undermined when he discovered that his assistant was being paid a higher salary than the manager and when he subsequently quit, six months after election, Gradi appeared the obvious choice to take the reins. But instead it was Bassett who was given first refusal from chairman Ron Noades. With an honest sense of acceptance that he wasn't yet ready to step into management, Bassett respectfully declined and Gradi stepped up, winning promotion to Division Three in 1978/79.

Gradi was another who recognised Bassett's value and offered his on-field skipper the chance to combine that role with the No.2 job. Bassett ummed and aahed, sought Batsford's approval and subsequently accepted. Juggling three jobs was deemed unmanageable, though, and Bassett subsequently wound down his day-to-day involvement with the insurance company he had set up while still working with Scottish Life.

By the time the invitation to step up and become Wimbledon's new manager came again, Bassett felt he was ready. Noades had left to take over at Crystal Palace and offered Gradi the chance to go with him across London. The Bassett era had officially begun. In came Taylor, to oversee the youth team, and Derek French later joined the set-up as physio. French combined his physiotherapy work with taxi driving to make ends meet but was far more than just a bucket-and-sponge man. Back then, he wasn't even that.

"I hadn't even qualified when I went to Wimbledon," French said. "I did my courses through the FA and had my final year at Lilleshall while I was at Wimbledon. Becoming a physio was a natural thing. I'd never trained to be anything in particular or went to university. I was just a hobo, really, enjoying my life. I had no experience at all until I went to Barnet as a physio. I wasn't a fool, don't get me wrong, and I found I quite liked it.

"The first time I met Harry was when he brought me into Wimbledon. I have no idea why he took me there! I don't ever profess to be the greatest physio in the world, so I don't know. Maybe it was my persona. I like a good laugh and I don't ever treat anyone badly. I did the best I could and I think he just trusted me. He was a workaholic even then, Harry, and he expects the same level of commitment from you. He hasn't changed. He's never got any money on him.

"He thought I'd take to it like a duck to water and that everyone liked me. I don't know if that's true, but I've always got on with people and people still talk to me, so I must be doing something right! He never actually told me what I had to do. I'm quite good at dealing with people and problems, and I think that helped me. I wouldn't say I'm a good football man, as such, but I know people. I know whether people have the right attitude, or if they're the right kind of person that Harry wants. So that will have helped, too."

It was at Wimbledon that the idea of Bassett's "heads" was coined. The manager was able to switch at any given moment between being "one of the lads," joining his players for a beer and a laugh, to the boss who commanded total and immediate respect. He had a contract head for when players used to go into his office and barter for minuscule price rises, and a downright grumpy head when he had the hump with something, or nothing, and those around him gave anyone they could make eye contact with the look that simply meant: "Stay away."

"He'd always be unhappy with someone in the club," French added, "but he'd never do you individually. He'd do a meeting on the Monday morning and go round and say what he wasn't happy about. He'd get to the one that he really wanted to have a go at and keep on them, but he didn't single them out. He made his point, but he made sure that everyone got some so that nobody felt picked on. He had a go at me for things I wasn't even involved in, because he wanted to have a go at someone else. He would test you all the time, but that was Harry. He would come down to my room when all the lads were in there and give me a bollocking about something or other. But then he'd come down 10 minutes later, after all the lads had gone, and have a laugh about something. I loved that about him. I think he's brilliant. Just a genuine man. But he's tough … he can look after himself as well."

Bassett's managerial career began midway through the 1980/81 season and that campaign, plus each of the ones that followed, tell their own story of the remarkable Wimbledon ride: promoted from Division Four, relegated from Division Three, champions of Division Four, promoted from Division Three, 12th in Division Two, promoted from Division Two, sixth in Division One. In between there was even time for surely one of the shortest managerial reigns in history, as Bassett accepted another invitation from Noades to join him at Crystal Palace before performing a U-turn four days later. There was something about him that belonged at Wimbledon, the team he had cobbled together on a shoestring budget that was on the brink of a fairytale rise to the First Division.

The unthinkable became reality in 1985/86 when Wimbledon finished third in Division Two behind Charlton and champions Norwich with a squad full of future Sheffield United players. It may not have been pretty but it was damn effective and stories of the Wimbledon "Crazy Gang" became part of football folklore – whether they were correct or, as some were, embellished over time. John Motson, the legendary commentator, likened the rise to a Sunday League side playing in the Premier League, while the media nailed their colours to the mast by christening Bassett *"Dirty Harry,"* in a reference to the popular Clint Eastwood movie series, and decrying the Wimbledon approach as "long ball." Unsurprisingly, Bassett rallied, arguing that there is actually no single right way to play the game.

"People have got different perceptions of what good football is," he reflected. "There's no rule saying the ball's got to stay on the floor or has to go in the air. I decided I wanted to try to be in football to last, but saying: 'We're playing the right way' and losing doesn't keep you in the job. Results keep you in the job and if you learn how to win football matches, then that's pretty important. When I was the manager of Barnsley and Nottingham Forest, we didn't play like we did at Sheffield United or Wimbledon. At Barnsley we played some fantastic football. At Forest we won the Championship and the ball wasn't in the air there. I didn't care two shits, to be fair. I ended up with more than 1,000 games and 20-odd years in the game, unlike some of the bullshit I read. 'We play the right way.' Well, fuck me, I think … you're third from the bottom."

The best kind of football, essentially, is winning football and Bassett's Wimbledon did plenty of that. Opposition teams were unable to cope with their relentless pressure and unwavering spirit and on top of that, they had footballers who could play as well. "Alan Cork was a great goalscorer, Glyn Hodges was a talented player, Kevin Gage was a talented player," said Bassett. "Nigel Winterburn was a talented player. So I had a meeting with them and decided to change the way we played. We did a fortnight's work on it and we won our next two games. If we'd lost them, then it could have been a problem. But credit to them, they got on with it and all of a sudden realised how good they could be. The opposition didn't like it because they were under constant pressure.

"Look at Pep Guardiola at Manchester City. He wouldn't like it; he believes in the way he plays and that's fair enough. But all this DNA shit from the FA worries me, playing the ball out from the back. Why does everyone want to play the same way? It's alright if you've got great players and can play like that. But if you've got, say, four good players that can do that, well, the other team has got 12 of them in their squad. So the odds are they are going to beat you every time. You've got to find a way to even the odds."

The Wimbledon school bred tough people as well as tough players. It was a sink or swim mentality and some – including Ian Holloway, who later became a manager in his own right, and future Liverpool defender John Scales – struggled with the demands. Those who stayed afloat enjoyed the ride of their lives and even 45 years or so on, Gage can still vividly remember his first encounter with Bassett. "I'll never forget it as long as I live," he laughed. "I'd been at Wimbledon about two months and I was 15. We had a Youth Cup tie against Spurs at Plough Lane and I was the only schoolboy playing. It was all apprentices and 18-year-olds. I played midfield in the game and I thought I'd done quite well, but we lost 2-0. After the game, we were in the changing room with the youth-team coach Alan Gillett and, all of a sudden, the door flung open.

"This bloke I'd never seen before, with a sheepskin-like coat on, burst in and his face was raging. He had a go at every player, starting with the goalkeeper. 'You were fucking useless, what were you doing there?' and so on. He went round to the number two, then three, four and five. I was number eight and it dawned on me that he was going through everyone. I was 15, I'd played Sunday League and school football and no one had ever spoken to me like that. I was trying to go through the game and think of anything I'd done wrong and as he came to me, I froze in my seat, thinking: 'Oh shit, oh shit.'

"He got to me and said: 'As for you … you did alright today, well done.' I honestly nearly fainted. He went on to slaughter the number nine and 10 and I think he even slaughtered one of the subs, who hadn't even got on the pitch! He walked out and I had to ask someone a few minutes later: 'By the way, who was that?' They told me it was Dave Bassett, the assistant manager. I wondered what I'd let myself in for."

The final chapter of Bassett's remarkable Wimbledon story was actually written in the Steel City, with a 2-0 victory over Wednesday at Hillsborough. He allowed his players a night out in Sheffield after his final game in charge, and they thanked him by scattering the contents of his room throughout the corridor of the team hotel. He had already resigned himself to leaving, and Bassett remembered the final straw being owner Sam Hammam's attempt to insert a clause into the manager's contract, giving the owner veto powers over team selection.

Bassett suspected that Hammam was jealous of the adulation given to the manager, rather than the owner, for the club's recent success. And as he walked around the pitch at an empty Hillsborough, his mind racing, the realisation hit him. "I thought to myself: 'It's the end of an era.'"

***

Described in its own promotion material as "quintessentially English," Chewton Glen country house and spa is a place of five-star opulent luxury. Sitting in 130 acres of lush Hampshire countryside, just outside the market town of New Milton, it dates back to the early 1700s and boasts a nine-hole golf course, as well as 17 award-winning treehouse suites. It was here, 180 miles south of Bramall Lane, that Dave Bassett's Sheffield United revolution began to roll into action.

United, managerless after the departure of Billy McEwan and with coach Danny Bergara in temporary charge, were at Dean Court to face Bournemouth that afternoon and Derek Dooley, United's managing director, has been forced to risk the wrath of his wife Sylvia by cancelling their planned weekend away. Instead, he travelled south with chairman Reg Brealey to meet Bassett, with fellow directors Paul Woolhouse and Michael Wragg following later. The board had already unanimously made up their mind that Bassett was their man.

But on the long journey down south, Dooley couldn't shake off his reservations. They were not of Bassett's qualifications, nor his suitability for the United job; but purely of location. Bassett was a London boy, born and raised, with a crafty Cockney reputation and a CV that had not taken him north of the Watford Gap, never mind as far as Sheffield. Bassett was unquestionably the best man for the job. Dooley's big doubt was whether he would want it. It was a fair concern, but one that proved unfounded. Bassett was realistic enough to appreciate that his short time at Watford may dissuade First Division clubs from giving him another opportunity so soon. And despite United's low ebb, he saw enough signs of life to make him think that the club was not beyond saving.

Bassett, who remembered the support of Unitedites who had travelled to Plough Lane to see their side battered 5-0 by Wimbledon in 1985, saw United as a club of "good standing and good fans" with the raw ingredients to build something special. The most important one that he needed was time.

"I just thought: 'Why not?'" said Bassett. "I *was* a London boy and I had made a mistake in going to Watford, but we'd played Sheffield United at Wimbledon on our way up. It was a lovely stadium, and it stuck in my mind. The potential was there. To be honest, I wanted to get out of London. I didn't have a clue about Sheffield; my vision of it was on the M1 going past Rotherham and all those grey cooling towers and Christ knows what else by Meadowhall.

"It wasn't exactly the most picturesque place and I thought: 'I'd best enquire about this to the missus.' I didn't realise the Peak District was just the other side. At the time it felt like going abroad! But I thought: 'Let's go for it.' I wanted to carry on working and the club had heritage and potential. If I got it going I knew they were capable of getting good crowds, which was a problem at Wimbledon. They were better supported than Watford, too, so it seemed ideal. The kids were young enough to go and the wife was okay with it. So I thought we'd go north and see how we did."

The Chewton Glen meeting was on Christine's birthday weekend and while Bassett spoke to the directors in one room, the wives of Wragg and Woolhouse worked their magic in an adjoining room – selling Sheffield to Mrs. Bassett, and assuring her that any prior conceptions about life in the north were wide of the mark. They didn't know that Christine was already on board following earlier conversations with her husband, who was impressed by the promise of the board that they were committed to getting back into the First Division.

Sheffield was a city with a deep-rooted passion for football, they said, which was something Bassett had never really felt at Wimbledon or Watford. There were no false promises about money to spend in the transfer market, either; Bassett still recalls to this day how Brealey had been up-front with him that there was none.

The chairman and his prospective new manager were wildly different personalities. Brealey was a religious man who held numerous positions at his local church and used to spuriously quote the likes of Rudyard Kipling and Theodore Roosevelt in his missives while Bassett was a more straightforward character, peppering his speech with rapid-fire swear words so often that they just became normal after so long and having the character and confidence to christen his boss "Steak and Veg," in Cockney rhyming slang. Brealey also didn't have Bassett's passion for football and during his time in charge of United, didn't once watch the full 90 minutes of a game – instead, taking the time to walk around Bramall Lane and check that all was functioning as it should behind the scenes.

But around the roaring fire, both parties had heard enough from the other to convince them that this could be a marriage made in heaven, even if Bassett had learned his lesson from Watford and did not accept the job there and then. That afternoon he was an interested (and paying) spectator on the away end at Dean Court as United gave their fans some welcome respite with a 2-1 win. Impressed with United's spirit and organisation after watching an hour, Bassett returned home to continue his due diligence.

Emlyn Hughes and Howard Wilkinson were amongst the respected football names who tried to dissuade him from taking the job. The club was broke, they said, and Bassett's reputation could be damaged further. But he followed his gut, and former England international Hughes' views on United didn't stop him linking up with Bassett to train with the Blades soon after. In the pre-internet age, the January 21 edition of the *Sheffield Star* broke news of the Blades' new manager to supporters. "IT'S BASSETT," the simple headline screamed.

An initial 18-month deal paid Bassett around half the salary he had been on at Watford, with various incentives sensibly built in, and with his side 18th in the Division Two table, the new Blades boss was under no illusions about the size of the task facing him. "If a club has millions, they send for Ron Atkinson," he said at the time. "If they are skint, they send for Dave Bassett." Dooley recalled Bassett's impact as not so much a breath of fresh air but a whirlwind, but that was exactly the shock therapy the club needed. As well as a squad that he admitted was "too old and couldn't run," Bassett had inherited a club on the floor and with a sense of impending doom lurking around every corner of Bramall Lane.

There was some relief when United went 1-0 up inside the first 30 seconds of Bassett's first game in charge, a rearranged clash at Portsmouth in the FA Cup, but they still lost and back-to-back defeats in the league hardly signalled a dream start for the new boss. Tony Agana and Wally Downes joined Bassett at Bramall Lane from Watford and Wimbledon respectively, and Agana's goal got the new era up and running with victory at home to Barnsley on February 20.

Agana arrived alongside Scottish midfielder Peter Hetherston as part of the deal that took Martin Kuhl to Vicarage Road, with Bassett also bringing in Cliff Powell from the Hornets on a free and signing Simon Webster from Huddersfield, plus Darren Carr from Newport County. His teammate from the Welsh side, Paul Williams – a Sheffield-born forward whose mum Betty won a Nobel Peace prize in 1976 – and goalkeeper Graham Benstead also arrived on loan as Bassett set about putting his stamp on a group he had assessed quickly, and simply. "It was a bad side," he remembered.

A 2-0 victory in their final game of the season, away at Huddersfield Town, was not enough to secure United's Division Two status and they entered a relegation play-off, facing Bristol City – who had finished fifth in the third tier – in the semi-final for a chance of survival. United lost 1-0 in the first leg at Ashton Gate and Colin Morris' goal – scored past his best mate and former United goalkeeper Keith Waugh – at Bramall Lane was not enough as the sides drew 1-1, with City advancing to the play-off final on aggregate and the Blades condemned to the third tier. To compound the misery, journalist Cynthia Bateman's match report in *the Guardian* then referred to United as Sheffield Wednesday.

Benstead remembers United being "resigned to relegation" when he arrived at Bramall Lane and the sight of Wimbledon lifting the FA Cup at Wembley, with a side effectively built by Bassett, the day before the play-off first-leg defeat was the sort of cruel irony that football so often delivers. Bassett was in the Wembley stands to watch his old pals shock the mighty Liverpool and afterwards Vinnie Jones and captain Dave Beasant lifted the famous old trophy in his direction, as a bit of recognition for the part he had played.

But all Bassett's focus was now on the future, rather than the past, and he was characteristically ruthless in a post-season clear-out. Later he would admit that relegation was the best thing that could have happened, allowing United to clear the decks. But still, there was uncertainty.

Bassett admirably did not shift the blame for United's relegation onto McEwan, fronting up his share of the responsibility, and even offered his resignation to Dooley with the promise not to seek any financial compensation. Christine and his family had not yet moved up from London to join him in Sheffield, the rebuilding job was substantial and if he would get only eight or 10 games of the next season to improve things before the axe fell, he would rather leave now. Dooley's response left him in no doubt. The board was fully behind Bassett, was the crux of Dooley's message; they had hired him to do a job, and now was the time to get on with it.

3

RELEGATION, REBUILD AND REBIRTH

Ask anyone who was around to witness it, in the 1980s and 1990s, to describe Dave Bassett's style of football and the answers would probably vary wildly. Some would probably label it prehistoric, a crude approach with players who lumped and bullied their way through games. Others would argue it was innovative and actually more technical than its detractors could comprehend. The difference in viewpoint likely depends on which side of the fence those expressing it sit; whether they were part of Bassett's remarkable rides at Wimbledon and Sheffield United, or on the receiving end of it.

For Bassett, it essentially came down to two distinct choices: "Do you want to look pretty, or do you want to win? Fans want to win. Are you worried about aesthetics? You can have a Rolls Royce car and a Mini, they both get to the same destination. We didn't have the Rolls Royce players. It's easy to talk about different ways you want to play when you've got the best players. It was labelled long ball because we upset the system. Wimbledon weren't meant to come up and finish sixth, beating Man United twice or Chelsea twice or Tottenham. Knock the cup holders Everton out and get to the quarter-finals.

"To play against Wimbledon and Sheffield United, you had to be fit and run about. The players nowadays are faster and fitter, but by Christ, our players were doing the same mileage as most of them back then. You had to get up and down the park and if you weren't fit and athletic, you had no chance of playing the way I wanted to play. If you weren't fit and strong, then forget it. It was demanding and it was hard work.

"We stretched the game. If we played today, we'd probably lose a lot of games but we'd score some goals and we'd cause a few shocks. We wouldn't be sitting back like a lot of teams we see, letting the other side have 65 per cent of the ball and only having two shots. We played against good sides who could pass it around at that time. But Liverpool could mix it up on their day. So did Everton. They knew what they were doing. But they got away with it because people looked the other way."

Bassett recognised that the side he had inherited, and then rebuilt, would not be able to out-pass opposition players. Assembling a team packed with technically-gifted players, who could play attractive football on the types of pitches in that era, would cost serious money, and Bassett had found that in as short supply in the Steel City as he had at Wimbledon. "Reg Brealey told me at the start that there was no dosh," Bassett remembered with a wry smile, "and he wasn't lying."

What he was able to do was trade his way into a position where he had a group of ruthlessly-hungry players who not only understood how he wanted to play, but were more crucially able to carry it out. Bassett's United played percentage football with a relentless pressure placed on their opponents. Some could handle it but many simply couldn't. Midfield players became like long-distance runners in terms of the ground they had to cover, both ways. Wingers had specific instructions – put in first-time crosses that create havoc – and strikers expected them. Demanded them. Later in the Bassett era, winger Paul Wood dared to not deliver a pass to striker Billy Whitehurst at United's training ground, and almost paid the price.

"It was before training had even started," Wood remembered. "I got the bag of balls and emptied them out on the ground. Billy just said: 'Yes', so I went to pass it to him and dummied it. I checked back, saying: 'No, it's not on Bill.' There was no one else around! He shouted: 'Not fucking on?' and just ran after me. I thought: 'Bloody hell.' He chased me. Not around the pitch … he chased me through the woods, over ditches, through the trees next to our training ground. It went on for about two miles. When training had started, we were still running through the trees.

"He was quicker than me, Billy. We would do 50m and 100m sprints and he would beat me. I was nippy but once Billy got going, he was quick. There was no point in me running round the pitch, because he would have got hold of me. So I ran into the trees and afterwards, I didn't go into the changing rooms to get changed. I stayed outside until he had gone. And then by the next morning I had forgotten all about it. I was getting changed and when he came in, he came over and just said: 'You'll pass that fucking ball next time, won't you?' And I did."

To try and pigeonhole Bassett's approach is difficult, because it meant different things to different people. Some players relished it, others tolerated it and a few simply gritted their teeth and got on with it. But it's a much safer bet to assume that few opposition players enjoyed the challenge and gradually, as the wheels of the United juggernaut began to turn, Bassett's players began to realise that they were becoming *feared*. There would be no easy ride against United, as some clubs may have experienced in recent years. They would have to run about, work and head the ball and tackle, just to even compete. Bassett smiled years later as he recalled certain players who picked up mysterious injuries in training, with United on the horizon, before returning to the opposition's team-sheet a week later. Some of those who did play against United weren't shy in voicing their displeasure, including a future United manager in Adrian Heath. "You're getting the game done away with," he once complained as he left the pitch, after his side had been battered and bruised by the Blades. It was music to Bassett's ears.

To survive in his team, players had to completely buy into Bassett's methods. It wasn't so much his way or the highway but players were told in no uncertain terms what was expected of them and if they didn't want to be a part of it, or felt they couldn't cope, then they were invited to voice their views with no hard feelings. "If half the team did their own thing, then what Harry did wouldn't have worked," said striker Peter Duffield. "It only takes one or two not to buy in and it all falls apart. If Jock Bryson crossed it to the back stick and you weren't there, then it'd be clipped and shown on video.

"'If you're not fit enough to get there, I can run you,' he used to say. And if he sensed that you didn't *want* to get on the end of it, then you'd be out. Glyn Hodges was probably the only one who got away with it, and that was because he was a genius. He'd just try to nutmeg you all the time in training and to be fair, he usually did. I had a real bad injury – a broken leg that actually left me 20 per cent disabled, which no one at United knows to this day. But for the time I was there, it was a real fun place."

But it was tough, too. Bassett earned the nickname "Harry the Bastard" from his players – presumably not to his face – because of his ruthless streak. "He could be horrible, don't misunderstand that," Duffield added. "Once we were on the coach to an away game and he asked me how many tickets I needed for my family. I said two, and he said: 'You'd better have one for yourself.' That was his way of telling me I wasn't playing. The problem was that my family were coming from Middlesbrough to watch me and it was pre-mobile days, so there was no way I could warn them. I was on a table of four and he dropped me like that, in front of the lads. He could be ruthless. But all the rest burst out laughing and so I couldn't really take the hump with him. He diffused a potentially awkward situation and made it into a funny one. He was so intelligent like that, both on and off the pitch."

At Wimbledon, Hodges and Wally Downes were initially reluctant to get on board with the new way of playing at Plough Lane but soon found that they wouldn't be in the team if they didn't and fell into line, enjoying the ride up the leagues as a result. Bassett insists now that he was not trying to recreate the Crazy Gang spirit at Bramall Lane – even though some of his players at the time disagree – but it was also no coincidence that so many former Wimbledon comrades followed him to Bramall Lane.

One who made that familiar journey north from Plough Lane to the Steel City was midfielder John Gannon, a trusted lieutenant of Bassett who many teammates eventually began to refer to as "Harry's son" because of their close relationship. "Harry was very good at getting people to buy into what he was trying to do, and to believe in it," said Gannon. "In fairness I think the success helped but you also had to get on board with Harry, or it just didn't work for you. It was as simple as that.

"People talk now about Pep Guardiola and his way of playing. He has requirements and if people don't fit into that, then they don't play. It was the same with Dave, even though they are a million miles apart in the way they want to go about things. If you didn't do what was required or stick to the plan, then you wouldn't last. It was as simple as that. You had to be committed. You had to put the team first and not yourself or your own ego. You had to be able to take criticism, definitely, and you needed to be tough. He'd challenge you and wanted to see how you'd bounce back. He'd put you down and see if you recovered and challenged it, either by words or actions. And if you couldn't, then maybe you weren't good enough for him, or what he needed."

Gannon joined United in February 1989, initially on loan, before his move was made permanent later that summer. His debut, as an 80th-minute substitute at home to Blackpool, saw him pick up a booking with his first tackle and score United's fourth goal with his second touch. But life at Bramall Lane was a test of character as much as anything else for Gannon, as he struggled initially to win over sections of the Blades fanbase. "I had some issues, absolutely. Some serious issues. But that was probably the making of me. It's amazing how these things come and challenge you, and you had to grit your teeth and get on with it. I was 22 years old and I'd only played about 50 senior games, so it was quite a lot to deal with at the time. But I dealt with it. I had to man up and move forward.

"Did I win them over in the end, the fans? I don't think anyone will ever win everyone over, completely. But I think that they could see that over seven years and 200-odd games I played, I added something. I think I did my bit. There will always be players who, when maybe things aren't going well and they perhaps make a mistake, will get it worse than maybe a Brian Deane did. And I fully understand that. There's going to be the odd day and odd moment when people get frustrated, and I was a target from time to time. But in football there were also a lot of people who gave me a lot of support.

"Those sorts of moments can be sink or swim, really. You could go under with that sort of stuff, but I chose not to. I chose to fight it. I remember a few years ago, watching Granit Xhaka at Arsenal when he got booed off by his own fans. It was interesting to see how the players manage, or don't manage, in that situation. We weren't as powerful as the players are at the moment. Xhaka could have probably just sat on his arse and felt sorry for himself and got another big-money move somewhere. Whereas being at United was my opportunity and I had to make it work. I couldn't just sit down, and I didn't want to. I had to pick myself up and keep fighting.

"I was a free transfer from Wimbledon. I wasn't a £30m player, and I wasn't the finished product by any stretch of the imagination. But there were certain things that I was good at and we were about the team. I could do some of the things my midfield partner couldn't do, and vice-versa. You weren't going to get complete players at the level we were at, so you had to find partnerships and find strengths in each other. Stick to what you were good at, and let others do the other things."

Gannon's steel-like inner strength had been forged in his younger days, when issues with his knees began to flare up thanks to hours and hours training on Wimbledon's concrete pitch as a youngster. "There's no other way to put it … that destroyed my knee. I was fortunate to get to 30-ish and find the right time to retire, otherwise I was in danger of really doing a lot of damage. I managed it really well, I think, but it can be difficult at times, especially when you're having to take tablets to be able to play. But I got through it and, touch wood, I'm still fit and healthy now.

"Unfortunately, the injuries were just something players of our time suffered more from. We were more tolerant and more prepared to put our necks on the line when not fully fit. It wasn't always fair on ourselves, but it was a generation thing. Nowadays all the kids train on soft surfaces and the grass pitches are wonderful, so they don't have the same issues. I have to be careful what I do now because of the knee but I can pick and choose what I need to do and stay fit.

"We all get tested, don't we, one way or the other? I was probably my own worst enemy when I was younger because I was constantly training, trying to improve. Sometimes you just had to grit your teeth and get through it when life wasn't comfortable. All players from our era did it, because we wanted to stay in the team and hold down our place in the team that we'd worked so hard to get. Did we do ourselves any favours? Probably not. But our hearts were in the right place."

Bassett's reputation in the game was such that United's players knew full well how his Wimbledon side had played when he arrived at Bramall Lane and in an early meeting, the new manager set his stall out to his players. This was how they were going to go about things, he said, and anyone who wasn't willing to get on board for the journey was welcome to say so. Mark Dempsey quickly realised that the new way of working would not be for him and Bassett respected the midfielder's honesty, allowing him to leave and join former boss Billy McEwan just over the border at Rotherham United. Dempsey was far from the only casualty of Bassett's revolution as the new manager ruthlessly reprofiled his squad, seizing the opportunity to release a number of older players and cash in on others to free up some room for manoeuvre in the budget. Of the XI that started the play-off defeat to Bristol City that confirmed relegation, only five began Bassett's first full season in charge in the team and by the final day – ironically against City again – only Martin Pike and skipper Paul Stancliffe had kept their places from 12 months earlier.

Peter Beagrie's £200,000 move to Stoke had bolstered the funds at Bassett's disposal and top of his wish list was another striker, with his search leading him just down the road to Doncaster. Bassett had been tipped off about a young striker called Brian Deane and had gone to watch him in action for Rovers. He didn't score, but stood out to Bassett because of both his athleticism and ability. Rovers were subsequently relegated to the Fourth Division and had scored just 40 goals all season. The young Deane had netted a quarter of those on his own but saw the resulting contract offer from Rovers as insulting, and had made up his mind to leave. United's offer of £30,000, rising by £10,000 with appearances, secured Bassett his man and was subsequently proven to be one of the best pound-for-pound signings in the club's history.

Bassett's Bramall Lane overhaul also extended to his backroom staff. One of the conditions of his arrival, on a contract that managing director Derek Dooley later remembered being worth "peanuts," was that he worked with the existing staff already in place from McEwan's tenure but it was an arrangement that couldn't last, especially when Bassett was informed that one of them had been talking rather disparagingly behind the new manager's back, about him and his methods. In came long-time Bassett acquaintances in Geoff Taylor and physio Derek French, who had left Wimbledon and was working on a building site when the call came to link up with his old manager again. Both were vital cogs in Bassett's wheel and the trusted inner circle was later boosted by the arrival of John Greaves as United's first full-time kitman. United's hierarchy initially knocked back the request to hire Greaves but Bassett brought him in anyway, paying his wages out of his own pocket until he could smooth things over with those upstairs.

"They were a massive part of it," Bassett admitted of his staff. "They were characters. I had known Geoff since I was 17 or 18 and playing non-league football. He was the voice of reason, totally different to me. A nuts-and-bolts man who was not interested in the flamboyant life. A non-drinker. Frenchy was a funny man, quick with the verbals and could come back with players. He was more than capable of giving back and we created a good atmosphere. We knew when we had to work and when we had a chance to have a laugh we did. Greavesy was ideal as well, he fitted into the situation.

"The girls in the laundry were part of the equation and the boys on the ground staff, we didn't disregard them. Andy Daykin, the commercial manager, and the people at the training ground. We spent time building it so it became their club. They felt part of the club. They wanted to make sure everything was right as a result. The girls in the office. The first Christmas we were there, we had a massive party. A real shindig. I don't know if they ever did that before. There was this atmosphere that we were all in this together. The players were there but not any more important than him or her.

"At Wimbledon there were different players but it was the same spirit we had there. Of course not everyone gets on but their differences go missing when they're working. When we're on the pitch, we were all one. Whether you like him or he likes you is fuck all to do with it. Is he doing his job properly? And if he is, then respect him."

French's bubbly personality and silver tongue had seen him sweet talk a local businessman into lending him a car soon after he joined Bassett in Sheffield. Later that summer, Bassett pulled French into his office. "He said: 'We're going to sign this kid from Doncaster called Brian Deane,'" French remembered. "'Do you think your mate will be able to sponsor a car for him as well?' I said I'd ask, and gave Harry his number. The next day Harry called me in again and said he needed to speak to me. 'Great news, son,' he said. 'Your mate is going to sort Deano out with a car. The only problem for you is, it's your car.'"

A one-man band for much of his United career, physio French did not ever actively encourage players to be in the treatment room but grew to enjoy his Sunday overtime sessions, which invariably ended with a game of head tennis in the ramshackle Bramall Lane gym before a few pints in the social club and a heckle of club stalwart Derek Newbould while he was calling out the bingo numbers. "It wouldn't happen now," French laughed. "We also used to go and have a look on matchday at who was playing for the other team, once they'd put all their kit out. It's obviously a bit naughty, but nothing too bad. Once, the Crystal Palace lads laid all their stuff out and then asked where the nearest fish and chip shop was. Me and Greavesy sent him around the corner and went in to have a look. They came back in and caught us red-handed. We just had to hold our hands up and say: 'Fair enough, son.' It was one of those things."

The final piece of the jigsaw was Downes, who was one of Bassett's first signings and remembered by Kevin Gage, a former teammate at

Wimbledon and a future colleague at Bramall Lane, as "Bassett on the pitch." Downes was crucial to Bassett's success at Wimbledon as a de-facto gatekeeper of the Crazy Gang spirit. "If you could get on the right side of Wally and cope with all the abuse he used to give you, you'd be alright," said Gage. "He was a very abrasive character and you either liked him or loathed him. He would verbally attack some players and leave them in bits."

Essentially, if you could cope with Downes then you could cope at Wimbledon, although his influence was largely limited to off-the-field after he followed Bassett north to Bramall Lane in February 1988. Of his 11 appearances in 1987/88 United lost eight and he was sent off twice, one for a challenge against Bradford City described in the Blades' *Who's Who* book as "probably one of the crudest 'tackles' ever seen" at Bramall Lane. The iconic *Flashing Blade* fanzine once said that Downes, the nephew of former world middleweight boxing champion Terry Downes, "makes Graeme Souness look like Mother Theresa" and Bassett still chuckles at the memory of being in the car with Downes and listening to the *Praise or Grumble* show on *BBC Radio Sheffield* after one of his red cards, in a 5-0 defeat against Leeds. A Unitedite called in and described Downes as the most hated man in Yorkshire – before having second thoughts and downgrading Downes to second place, behind the *Yorkshire Ripper* Peter Sutcliffe.

Goalkeeper Graham Benstead had briefly experienced the original Crazy Gang at Plough Lane as a youngster, before being released without making the grade. Good enough to have been capped by England at both youth and semi-professional level, he moved to United on loan before making the move permanent in the summer after relegation.

"The original Crazy Gang, with Wally, Dave Beasant and those types, was quite intimidating," he recalled. "I was young and naïve. Progressively over the period of a year or so they got rid of me. I got released. I remember they used to call me Gary Sprake. I've got nothing against him, he was a good 'keeper, but apparently he was liable to the odd clanger now and then, which is what I used to do in training. So Wally Downes stuck that on me. Everywhere I went it was: 'Sprakey this, Sprakey that.' With Wally, you either stood up to him, or you cracked. Harry wanted strong characters, people to do the job he was sending them out to do and, looking back on that, I really admire it.

"Over the years I matured and stuck up for myself, you grow up. I always remember walking into the dressing room at Sheffield United, not long after I'd signed. All the lads were in there, like Chris Wilder, Agana, Paul Stancliffe. Wally was late as usual – he'd had a bit of a late night, I think – and when he saw me, he said: 'Sprakey, what are you doing here? I don't fucking believe it. You are the worst goalkeeper I've ever seen. What a waste of money this is!'

"All the lads were looking at me in a bit of shock but I knew what Wally was like and told him to go and do one. He looked at me, laughed and gave me a wink and from then on, we were best buddies. Harry liked big characters in his team. He could trust Wally, who was a good player too. They had a relationship a bit like Alex Ferguson and Roy Keane, just on a different level. Wally was there to make or break players. Sink or swim. I'm not saying Harry released players on the strength of that, but he was a good judge of character. And with the style we played, and the situation we were in, you had to be strong mentally."

One of Benstead's most vivid memories of his early days at United was being ordered to pick up Downes in his mum's car and drive to one of the sketchier parts of Sheffield. Benstead may have been green and a little wet behind the ears but it soon dawned on him that they were in what looked suspiciously like a red-light district, with Downes bursting with laughter. It was a test, rather than anything more sinister, and the young man passed by putting his foot down – literally and figuratively – and driving quickly off. One wonders how often Keane put young players through similar initiation tests at Old Trafford.

A broken ankle sustained in pre-season limited Downes' appearances in a United shirt and he later took up a coaching role under Bassett. Players from the time remember him adapting his approach to become a bit more mellow than he had been in his own playing days, but he was well-regarded as a coach. Striker Bobby Davison remembered his sessions at United as "excellent" and Downes later offered a fresh dynamic to a staff that Bassett kept deliberately small and tight-knit. Taylor was well-respected as an "elder statesman" who was fondly remembered for his coaching prowess while Bassett was a master man-manager and motivator. "It was very much good cop, bad cop," said Gage of the pair's dynamic. "Geoff wasn't one for screaming and shouting, picking on players and having a go at them. He was a bit more constructive, taking players to one side and putting his arm around them. All the players respected that from Geoff. He'd served his time in football and talked a lot of sense. They were a very good combination."

Bill Shankly and Brian Clough, two of the finest coaching minds that the British Isles have produced, were both of the opinion that football is fundamentally a simple game and it was a theory to which Bassett also subscribed. In the early days at United there were no wild tactical innovations, to the level of inverted full-backs and false nines that have permeated the modern-day game. United were set up in a 4-4-2 shape, with strong defenders, balanced midfielders, reliable wingers and capable strikers, and the focus was on what would bring success with the group they had at their disposal, rather than looking to reinvent the wheel. The approach may have appeared simple but as the results show, it was devastatingly effective.

That's not to say that Bassett didn't know his stuff when it came to tactics, or was afraid to think outside the box. Decades before Sir Dave Brailsford transformed the fortunes of British Cycling with his "marginal gains theory," Bassett was already hard at work trying to eke an extra one or two per cent from his players by any method he could. A fitness consultant by the name of Ed Baranowski was enlisted to offer tailored strength and conditioning sessions to players – at a time when most of football's idea of fitness work was a long cross-country run – while the Olympic bronze medallist and Commonwealth Games gold-medal winner Joslyn Hoyte-Smith led United's players in some stretching work to help mix things up.

In his first season at Bramall Lane Bassett found some budget for a part-time video analyst to cut up clips to show to his players, an innovation he had successfully introduced at Wimbledon. It acted as both a preparation and motivational tool; Vinnie Jones in particular used to worry about making a mistake at the weekend because he knew it would be clipped and played on Monday in front of his teammates, who would not hold back. Bassett even remembers one player at Plough Lane claiming it hadn't been him that had made a mistake, despite the grainy evidence being captured on VHS for all to see.

Showing Third Division players clips of AC Milan's iconic defence caused a few eyes to roll at the time but United's players mostly bought into the innovation, even if their patience was tested while Bassett and

Taylor constantly rewound and replayed certain clips with the clunky remote control. The long days weren't confined to the video room either, as Bassett placed real emphasis on set-pieces as another area that his United side could gain an advantage. One year Bassett had calculated that for every 12 corners – 12.6, if he remembers correctly – United scored a goal. In the first half of the 2023/24 Premier League season Arsenal were the most efficient, scoring a goal for every 16.4 corners. Manchester United netted, on average, once from every 67.

As a result United dedicating much of their pre-match preparations on Thursday and Friday before a Saturday game to corners and free-kicks, with Bassett keeping his players on the training ground for hour after hour until they got their routines spot on. And if they didn't, it'd be a case of reset and go again. The practice mostly paid off but football is also not an exact science and Bassett still remembers vividly a game at Gillingham in his first full season, rattling off the statistics 35 years on as if he was recalling his London Underground journey earlier that day.

"We had 28 shots at goal and they had two, and beat us 2-1. Early in the year Chesterfield beat us at Bramall Lane and the figures were similar. We had something like 17 corners and they beat us 3-1. There were a couple of games I remember where we went away and won with two or three shots ourselves, though, so it does work out over the season. Basically you need an average eight shots on target to get a goal. I'm not talking about a tricky shot; it has to be a decent one on target. Sometimes you have 16 and don't score but then you'll have four and score twice. That's the random element of the game."

Entry into Bassett's inner sanctum was earned, not given, and another man welcomed into it with open arms was the great Derek Dooley. A genuine Sheffield sporting legend, Dooley scored 46 goals for Wednesday in his first season in professional football and his career was destined for superstardom when it came to an abrupt and devastating end in the cruellest of fashions. It was Valentine's Day at Deepdale in 1953 when Dooley collided with Preston goalkeeper George Thompson and badly broke his leg. As he prepared to leave hospital and return home, a nurse realised that Dooley couldn't feel his toes and it was discovered that his leg had become infected. Gangrene had set in so severely that his life could have been in danger on the journey back across the Pennines and as Dooley battled a situation he remembered as more likely to affect wartime soldiers with shrapnel wounds than a professional footballer on a pitch, the headline of the *Sheffield Star* that night said it all. "Doctors fight for life of Dooley."

Dooley, whose passing in March 2008 at the age of 78 was mourned on both sides of the Steel City, later spoke of the shock of waking up from an operation and feeling for his injured leg, only to realise it was missing. The decision had been made to amputate his leg to save his life, at the obvious cost of his footballing career. His first reaction was that doctors may as well have taken him outside and shot him. But he bounced back to return to Hillsborough in a behind-the-scenes role before his promotion to first-team manager, which was cruelly curtailed by a heartless sacking on Christmas Eve in 1973. Bruised by the humiliation, he defected to Bramall Lane and had risen to the position of managing director, his crucial experience of the football world bringing real value to the Blades board. And especially to Bassett.

"I was very lucky with Derek," Bassett said. "He was a football man, he understood how it worked. He'd been in dressing rooms and knew how the game went. He was very supportive and I think he was impressed with what we did. With me, Geoff, Frenchy and Greavesy, Derek saw something I don't think he'd seen before. I could go to him and it was good for me. If I wanted things done, I'd ask him to speak to the directors for me, so I didn't have to waste time. I'd go to board meetings and Bernard Proctor was a lovely man, but he used to ask silly questions. Derek would say: 'Bernard, please don't ask that … it shows you know bugger all about football and our manager's not here to talk about that.' He could do things like that, even with the chairman.

"He loved it and became part of the team. He loved our Friday nights away; we'd have our meal and a few drinks after and he loved the football stories and the banter. He was a good man, he understood as a player and a lot of things that people who haven't played football don't understand. They like football, there's nothing wrong with it, but I come across a lot of people and think: 'You are fucking clueless.' They talk with authority and I look around and think: 'It doesn't surprise me that that club isn't doing well.'

"Derek said to me once that our eight-year period was the best years he had in football. He loved it. Derek was part of the team. He came on the team coach with us, and on pre-season. It was important in that he understood where I was going, and how I wanted to get there. He was a great man."

***

In many ways, Mark Todd was a quite atypical Dave Bassett footballer. He was diminutive in stature, at least compared to many of the other physical midfielders the manager brought in during his time at Bramall Lane, and brought up in the refined finishing school of Manchester United rather than the muck-and-boots life in the Southern League with Wimbledon. But whatever physicality Todd may have lacked, he more than made up for in terms of heart, desire and tenacity; despite being left out of the travelling party for the pre-season trip to Sweden, only four players ended Bassett's first full season in charge having made more appearances.

A Belfast boy who moved to Manchester at the age of 16, Todd had clubs in the north and south interested in signing him after he was let go before deciding to move to Sheffield United. The proximity to his life just over the Pennines helped, as did the bizarre fact that the then Blades boss Billy McEwan's wife was from Northern Ireland and actually knew Todd's auntie. As a fellow youngster, Chris Wilder was enlisted to take Todd out and acclimatise him to life in Sheffield and the two became close friends. A pal of the pair remembers Todd as "a scruffy little get" and the trio being thrown out of Josephine's nightclub for singing United songs. The two players then took turns trying to throw each other in the fountain at the top of Fargate before both ended up in the water, with Todd emptying his green flash trainers in the back of a taxi.

"Harry revolutionised that club, into what it currently is," said Todd, speaking over three decades later. "I think that, without the reset after Billy went, the club wouldn't be where it is today. At the time there were about nine or 10 thousand people turning up some weeks. The dynamic of Harry's group was that he didn't restrict your personality. He knew to express yourself on and off the pitch was very important and fitting into the group. And we had some characters! It's not like that now. There are no magic personalities. There is no Billy Whitehurst, or Vinnie Jones or Paul Gascoigne. It's all a bit samey.

"Harry was a very intelligent guy and also a very intelligent manager. How do we get success from this group that cost very little, certainly in the first seasons he was in? With a bunch of, how to describe us …

46

misfits? Possibly. What did we need? And he went and got it. There was a way to play, which I'd been taught for three years at Man United, but there was a way to win. Under Billy Mac, we were terrible. I don't know what we were. We were poor. The crowds were poor. The mood was just poor, generally. The squad needed sorting out and we needed someone of Harry's mindset to do it.

"When he signed me, Billy said I had wing mirrors. I was always scanning. But under Harry, my whole game with the ball had to change. I still tried to be myself in my short game, with a good first touch. I think that's why he picked me, because I could play with one touch. Tony Agana and Deano knew that I wasn't going to mess about and my technique wouldn't let me down, so they could be on their way. I trusted my technique, and so did they. Harry knew at some point the game would become technical, so he didn't mind it. It was learning a different way to play, but it was learning how to win as well. All the adulation, the moments of being involved in a successful squad … that's what you're in it for. You don't climb the mountain with playing style. You do it by winning games."

There was plenty of that and steadily, the Blades ship began to right itself. Unitedites who had voted with their feet during the apathy of the seasons previous were steadily goaded back and although it wasn't a process that happened overnight, the feel-good factor was gradually returning to Bramall Lane. Sheffield was still recovering from the effects of the miners' strike earlier in the decade and its reputation as an industrial city saw the Tory MP Michael Fabricant describe Sheffield as "not sexy" and "old and dirty" in 2001. As the landscape in the city began to change, thousands of coal miners and steelworkers lost their jobs and for many, football became a luxury that simply could no longer be justified.

Football in the 1980s also wasn't the family-friendly experience many enjoy today, with hooliganism still rife and fans packed onto standing terraces and penned in by barbaric fences that were only ripped out after the tragedy of the Hillsborough Disaster in 1989. Facilities, if you could call them that, were basic at best at most grounds and there was an overt sense of distrust of football fans from the authorities. The Margaret Thatcher government even wanted to impose ID cards upon those supporters whose only crime was to follow their team. The many were at risk of being tarred by the actions of the few.

For all the advancements in football, and society, in the years since, there are many who miss elements of that era; the rawness, the camaraderie, the standing, the singing. Saturday, 3pm kick offs. No *Super Sunday* or *Monday Night Football*. No social media campaigns for a manager to lose his job after a couple of defeats, or 24/7 rolling TV news covering mundane transfer gossip. The bloke who used to put the scores of games elsewhere on a big sign that corresponded to a number in the programme. Actual, proper programmes, not glossy matchday magazines. Players who were normal people, on semi-normal money, who saw falling to the ground as a sign of weakness rather than an opportunity to get opponents into trouble. Pay-on-the-day ticketing and no loyalty point systems. No half-and-half scarves. And certainly no VAR.

"We were scoring goals and the fans loved it," Bassett said. "The season before their team were bottom of the league and relegated, they were shit, and all of a sudden they were excited. Because it *was* exciting. On a good day. Of course there was passing, we just didn't fuck about. I think what endeared me in a way to Sheffield United fans was that, when they were leaving the church of Bramall Lane and they were going home, and we had been shit, I wasn't saying that we were good. 'We did this or that.' I said that we were shit, or: 'That ain't good enough and the players are training tomorrow.' So they felt better going home, because they felt I'd seen the game that they saw."

A healthy relationship with the local and national press was also something Bassett sought to cultivate at United. Some of his experiences with the media at Wimbledon and Watford had left him feeling a little persecuted, but he recognised the importance of playing the game with journalists and broadcasters who, with Bassett in situ, were certainly never short of an entertaining line or quote to take back to their editors. One press man with fond memories of Bassett is veteran writer and broadcaster Alan Biggs. "Dave was a joy to work with," he said. "An absolute delight. Although some people may say he was the classic crafty Cockney character, because of the colourful language, he is one of the most honest and genuine people that I have ever met in football. Very unusually for a manager, he was one of a very few that became a friend.

"Before he took over at United, I was one of several journalists who rang him at home. These days that is unheard of but he was honest enough not to distance himself from the United job, or deny it. He didn't confirm he was taking over but as good as. He then came in like a whirlwind, swearing habitually every other sentence to such an extent that it just blended in and you didn't notice it. He called everybody "son" – whether they were young or old – including his boss, the chairman Reg Brealey. I remember after one match, Reg came past us when a few of us were talking to Dave and he said to his chairman: 'You alright, son?' Reg did his middle button up and carried on. He must have been thinking: 'What have I got here?'

"Harry was also a man of principle. He felt he had failed when the Blades went down after his first part-season and I am sure his offer of resignation was genuine. He then absolutely threw himself into a massive shake-up and one of the outstanding things about him was his energy. He was 100mph; not just in the way he spoke but in the way he behaved and the way he acted as well.

"His energy was such that he would often do a day's work here and the next thing you would ring him and he would be like: 'I'm on my way to London, son, to do a motivational talk at a dinner.' Then he would be back at work in the office at nine the next day. But he would always talk to you. It might take five phone calls before he was free, and he might say: 'I'm just on the other phone, son, can you give me five minutes?' But he would always speak to you.

"It was totally informal. He would be characteristically late, not because he was rude but because he would be running late at a meeting with the players or doing something or the other. He was seldom punctual in terms of the time you would see him but you would go into his office and it would be like a social gathering, with four or five regular local journalists like Mike Morgan, Peter Ferguson, Keith Farnsworth, John Edwards and myself. There would be cups of coffee and a chat. Some off the record, some on it, and much of it hilarious. There would be ups and downs in the relationship. He would say what he thought at the time but then you would move on, he wouldn't hold a grudge."

One memorable incident saw Biggs banned from Bramall Lane. "I had a few run-ins with Reg, mainly through taking Dave's side about lack of funding for players. I was always sailing close to the wind. One day, the weather was lovely so instead of going inside to wait for him, we congregated in the car park. A few of us chatted while we waited for him to finish his lunch in the social club. When Dave came out, he came straight up to me and said: 'I'll think you'll find you are banned, son!'

"I asked if that was the case and he said: 'Yeah, they've decided it at a board meeting today. So we are having this press conference out here in the car park. Is that alright?' He did that, especially for me. I thought that was a nice thing to do. He was great with us. He did have a few run-ins with the national press, London-based journalists, who would decry Sheffield United's style of play. Dave would say that there was a lot more to it, which there was. It was exciting, the ball was constantly in the other team's penalty area. He got no stick from Blades fans or us locals for that.

"He commanded loyalty. That was a part of it. You really didn't want to let him down. And that was us, so I can imagine for the players that was 10-fold. He has been the best manager to deal with here. Neil Warnock was brilliant, Chris Wilder exceptional, but Dave he was by far the best. It was a great time for a journalist. Fridays would be very busy. We'd also have Ron Atkinson or Trevor Francis at Hillsborough and we had all this work to do, to write these stories up. I'd be sitting in Bassett's office and thinking: 'I need to get out.' But you also didn't want to leave, because his company was so good."

***

As he sat down in a London restaurant to reminisce about his colourful career, Dave Bassett acknowledged a crick in his neck. It is not a consequence, as some of his detractors may unfairly claim, of watching his teams kick the ball long, but instead another reminder of the unorthodox managerial methods that anyone would struggle to find in an FA coaching manual. "I'm convinced it's from when we were on the love boat from Sweden to Finland," Bassett said. "Me and Carl Bradshaw must have wrestled for about an hour and a half and he had me in a headlock.

"I've still got a dodgy neck to this day and I'm convinced it was from that headlock. But it was all part of the craic. I liked them all, my players. People would say: 'You can't manage like that' but the players knew when we were being real. I didn't mind them calling me Harry or whatever. I grew up with many of them at Wimbledon so they knew me anyway. It was a difficult way to manage but it worked for me and it helped build things. You've got to be in control and they've got to know when you're playing and when you're not, but it's about accepting that people have characters."

Bassett was routinely jumped by his Dons players as he ran around Wimbledon Common, and thrown in puddles, while physio Derek French still remembers all too vividly the experience of being hung over the side of a boat on the way to Finland. Years later, new signing Alan Kelly had a rumble with his manager to help get out the frustration of an error in a reserve game the night before. "We were on the coach to a Premier League game and Harry got on, slapped me around the back of the head and asked: 'Do you want some?' I said: 'Yeah, actually I think I do … bad result last night," so we had a quick two-minute scrap. He'd often appear at the back of the bus with his hair ruffled and clothes all over the place because he'd been kicked from pillar to post by Brads and the rest. It was just cute management, for me. All about fostering team spirit."

Another player remembered Bassett coming onto the team coach a bit tipsy after sampling a whiskey or two in the home boardroom, "so a couple of times the lads took him to the back of the bus and beat the crap out of him. They were shit coaches with a bed at the back, which Deansy used to lie on, and Harry got beat up on them a few times." Once, on the way to an away game at Liverpool, Bassett was late onto the bus and was subsequently stripped by some of his players, who threw his clothes through the skylight in the roof somewhere on the M62. "He had the hump with us after that," laughed striker Peter Duffield. "I think he had one sock left, his boxers and a shirt with one button left. I think we stayed at the Hilton but wherever it was, he walked into the lobby with his briefcase, in his boxers and with one sock on. Can you imagine that now?"

That wasn't Bassett's only punishment for keeping his players waiting on the coach, either; he was also hit in the pocket. Fined by the minute if he was late, there was often a considerable sum finding its way into the pot as the coach snaked back towards Bramall Lane from an away game, usually via a fish and chip shop and an off licence. Another of French's many jobs was to collect the coach's food order and one can only imagine the horror of today's sports scientists at the thought of professional footballers scoffing fried chicken or fish and chips – with mushy peas, of course – in the early hours of the morning on the way home from an away game.

Hours earlier, French had helped fuel the players pre-match by ordering a round of ham and cheese sandwiches from the legendary Bri and Irene's sandwich shop on the corner of Shoreham Street and Cherry Street. "That was another one of my jobs," he smiled. "There was no one else to do it. Now, you see teams with so many members of staff… I don't know how they all fit on the coach."

Bonding Bassett's group was not a process that happened overnight though, with something of a north/south divide opening up between some of the players. In one corner were the local and northern lads, in the other the cheeky Cockneys who had been brought up by Bassett, and in the early days some players remember a squad that was rather fractured. Things came to a head on one of the frequent army camps that Bassett organised to bring his team together, as French remembered a physical altercation between two players. "It was really quite scary at the time," he said. "Then on the way home, we stopped to get some fish and chips and everyone just suddenly started laughing at something one of the lads had said. Everything just calmed down from that moment on. Me and John Greaves have scratched our heads ever since and we don't know exactly why."

In a way it didn't matter as the end goal had been achieved, although it didn't stop the north-v-south training matches on Friday afternoons being contested as if the players were in an FA Cup final. The only miracle is that more were not ruled out of the weekend's game with injuries sustained from a full-blooded tackle from a teammate. But Bassett loved every minute, going from one team to the other beforehand and winding them up. "These Cockney wankers all think they're better than you," he'd say to the northerners, before wandering over to the other side. "I've heard the northern boys are beating you up … are you really going to let that happen?"

Goalkeeper Simon Tracey was one of the southerners to make the trip up from SW17 and integrate into the United squad. "Harry wanted the group to be together," he said. "You've got to remember that a lot of people had come up from London and a lot were single or had time on their hands. We didn't have many friends or knew a lot of people up here, so our friends were the players. In training, you'd have to earn your day off, because Harry was massively into his fitness. He didn't have the greatest bunch but he knew we had to be fitter than the opposition.

"So we had Wednesdays off but you wouldn't be out playing golf because you'd be recovering from the work you did on the Tuesday.

Thursday and Friday saw a lot of tactical work, a lot of standing around and the last thing on Friday was that little game of north-v-south. Players didn't hold back; we were let loose for like five or six minutes each way and you wouldn't believe how quickly it would go. But it was probably for the best because if it lasted for any longer, Harry wouldn't have had any players for the Saturday. The outfield players would kick lumps out of each other."

The state of United's training ground was one of the big culture shocks from Bassett's move north. United trained at the Ball Inn sports ground and Bassett remembers it as a "mudheap," quickly orchestrating a move to the University of Sheffield pitches at Warminster Road. The wind up there could be biting on a cold day but the surfaces were much better than the Ball Inn, which Bassett rated as worse than Wimbledon's facilities at the time. "We looked after the groundsman at Warminster who always found a pitch for us, and it became an improvement," Bassett said. "We changed at Bramall Lane and drove there. But a lot of clubs in those days did that. There was coaching, but not a lot of coaching. There was a lot of physical running so if it was wet the players just did a physical session, rather than working on structuring a team on set-plays and things like that with a full pitch."

Kevin Gage couldn't believe the state of his new club's training facilities when he joined United later in the journey from Aston Villa. "They were absolutely dreadful," he said. "We used to take it in turns to drive up to Warminster Road after getting changed at Bramall Lane, four in a car, in your little car schools with the same people. We'd drive down this rickety little track and park on a verge, so people could get past and park after us. It was like a park pitch, on a hillside as well that sloped. The grass was too long for proper football training and there were areas that we couldn't use, but we used to get on with it. There were rugby pitches there as well but they were marked out all over the place, not in straight lines or anything, and we couldn't use that either. The rugby pitch was on the second level and on the top level was the best pitch, because the rain used to drain down the hill. I must have trained on that top pitch half a dozen times in four years.

"We weren't allowed on there often because it belonged to the university. So we'd drive past the best pitch, which we couldn't use, and then the rugby pitch, which was nice too. Then down the end of this track to where we had to train, on this park pitch. At the end of the session we were caked in mud and sometimes soaking wet, and had to climb back in the car to go back for a shower. If someone hadn't had the foresight to put some towels in the car then all their seats would be messed up. It was just horrendous. Bassett used to sometimes go on about the fact that no one stayed behind and did extra training, but it was impossible. You wouldn't get a lift back, for starters, because your car school would have gone! So it didn't work.

"We shouldn't have been successful, really. If the weather was too bad, we used to go inside the sports hall, which was at the top of the Bramall Lane car park. To say it was dilapidated would be a massive understatement. These days it would be astroturf but back then it was carpet on the floor, which was all uneven and roughed up and not fitted properly. The roof leaked so there would be puddles of water everywhere if it had been raining. It was horrible, but it was indoors and you could get a bit of training done if the weather was rubbish. Looking back, I'm surprised we were allowed to go in there at all. I'm sure health and safety would have condemned it in an instant if they'd seen it, and it was probably full of asbestos for all we knew. So we had no training facilities whatsoever, really. It's amazing we had the success we did.

"At Wimbledon we used the council facilities to train but they were fantastic. We all had our own changing areas, there was a little café next door and a little meeting room upstairs where we used to watch videos and stuff like that. The training pitch itself was not fantastic quality but it was certainly good enough. Then at Aston Villa, Bodymoor Heath had state-of-the-art facilities. The cafeteria, gym, a little five-a-side pitch. Wonderful facilities. And then I went to Sheffield United and it was like Sunday League football. When you look back, it's unbelievable. You think: 'Fucking hell, did we put up with that?'"

***

As a young man obsessed with all things Sheffield United, Steve Thompson can still vividly remember being mesmerised by the glow of the Bramall Lane floodlights as he arrived at college on Granville Road on Tuesdays. Their lure proved so strong that he eventually quit his course so he could go and watch his beloved Blades, who later released him after an unsuccessful trial and before his football career began in non-league. But he bounced back and by 1988, three months after his 33rd birthday, he was under those same floodlights as a United player, having been brought in from Leicester City's reserves by manager Dave Bassett as extra defensive cover.

Less than a decade later Thompson was back at Bramall Lane again, this time as a coach, and after a period of turmoil which saw the resignation of Nigel Spackman in 1997, he took caretaker charge of his boyhood club for their FA Cup semi-final defeat against Newcastle United. Walking out at a packed Old Trafford, the sight of thousands of Blades supporters behind one goal brought tears to Thompson's eyes. "Playing for United and then managing them … I can die a happy man," he said. "Get me in City Road cemetery. I'll be alright."

Thompson's delight at signing for United under Bassett was short-lived. Driving in on his first day he stopped for a newspaper from the local stand before making his way into the Bramall Lane car park, followed by a policeman on a motorbike who noticed he wasn't wearing a seatbelt. "It was only across the road," Thompson pleaded, to no avail. As a last throw of the dice he mentioned he played for United, but the policeman was a Wednesdayite and Thompson was fined and got three points.

Later that day he was returning to his mum's house when he was cut up by another car on the Parkway and swerved to avoid it. A police car pulled him over and Thompson told the officer that United were playing Fulham the following night. "Looks like you've got your three points a day early, then," the policeman said. Another Wednesday fan. Six points in a day. At least Thompson could raise a smile as he watched his new side beat Fulham 1-0, with Brian Deane on the scoresheet.

Thompson's only United goal came in a 2-1 win over Northampton on April 15, 1989 – a day seared into Sheffield football infamy as 97 Liverpool fans were killed at their FA Cup semi-final against Nottingham Forest at Hillsborough. It is a sad footnote to what should have been a joyous memory for a man who was no stranger to tragedy.

Thompson was playing for Lincoln City on the day of the Bradford City fire on May 11, 1985, which claimed 56 lives and caused 265 injuries. Ignited by a lit cigarette dropped onto paper and debris underneath a wooden Valley Parade stand, the fire spread rapidly with burning wood and other flammable materials falling from the roof onto the crowd below. In less than four minutes the entire main stand had been engulfed in flames as Thompson and his fellow players watched on in horror. "They ushered us off the pitch and there was a local pub just opposite the ground, where we all sat in our kits," Thompson recalled.

"The Bradford lads were obviously all concerned for their relatives that had come to celebrate and we were watching the flames on the TV. We travelled back to Lincoln on another team bus because ours had been burnt by the fire and we kept hearing: 'One's dead, now two are dead.' It kept rising and rising. Two of the guys who died were from Lincoln, Bill Stacey and Jim West, so Lincoln named one of their stands in their memory. You don't expect people to die at football matches."

Just over a fortnight later Thompson experienced another brush with death. Lincoln's squad had travelled to Magaluf for a post-season trip and after a cable in his apartment lift snapped, Thompson was on the British Airtours flight that overshot the runway at Leeds Bradford airport and crashed into an embankment with more than 400 people on board. "They used to call me 'Lucky Jim,'" Thompson said ruefully. "Now they just call me 'Jim.'" At the time of the interview, he hadn't stepped foot in a plane in 10 years.

His time at United offers better memories. "Harry liked a beer but he knew when you'd been out," he laughed. "He'd come over in training and go: 'What was Josephine's like last night, Thommo?' You would run through brick walls for him and he fostered this spirit where we knew that if anyone did beat us, they had to be really good and really earn it."

Thompson had to be patient but got his chance towards the end of the 1988/89 season and at one point played 21 successive games, including a man-of-the-match performance in a 4-1 win over Blackpool on February 25. In the build-up to the game Thompson was involved in a car crash and had to have 15 stitches in his head. "Nowhere that will harm you, then," said Bassett when Thompson told him. He was cleared to play against Blackpool and partnered Paul Stancliffe at the heart of defence as United eased to victory. "Lads who had been man-of-the-match before had been getting crystal decanters and things like that," Thompson smiled. "They announced my name in the VIP place and I went up and got a Halford's car set."

4

PERFECT 10

As he passed away his Saturday nights collecting glasses in a nightclub in Leeds, ruing the devastating injury that he thought had ruined what had promised to be a promising football career, dreams of First Division football and England recognition were exactly that for a young Brian Deane. "I used to sweep a petrol station as well," he recalled. "They were very harsh but good lessons. It made me really want to succeed. I wouldn't say I'm massively religious, it's a very individual thing, but I have an unshakable belief that I am here for a reason and my faith, going to church, really helped me. I had something to focus on. I was either going to make it or I had to do something. I had to believe that I was going to be somebody."

His lasting legacy at Sheffield United, the club 30 miles south of his birthplace in Chapeltown, Leeds, shows that the faith was not misguided. Three spells, 275 games, 119 goals. Three England caps, two promotions, the first-ever Premier League goal. A world away from those early days.

But it could all have been so different. Deane was a teenager playing for Yorkshire Amateurs when he broke his tibia and fibula, and dislocated his ankle for good measure. The injury came against a club from Chapeltown, Mandela, and Deane can still remember grown men in their fifties on the sidelines, seemingly angry that he had "moved on" from his hometown club, offering wagers to anyone who could break his leg. As fate transpired a bad tackle, from behind as Deane raced away on goal, ended up doing exactly that, although Deane bore no malice to the perpetrator. What followed was eight months of rehabilitation, with four months of a pot up to his hip, and the growing realisation that his career could be over before it had even begun.

Deane's story began at St James's University Hospital, commonly known as *Jimmy's* after the long-running *ITV* documentary filmed at the hospital between 1987 and 1997. He attended Allerton Grange school in his home city, with David Batty in the year below and the celebrated artist Damien Hirst also amongst its notable alumni. Allerton Grange was primarily a rugby school but the young Deane found the sport boring and instead concentrated on football, with an interest in athletics and table tennis on the side. The early football focus caused some friction when he had made the Leeds Boys side and, with a headstrong mindset from young, threatened to leave the school before his mum smoothed things over.

Mr. and Mrs. Deane came over from the Caribbean in the 1960s and settled in the UK. There was no pressure on the youngster's shoulders from his parents, despite his early promise, and he was fortunate enough to be able to view football as more of a hobby than a chore. Even when he made it as a top-flight footballer Deane's mum still worried whether he was eating enough, while his dad could not contain his pride at reading about his son's exploits in the newspaper. A signed photo on the wall of the family home in Chapeltown thanked his parents for their support, while Deane never liked his mum coming to games at night, worrying she would be too cold. Instead, she listened to many games on the radio, pacing around with nerves, and sometimes felt like calling into *BBC Radio Sheffield's Praise and Grumble* phone-in to correct anyone who dared criticise her son. His mum sadly passed away on one of Deane's birthdays, a tragic occurrence that has had a profound effect on him in the years since.

Family was, and remains, incredibly important to Deane, and as a youngster he was also heavily influenced by his older brothers Steven and Tony. The three played football for hours on a small rec near the family home and at first, the older siblings told Brian that he wasn't big enough to play with them – something that soon changed when he grew up to become a 6ft 3in adult. Tony's advice, to use a tennis ball to develop his use of either foot, also stood Deane in good stead and goals galore for Leeds Boys and Yorkshire Amateurs had him dreaming of a career in the game. The next step was a trial at Leeds but, at 13, he was one of the youngest hopefuls and subsequently stuck on the wing, unable to show off his prowess in front of goal. Then, after the broken leg, he feared his chance had gone.

"It wasn't an easy time," Deane admitted. "I'd stayed on in school and was collecting glasses. It gave me a real hunger to do more. People don't always mean it but sometimes the way people treat you when doing a job like that … it gave me a humility as well, to treat everyone the same. It made me realise I had to give everything I had to be in control of my own destiny."

Deane refused to give up hope completely, but combined his football with a BTEC business diploma at Leeds City college before writing to Doncaster Rovers to request a trial. Dave Blakey, the scout at Leeds from his first try-out, was by that point working for Rovers and invited Deane over to Doncaster. Doubly determined to seize his second chance, Deane this time shone and was offered a professional contract at 17 by new manager Dave Cusack, who he still regards as one of the biggest influences on how his life panned out. "I'm very lucky to have someone like Dave," said Deane – even if his mentor did feel the full force of the striker's elbow in an early training session.

After what he described as a "nightmare" debut, in which he felt like collapsing after 10 minutes because of nerves, a teenage Deane got to grips with life at Rovers and of the 40 goals they mustered as a team in their 1987/88 Third Division relegation season, their young striker had scored 10 on his own. The contract he was subsequently offered to stay did not tally up with Deane's standing in the side, he felt, and he turned to Cusack, who had by that point left Rovers, to help guide him in his next steps. "We didn't have agents then and all that rubbish," said Deane.

"There was no U21s football either, where kids get spoon-fed and looked after. It was chucked in the deep end stuff. It was a big man's league, the Third Division, and it was a great development for me. I was a tall, skinny, rangy kid and I was only going to get more physical as I got older and a bit more mature. Dave prepared me for what a senior changing room was going to be like and told me that I had to deal with it. If I'd gone to Sheffield United having been spoon-fed, then it would have been a rude awakening."

There was a flirtation of interest from Sheffield Wednesday while Deane was at Rovers and it was in the Steel City, albeit on the other side, that he would make his footballing name, after Cusack had assured Bassett that Deane was better than his former Wimbledon striker John Fashanu. A partnership with Tony Agana began with three goals between them in an 8-1 friendly victory at Skegness Town on their first experience of playing together and they didn't look back, taking Division Three and then two by storm to reach the top of the football pyramid.

"I just felt that I wasn't going to settle for nothing. That's what it was, I think," Deane said. "Having goals means ones that are achievable as long as you don't set the bar too high. They've got to be realistic and you can use them as stepping stones. You don't aim to go from zero to 100 straight away and one of the things that's an issue nowadays is that people set unrealistic goals in life. They look up to the wrong people instead of looking at what is realistic for them. It's all relative but I do feel that there's been a disconnect somewhere. We're not always as realistic as we should be.

"But, looking back, I am blessed to have played at the time I did. We did some fantastic things and when I speak to people of the similar age group or a bit older, they've had kids who've told their kids and they might have seen bits and pieces of me playing. And it's always nice, I'm not going to lie. I've got two young kids myself, and they're not old enough to really understand that I used to play football so it's a little bit strange for them. I look back and wish I'd kept certain bits of memorabilia. I managed to keep a lot of my shirts; my mum kept a lot of clippings and you can see some of my goals on *YouTube*."

Even before such technological advancements Deane clipped up videos of his best moments on VHS, setting them to music and replaying them before games. Perhaps it was a tactic to try and counter the imposter syndrome that punctuated his career. He can vividly remember watching back footage of his iconic hat-trick in United's hammering of Chester City in September 1988, and seriously expecting to see someone else on the tape.

That 6-1 win, which also saw strike partner Agana score three as a formidable strike partnership began to form, was a turning point for Deane. "The kind of game where me and the fans became married. Those goals, you don't see goals like that now. That was *me* scoring them. *Was that really me who did that?*

"That's why I look back and think I could have achieved more. That's not me being greedy or being bitter; I just never believed in myself as much as I should have done. I think a lot of that goes back to being younger, when I didn't get a realistic chance before I was dismissed. I'd written to clubs for trials, I'd been rejected as a kid by five or six clubs, and that doubt followed me. Even when I was achieving. My brother met Gary Pallister once on holiday and he said: 'I don't think your kid knows how good he can be.' That was after I'd played for England and all the rest. So that's why I look back with regrets. My brother is more of a showman and maybe if I had some of that in me, that charisma, I perhaps could have achieved a lot more.

"I really wish I could have had Dave Cusack all the way through my career, just as someone on my shoulder to say: 'Look Brian, you're better than you think you are.' Even when I was playing with England, there were times I didn't believe I belonged there. Some of that was because you had five players from Arsenal and five from Man United, and no one talked to each other. So a lot of times you'd be left isolated. You'd go down for your dinner and no one would talk to you. So it could be difficult.

"It was also the time when Paul Gascoigne was coming in, and he was a huge star. All the focus was on that, so anyone on the periphery just faded away. I was in a lot of squads and a lot of stand-bys but it just didn't materialise. And some of that was because the press and journalists were very big-club centric at the time. I look back with a bit of bitterness at that, because I think they were lazy. Because I played for Sheffield United, they thought I couldn't be any good. But it is what it is.

"I was just doing what I did and because of the way I was brought up and the values my parents instilled in me, I was just trying to give everything all the time. Everybody's different and that's not a criticism of anybody. I played until I was 38 and there are still times I look back and think I could have given more, and I regret those times. But that's just me being hypercritical of myself."

If Deane still ever has moments of self-doubt, he could do worse than speak to any Blade fortunate enough to have witnessed his first spell at Bramall Lane and soak in the adulation that would inevitably follow. Plucked from the relative obscurity of the Third Division, he became a genuine Lane legend with the ability to score all types of goals – making a mockery of the unfair and lazy "big man" tag. There were headers, as you'd expect from a player of his stature, but also a great hold-up and finish against Mansfield, a superb flicked finish over the goalkeeper from a near-post cross against Bury. Had his remarkable 45-yard lob against

Liverpool in 1991 been scored by Gascoigne or another, more "fashion-able" player of the era, it would still be shown on an endless loop to this day.

"Every goal was such a fantastic feeling, wherever it was. I never took anything like that for granted. I was happy. I do believe that footballers are happy in life when they're playing well. All the material stuff doesn't really matter; if you're playing well and scoring goals, that's all you want to do. I could be wrong, but I'm romantic and I like to think that most players are still the guy scoring in his U10s or for his school team. That's what it means.

"I'd look at the opposition before the game and think: 'Blimey, he's big or an experienced defender' but a lot of the time, they were probably looking at me and thinking: 'What am I going to get from this kid?' And I was gone. I was relatively quick and because I could use both feet, you couldn't just keep me on one side. I could go either way and I could shoot, so it was a problem."

A total of 22 league goals from 43 games in his first season at Bramall Lane was followed by 21 in 45 the following campaign – including one on the unforgettable promotion-clinching day at Leicester – as United sealed back-to-back promotions to the First Division. It got to the point where a cross would be met by a roar from the fans before it had even met the head of United's iconic No.10 in the box, such was the confidence that Deane would make the most of the chance. Even as Agana's powers began to wane, Deane continued his potency in front of goal and finished four consecutive seasons as United's top scorer.

Did the pressure of being United's main man ever weigh heavily? "It didn't really bother me. As long as I knew I had the support of the team and the manager, that was fine. There were times when that was strained, when I think I took more on and I think others should have done more. But people hide sometimes. When it's a bit tasty they think: 'It's not for me … he'll deal with that.' Sometimes you look around and there's no one there. So from that point of view, there were times when it took its toll. And I think that the lack of a plan for the next season was one of the reasons why I left. I couldn't just keep going on like that, with people taking potshots at me in the press or the odd fan saying I'm not putting it in. I'd rather be a big fish in a big pond. It's too easy to point the finger at me and everyone else can say: 'Not my problem.'"

It was the summer of 1993 when United sold the family silver for just under £3m, allowing Deane to follow the path of Mick Jones, Tony Currie and Alex Sabella before him by moving up the M1 to Leeds United and effectively signing their own Premier League death warrant in the process. At his boyhood club Deane played in the UEFA Cup and in the 1996 League Cup final at Wembley, a 3-0 defeat to Aston Villa in front of 77,000. But despite the emotional ties of being back in his hometown he could not establish the same connection with Leeds that he had enjoyed with United, and returned to his footballing spiritual home in the summer of 1997. His partnership with fellow striker Jan Åage Fjørtoft spearheaded a promotion push, before both strikers were sold on a day still known to Unitedites as "Black Thursday." Boss Nigel Spackman resigned in protest after his promising side was steadily dismantled and United, unsurprisingly, didn't recover.

Fittingly, Deane's playing career came to an end at Bramall Lane, after a third spell in 2005/06 and a cameo role in the Blades' promotion back to the top-flight for the first time since his first stint. "I didn't contribute as much as I'd have liked to, the third time round, but it was a fitting end," Deane said. "I wouldn't have wanted to finish my career anywhere else, so I'm very grateful for that. But I also feel like I made a huge contribution to the foundations of the club as well. So we all got something out of it.

"It sounds corny but I just try to be a better person every day. When you've had the sort of experiences someone like me has had, it's not good to bottle all that up. I've spent time with some of the biggest managers and played with some of the best players in the world. But I know the door is always open for me at Bramall Lane, and that's nice. I'm a servant of the club. I look at it that way. I'm always grateful to come and do things. I've been blessed but I'm also grateful that I had the opportunities. If it wasn't for football then it would have been very difficult for someone like me, growing up when I did, to get to the top of whatever. For different reasons. So being empowered by the gift that God gave me, and being able to express myself and have a good passing of time, has been very important to me.

"Sheffield United was the happiest time of my playing career. When I was there at 20, I was just living the dream. Literally. Then you get a bit older and other things start coming in, but that whole era was just fantastic. The manager was good, the players were good and the staff were brilliant. We were one big happy family, and the fans have always been really good to me. I felt as though I knew every fan, and every blade of grass at Bramall Lane."

Being a prominent black footballer in that era was not all plain sailing however and when asked about his experiences of racism, Deane took a heavy pause to collect himself. "Yeah, it was tough," he said. "I remember going to an England get-together with Ian Wright and Les Ferdinand and talking about it. They were saying we had to be better to get anywhere. It was like being in a boxing match and having to knock someone out to get a draw. Black players leading the line wasn't something people wanted to see at that time, I don't think. People will ask: 'What's he on about?' but I know it, because I lived that life.

"It was difficult at times. But we were more resilient I think, because of what we'd gone through in the 1980s and as kids. It affected us less. You had to have rhino skin, with some of the things that used to be said and all the rest of it. Even some of the unconscious bias and prejudices at the time, we had to deal with it. It was simple. A lot of the time it was about controlling but it is what it is. I firmly believe that you get dealt a hand, and you have to make the best of that hand sometimes. The only person you're going to harm is yourself if you don't get the best out of your career and life. You can't get time back. It was tough, but do you know what? I'm proud of what I am. I've always been extremely proud to be a black man."

In 2024, every player in the top four English leagues carried an anti-racism or anti-discrimination message on their shirts, while the Premier League runs regular education efforts aimed at eradicating racism from the game. Fans are encouraged to report abuse and specialist charities like Kick It Out work towards positive change. Players have begun simply walking off the field if they are subjected to racist chanting; in February 2024, a 24-year-old so-called football fan called Ryan Ferguson was jailed for nine months after pleading guilty to racially abusing Forest Green Rovers winger Jordan Garrick.

Society still has its share of knuckle-dragging neanderthals but football at least seems to have come a long way since the 1980s, when photographer Bob Thomas captured an unforgettable image of Liverpool's John Barnes kicking away a banana thrown at him by an Everton supporter.

The emergence of Deane and Agana as terrace heroes, as well as contributions from the likes of Francis Joseph and David Barnes, undoubtedly helped break down barriers at Bramall Lane but in a decade when far-right groups used football as a mechanism to spread their hateful message and attract new recruits, boos and vile chants aimed at black players were frequently heard at away grounds.

Deane's first negative experience came much earlier, as a teenager after a game for Leeds City Boys in the north-east. The youngster had just walked into the local working men's club and was quickly noticed by a man playing pool. "He just looked up and said: 'You black bastard,'" Deane recalled. "I was just a small kid, and I just froze. Everyone else in the room was white, and those things used to happen. Regularly. The one way you could pay people back was by scoring goals, dominating the opposition. It doesn't make it right but the problem is that there are people out there in wider society, with these unconscious biases that people don't want to face."

Deane had a crack at management in Norway, with newly-promoted Norwegian top-flight team Sarpsborg 08, and kept them up in his first season before reaching the semi-finals of the Norwegian Cup in his second. He was thrown in the air by his jubilant players after victory in their final game and, keen to continue his managerial career, he returned to England. "No one would talk to me," he said. "Even after my experiences of playing abroad with Benfica, going abroad to manage, playing for all these clubs and having a decent CV ... I rang a chief exec to ask if I could be considered and he gave me lip service. I thought: 'Do I want this for the rest of my life?'

"We'd better get real, because these are the questions that people need to reflect on. Try putting yourself in someone else's shoes and understand what their journey is. There are some harsh questions but at the end of the day, someone like myself and others have been lost to football because someone doesn't like the way I look. I haven't had a chance to go into a boardroom and tell people my views. I've not had the chance to show them that I'm the same as them, except in colour. Because people don't know how to deal with it and they're scared of what they don't know.

"To caveat that, I'm comfortable in the skin I'm in and with where I am at. I'm not here to challenge anybody. I know, when I'm with somebody, whether or not I'm the right person for them and a lot of the time I understand why that is. To fix it, I think it has to be a top-down approach, not bottom-up, and the people who have reached those heights have probably done so without having to look at too wide a spectrum.

"So usually they'll just have to look directly in front of them and think: 'I tried hard at school, I worked hard, I married the girl, I've got 2.4 kids, I'm the CFO,' or whatever it is ... they've not realised that, sometimes, the platform is set up for them to succeed more than it is for somebody else who might be different culturally. It might be gender, it might be colour, it could be even someone who's not able-bodied. We have to be more inclusive, otherwise we'll just keep getting the same people making decisions at the top. My thoughts are my own, based on what I've had to deal with in my life. It's as simple as that."

5

THE BLADES BOUNCE BACK

As Brian Deane turned the corner of Cherry Street and squeezed his brown Opel Kadett through the narrow entrance and into the Bramall Lane car park, he instantly fell in love. One of his first football mentors, Dave Cusack, was in the passenger seat with him to see a man who would become another big influence on his life. "I'll never forget it," Deane said. "It was a magical moment."

At the time Bruce Springsteen was preparing for his legendary Bramall Lane concert and Deane knew that Sheffield United was where he wanted to be. Manager Dave Bassett, searching for a strike partner for Tony Agana, had been tipped off about Deane and liked what he had seen when going to scout him. Deane was 20 years old and still very raw, but the potential was obvious. And after overcoming the setbacks he had to reach even that point, he was determined to eke every ounce out of his career.

"If I didn't sign for the club there and then, I'd have been so gutted," he said. "I'm the kind of person who has always bought refurbished houses to live in, and this was like going into a brand-new house for me."

Deane made an early return to Doncaster Rovers not long after signing for the Blades, coming off the bench in a 0-0 Yorkshire and Humberside Cup draw that prompted chairman Reg Brealey to express his concern to boss Bassett about where the goals were going to come from that season. As the Deane and Agana partnership clicked into gear, and Unitedites hailed their new heroes with a new terrace anthem to the tune of *The Magic Song* from the Disney film *Cinderella*, Brealey soon got his answer.

Brian Deane and Tony Agana, bibbidi-bobbidi-boo ... Put them together and what have you got? Top of Division Two...

The pair became the most iconic strike duo in United's recent history, with the subtle varieties in their game perfectly complementing each other. The left-footed Agana was a little shorter and quicker, with his pace and power seeing him utilised as a left winger at Watford before being banished to the reserves after Bassett's departure, while Deane, at 6ft 3in tall, was more physical, albeit with more technical ability than he was given credit for and was stronger on his right boot.

Agana was almost four-and-a-half years Deane's senior but had made his Football League bow late, at 23 after coming up through non-league and working for an insurance company, while Deane had earned his Doncaster Rovers debut as a teenager and was actually more experienced in terms of first-team football. That led to the situation where the elder statesman was often asking for advice and pointers from the younger buck, only further boosting Deane's confidence and strengthening their bond.

Deane was well aware of Agana's exploits and qualities from his time at Watford, reading about him in *Shoot* magazine, while Agana didn't know a thing about his new strike partner. But they soon hit it off with a partnership that delivered 72 goals in its first season, becoming synonymous with the Bassett era – despite not actually being the manager's first-choice pairing.

Bassett initially played Deane alongside Francis Joseph early in the season but the former Wimbledon man suffered an untimely injury on his league debut for the Blades at Reading, after he had scored. Deane and Agana got the nod for the first time together in a competitive game in United's next outing, a League Cup tie in front of just over 2,000 fans at Hartlepool, and both found the back of the net. It was the start of something truly special.

"It was almost by default, really, that me and Tony got together, because of Joe's injury," said Deane. "And then we just kind of clicked, frighteningly. It was perfect because he was left-footed, I was right-footed, he was extremely quick and he could score goals. If you're a forward and not scoring, it's good if the other one is because it takes the pressure off you a little. We complemented each other. He flicked stuff on for me and I flicked stuff on for him. I liked to go wide and cross things in and he did the same. It was like a mirror.

"I learned a lot from him. I was still growing into my body then. A couple of years later I went on the weights and got a lot stronger and more powerful, but Tony had that all-round balance.

"There were times when he was unplayable. He was unpredictable and it just worked. Teams couldn't cope with us. We had a lot of joy. We could see that it was mentally draining for defenders to be up against us and that was a new sensation for me. At one stage in that first season I'd scored more than Tony but for the last 10 games, he basically carried me. I had just turned 21 and I was still developing. My personality was still immature and Tony, for those last few games, was immense."

The pair were – and remain – great friends as well as teammates but the friendly rivalry also drove both men on. In the September of that season Deane had endured something of a dry spell, going four games without a goal and watching his pal net three in the same period. Bassett had noticed a bit of tension in his young striker and after pulling him to one side, told Deane to just go out at the weekend and enjoy himself.

There were some slightly harsher words from Deane's brother Steven, who told him to get his finger out and that he had to keep scoring. Deane remains unsure whether it was the carrot or the stick that did the job but he ran riot in his next game, scoring a first half hat-trick against Chester City and missing three easier chances to potentially walk off at the break with six goals to his name. Not to be outdone, Agana scored three times as well in the second half as United ran out 6-1 winners on one of the most memorable days of a remarkable season.

It was far from a two-man show, however. Bassett's ability to spot a bargain saw him bring in winger Ian Bryson in the summer, the flying Scotsman who was juggling playing part-time with Kilmarnock with working on his parents' farm, while Alan Roberts provided ammunition from the right. "I was on trial before I signed and we went to Sweden," Bryson said. "The likes of Wally Downes and some of the other old Wimbledon boys were around, and the stuff they were doing was unbelievable. One night Harry left his hotel key lying around and everything in his room ended up in one of the lifts.

"I remember thinking, as a very naïve 25-year-old Scotsman who had just come down: 'What the hell is going on here?' I had never seen anything like it. To be fair, a big centre-forward called Paul Williams half warned me, and said: 'Keep an eye out and keep yourself to yourself.' It was good advice. As you went on you came to understand that that was part of Harry's philosophy of keeping everyone together. We worked hard together and enjoyed the off-field stuff as well. He always said he wasn't bothered what happened during the week, as long as we turned up on a Saturday and performed. And he was true to his word. That's how he got the best out of his players."

Defender Steve Thompson remembered Bassett having a habit of bringing off Roberts late in games, much to the winger's annoyance. Until one game. "I looked at the Bramall Lane clock in one game and said to Rob: 'Off you pop, it's your 15 minutes left.' He smiled at me and said that it wasn't. It was the days before the electronic substitution boards, when they had cards in wallets, and would put his number seven up. But that day he'd put the number seven card in the boot of his car. I told him they'd just go to the away dugout and use that one instead. 'No they won't,' he replied, 'because I took that one as well!'"

Eight wins and 28 goals in their opening 10 games saw United top of the table. At the other end of the pitch captain Paul Stancliffe, who was one of the few players to have survived the close-season Bassett cull, was establishing himself as a key figure, while another familiar face to the manager from Wimbledon, Graham Benstead, began the season as first-choice goalkeeper.

"We were all on three, four or five hundred quid a week … all on the same level and singing from the same hymn sheet," Benstead remembered. "There might have been a couple of hundred quid between us but not a lot of difference. Now there'll be lads on £50,000 a week and others on £100,000 which, in my opinion, can lead to a bit of resentment. The money side was well down the list in my day."

Not that it didn't matter. Most United players' contracts, like that of their manager, were heavily incentivised for positive results, and one first-teamer from the time readily admits now that a good run of wins made a big difference in their pay packets at the end of the month. In 1988, according to the Office for National Statistics, the average weekly pay for a male in the UK between the ages of 25-29 was £225 – so United's players were not quite on the comparative breadline but were hardly drowning in riches, either.

They were a group of hungry young men, drilled to within an inch of

THE BLADES BOUNCE BACK

their lives to become a relentless and effective unit. They had discovered the taste of success, of adulation from a crowd who were steadily rediscovering the bug. And on top of all that, three points at the weekend meant a few more quid in their back pockets. It was a dynamic that saw a group already hungry for points become, as the season rumbled on, positively ravenous.

***

As he tossed his gear into a bag and made his way out of Griffin Park, Bob Booker's head was spinning. His Brentford side had just been on the wrong end of a 4-1 home defeat to a rampant Sheffield United and Booker, in his 31st year and battling a perennially-troublesome knee injury, had struggled badly against United's midfield pair of Simon Webster and Mark Todd. Tony Agana had netted twice to take his tally to seven in five league starts for the season, and United – top of the early table with five wins from their opening six league games – were flying.

Booker shared a journey home after the game with his long-time friend and United physio Derek French. The two had grown up in the same area of London and played for the same amateur side, Bedmond Social FC. "We just chatted away in the car and I said: 'You've got a hell of a team there,'" Booker said. "We got smashed that day.

"They just got the ball forward … Deane and Agana up front … Alan Roberts and Ian Bryson on the wings … Toddy and Simon Webster in the middle … Stancliffe, Chrissy Wilder, Martin Pike … it was a formidable team, and they were on fire." There was a brief boost in Booker's mood when French told him that Bassett had earmarked him as the Brentford dangerman from set-pieces. "Got that one wrong, didn't he?" French added, bringing his old pal right back down to earth.

How quickly things can change. Later that year, United travelled to Mansfield for an FA Cup tie and Webster suffered a horrendous broken leg after dangling it into a teammate's tackle. Todd can still remember the shocked look on the "daft enthusiastic chuff's" face as he lay stricken on the Field Mill turf, with all around him avoiding the temptation to look at his badly mangled leg. French described it as one of the worst injuries he had ever seen in football. Webster had nine pins inserted to strengthen the double-fracture and then suffered an issue with his blood

circulation which, in a process which sounds more like a medieval tor-
ture method than a legitimate treatment method, saw doctors cut open
his calf muscle and leave it exposed for two weeks, before closing up the
wound using skin taken off his thigh.

At the time Bassett liked a balance in the middle of his midfield – one
physical player, like Webster, and one more technical like Todd. The
absence of Webster, a six-foot tall midfielder signed by Bassett from
Huddersfield who had been a virtual ever-present until his injury, meant
United had a hole to fill. Scanning the leagues and dusting off their well-
thumbed contacts book, United's coaching staff settled on the name of
Booker.

Bassett had tried to sign Booker before, when he was in charge of
Wimbledon, and decided to have another go, with French tasked with
making contact this time and exploring whether his old friend would be
interested in coming up to Sheffield for a chat with Bassett. "What for?"
was the initial response. Booker, based on both his own situation and
French's reputation, thought his mate was on the wind-up.

"We didn't have agents in those days so I jumped in the car with my
dad," Booker said. "I pulled into Bramall Lane and it was a bit daunting,
to be honest. No disrespect to Brentford but it was a small ground in a
built-up area and when you turn up at Bramall Lane, it was something
else. It knocked you back. Mick Rooker, who I ended up being very good
friends with, came out and met me in reception and took me through
to Harry's office. I went in and me and my dad sat down and Harry said:
'How do you feel about coming and joining us?'

"I remember saying: 'Sorry, Harry?' He just said again that he wanted
me to come and join them. It was all very flattering but I just said: 'My
knee, Harry.' He said: 'Don't worry about your knee. I'll get Frenchy to
look after you, get you some one-on-one. We'll look after you and get
you fit.'"

Booker remembered in his biography that he earned £225 a week at
Brentford, plus bonuses, at the time and the United offer was £350 a
week – rising automatically to £375 if the Blades were promoted – plus
a £12,500 signing-on fee, paid in four instalments, and a £2,000 promotion bonus if United went up and he had played 15 games. On top of that
he would receive a goal bonus of £50 if he scored, and £25 if United kept
a clean sheet. There was also a travel and accommodation allowance of

£100 per week, for 25 weeks, plus up to £1,000 in moving costs. Booker had earned £60 a week from his first Brentford contract, and worked during the summer for a mate who owned a builders' yard to top up his income. Once he unloaded a ton or so of sand onto a customer's drive before discovering it was the wrong house and had to shovel it all back onto the lorry again. Suddenly, with one phone call, his life had taken an altogether different turn.

"My head was spinning a little and I asked Harry if I could go and have a chat with my dad," Booker added. "We walked down the tunnel, looked out towards the Kop and the hairs on the back of my neck went up. There was a bit of silence and then it was a bit like the scene in *Only Fools and Horses* when Del Boy and Rodney become millionaires. I asked my dad: 'Do you want to go first or me?' and he said: 'Let's go together.' So we just hugged each other, and I started to bawl my eyes out like the soppy git that I am. He said: 'Listen, son. You've been in the lower leagues all your life … get in there and sign that contract.' I went back and said: 'Harry, I'm all yours.'"

Booker joined a United side that had comfortably been in the top two for much of the first half of the season, before a mini-wobble around the turn of the year saw them lose three in four and allow Port Vale to edge them out of the automatic promotion places. Their only win over the festive period came on Boxing Day and even that 4-1 victory over Notts County came at a cost, with Brian Deane sent off for lashing out at defender Nicky Law. It was an uncharacteristic moment for a player seen as something of a gentle giant, and all part of the learning curve for a young striker still finding his feet at senior level.

"Nicky just kept coming through the back of me," Deane said, "and I just got sick of it. He went through me one time too many and I just smashed him with an elbow, and got sent off. I wasn't proud of myself. I thought I'd really let the boys down. But it turned out we'd won 4-1, so I didn't feel as bad. I didn't get fined, either, because it wasn't worth being fined in those days!

"Looking back, I tend to be grateful that I played in an era when defenders were proper defenders. They defended, and you had to be a character to deal with the way they did that. Teams who are watching you will try to label you with this and that, saying things like I don't like it when I get kicked, and then I'd just get kicked more and more.

"So I just thought: 'Nah, this isn't happening anymore.' I decided to give as good as I got and then, when you start getting a reputation like that, as someone who can't be messed with, you're allowed to play again. Because no one wants to try and take liberties. So it made me more feared, for sure."

United kicked off their centenary year of 1989 two points adrift of second-placed Vale but the Bassett juggernaut soon returned to its relentless best, as a 10-game unbeaten run, bookended by defeats to local rivals Chesterfield, saw the Blades rediscover their previous promotion form. They also reached the fifth-round of the FA Cup before bowing out with credit after a 3-2 defeat at Division One side Norwich, who would go on to reach the semi-final. Agana and Deane, who had his hotel room minibar raided the night before by Wally Downes, were both on target to show once again that they had the ability to trouble even top-flight defences, with Bassett made aware that his former chairman at Wimbledon, Sam Hammam, was willing to pay £1m – a huge sum back then – for the pair.

They were going nowhere, though, and Bassett instead turned his attention to the other end of the pitch. Wolves had seemed like runaway league winners for some time now, with the battle shaping up between Blades and Vale for who would join them in the Second Division. With six games to go, United were three points ahead in the race for second place and Bassett made a big call that could have defined the promotion battle. Benstead, No.1 all season, was out; Simon Tracey, an inexperienced 21-year-old from Wimbledon, was in.

Looking back now, Benstead can't deny that he was upset to be dropped at such a vital part of the season. "You hold your hand up if you make the odd mistake," he admitted, "but my performances over time were better than average performances. I don't think I let the lads down. When it came down to the nitty-gritty, and the shit hit the fan, and you had to go somewhere and win when the pressure was on, maybe Harry thought I couldn't take it.

"He said: 'I'm bringing Trace in, because I think he adds a bit more to this than you do, but you have a bit more of that. At this present time I want to play Trace.' He explained it to me but I was quite upset, to be honest. You never know, I could have played and done just as well as Simon had done, but I wasn't given that chance.

"I don't hold anything against him for it, though. He made the difficult decision at the time to go with Trace and as it turned out it was the right one. He did really, really well. He was brilliant. It's just one of those things. I have no grudge against Trace. Me and him sang *Bridge Over Troubled Water* at a Christmas do once.

"We'd had a couple of drinks too many and it was an absolute debacle. I think it's the only time the both of us had been booed together. But that's what we were like, and I don't have any malice against Trace. Life's too bloody short and if I'm being honest, which I am, it was the right thing to do at that time."

It wasn't a decision that reaped instant rewards, with Tracey conceding four times in his first two games as United's new first-choice and United failing to win either. But Vale failed to take advantage and overtake the Blades, who were still in pole position for promotion. Looking back years later, Tracey admitted it was a brave call from Bassett but offered his view of why it may have been made. "I had to bide my time when I first came up to Sheffield," he said of his bargain £7,500 move. "I played the odd game for a suspension or illness.

"Harry really liked the strength through the spine of his teams, so to put an inexperienced goalkeeper in for the last six games ... I thought that was a very brave decision at the time, especially when he already had an experienced No.1. We had a little bit of a wobble, too, but he felt that it was an opportunity to put me in. One thing that Harry knew about me was that I am a laid-back character, so whatever the situation I was in I never really got fazed by that. That was probably one of my strengths."

Promotion by that point was still United's to lose and they had one foot in the Second Division when they beat Aldershot 1-0 on May 1, with Vale slipping up at home to Northampton. A 5-1 thrashing of Swansea then left United needing just a point against champions Wolves in the penultimate fixture of the season. Goals from Paul Stancliffe and Agana saw the scores level at 2-2 in the dying minutes when the referee blew his whistle for a foul.

Mistaking it for the final whistle, several United players, including goalkeeper Tracey, ran to their supporters to celebrate – leaving Bassett and Co. rather panicked on the sideline. Luckily, the potential crisis was averted and both sets of fans and players could celebrate promotion when the referee actually blew for full-time. The Blades were going up. *Surely?*

A 12-goal swing in Port Vale's favour on the final day would have seen them remarkably pip United to second place and although Bassett was sure it wouldn't happen, that didn't stop him naming Benstead as a substitute just in case anything happened to Tracey at Bristol City. It didn't, and a 2-0 defeat didn't matter a jot as United's return to the second tier at the first time of asking was officially confirmed. Peter Duffield was the unfortunate fall guy, losing his place on the bench an hour before the game after Bassett had already named his squad and the forward was in it. "I can't blame him at all," the striker admitted. It was one of the few games he missed for Bassett while available.

Agana was named fans' player of the year in a season which saw him score 37 goals in 68 games in all, two more than Deane's tally from 64 appearances. The two netted 30 apiece in competitive games but Agana was keen to share the praise. "We had a good side, all in all," he said at the time.

"If you look at the 60 goals, probably 10 were individual goals; the other 50 came about by great teamwork, great wing play, midfield play, out from the defence, out from the 'keeper. Through everybody. We were playing very well as a team going forward and there were times when me and Brian weren't scoring and we had to shore it up at the back. And we did well there. It was a great season all-round, team-wise."

United's end-of-season celebrations took them to Magaluf, with Downes reporting for the airport with the clothes he was wearing and some essentials in a carrier bag. If he needed anything else in Spain, he reasoned, he'd go and buy it. The rules for United's players staying in Downes' hotel room during the trip were simple: when the sun came up, they would start drinking alcohol and they weren't allowed anything else until the sun went down again. No soft drinks, no water, no tea and no coffee. Benstead remembers fellow goalkeeper Tracey's "party piece" – downing a pitcher of wine in one go by tipping it upside down in his mouth. "I think that's what living with Wally, Francis Joseph and John Gannon does to you!" Benstead laughed.

But there was a serious side to the boozing culture of the time and more than one figure from the era independently referenced one player, still working in football all these years on, who had a drinking problem which began to affect his performance. Things came to a head when physio Derek French told Bassett, with the angry player reacting by grabbing French by the tie in the Bramall Lane social club and tearing the arms off his jacket. French remembers feeling fortunate that Billy Whitehurst was on hand to prevent the situation escalating further.

"I thought I was going to get taken apart," French admitted. "We knew he liked a drink but it was starting to affect him and everyone else was starting to talk about it, so it would have got to Harry eventually. There are certain things you have to tell him about. If someone came in in the morning after a big barney with their missus and they were going to split up, you'd have to try and be as clever as you could to try and get them through it. I wouldn't tell Harry about stuff like that … he didn't need to know unless it was affecting performance."

While his players soaked up their success in Spain, Bassett had turned his focus to reshaping his squad for another crack at the second tier and had another ex-Wimbledon man in his sights, in the shape of defender Mark Morris. The unlucky fall guy was Steve Thompson. "After promotion we went to watch Yorkshire play cricket, up at Abbeydale," he said. "I was standing on the pavilion with Harry and I said to him that I thought I'd seen Mark Morris coming up the drive. He said: 'Oh yeah, I forgot to tell you … he's taking your place and you're going back to Lincoln.'

"I asked him when he planned on telling me. 'Ah,' Harry said. 'I thought the cricket match was the best time.'"

"My goalkeeper has the brains of a rocking horse. I thought there was mad cow's disease out there."

– Dave Bassett

6

THE ADOPTED NORTHERNER

It has been well over 35 years since he received the phone call that changed the course of his life, but Simon Tracey remembers it like it was yesterday. He was 21 years old, still enjoying the comforts of living at home and on the way out of Wimbledon. A London boy who had never been north of Watford, he was mulling over an offer to join Leyton Orient when the invitation came to "have a look around" Sheffield. He drove up for the weekend and liked what he saw. That was in 1988 and to this day, Tracey remains a proud resident of the Steel City.

"I had no idea what to expect," he admitted. "If we had a family holiday when I was young it would have been down Cornwall way, or the Isle of Wight or somewhere down there. I didn't know what the north was. If I'd gone to Orient, I could have stayed with my parents. I didn't have to do anything at home. I couldn't wash, I couldn't iron. I couldn't cook. I'd never had to; I got everything on a plate. My mum did everything for me. But I saw it as an opportunity to grow up and be independent. To go and see what the big wide world was all about."

It was a decision that paid dividends, both professionally and personally. Sheffield United paid Wimbledon an initial £7,500 fee, decided by a tribunal; Tracey agreed a deal worth less than he had been offered by Orient, and what proved to be a long marriage was underway. "It wasn't about money," he reflected. "I didn't have an agent or anything – Wimbledon paid for a taxi for me to go and look around at Orient. I could have got more there, but it was about the opportunity and where I felt would give me the best chance to be successful."

The sight of Bramall Lane certainly helped sway Tracey's decision, with his former Wimbledon boss Dave Bassett setting out his ambition to get United going again. United had just been relegated in Bassett's first half-season in charge and Tracey was one of many familiar faces he turned to in a bid to kickstart his Bramall Lane revolution. Tracey may have been young but was not completely green, having been handed a baptism of fire senior debut in the 1988 Charity Shield at Wembley. It was a repeat of the previous season's FA Cup final, which had seen the Dons shock the mighty Liverpool to win the trophy, and Dave Beasant's subsequent sale to Newcastle had opened the door for 20-year-old Tracey to step in. He didn't disgrace himself in a 2-1 defeat, beaten twice by John Aldridge in front of almost 55,000 at Wembley.

Tracey's subsequent league debut in the first game of the 1988/89 season became his last appearance for the Dons – at least until a one-game loan spell in 1995. Wimbledon went 1-0 up against Arsenal through John Fashanu, but Tracey carried future United teammate Brian Marwood's cross over his own goal line for the equaliser and from there the Gunners ran riot, with Alan Smith scoring a hat-trick in a 5-1 victory. Tracey was out of the side and, amid a contract dispute, on his way north.

"Bobby Gould offered me a contract after the Charity Shield and I didn't think it reflected where the football club was. Really, for a club in the top division I thought it was pitiful and probably someone trying to exploit me, thinking I was desperate. I trusted that if I didn't get anything there, then I would somewhere else. I had enough belief in my ability to go somewhere else and start again, if needed. I think I had to play 50 games in the top division before I got an increase or any signing-on fees, which was ridiculous. So I made up my mind to turn it down and after the Arsenal game Bobby hung me out a little bit, saying: 'I bet you wish you'd have signed that contract now.'

"But I told him I wouldn't be and had no intention of signing it. I went to look around Orient and then the call came about United from Geoff Taylor, who was with Harry at United and who I knew from Wimbledon. At first I went in digs after I signed and then bought my own house. John Gannon, who was an apprentice with me at Wimbledon, came up a bit later than me and moved in. There were quite a few Londoners around, so that was a good thing for us."

Being a goalkeeper was never the plan for Tracey, who grew up in Woolwich dreaming of scoring goals for Charlton Athletic rather than saving them. The turning point was the typical story of so many goalkeepers – a boy's side lacking someone to go in goal and someone volunteering to give the gloves a go – and Tracey never looked back, joining

Wimbledon on a YTS contract before landing a professional deal under Bassett. A total of 383 professional United appearances represented exceptional value for money for the Blades and Tracey's total would have been even bigger had he not spent much of his Bramall Lane career competing for the No.1 shirt with another of the greatest 'keepers in recent United history, Alan Kelly.

In his early days, however, it was Graham Benstead who was Tracey's main competition and the youngster had to bide his time for a chance, before Bassett's big decision to change goalkeepers with the Blades going for promotion in 1988/89. A year later United repeated the trick with a famous day at Leicester City, Tracey playing every one of the 46 league games as Bassett's men secured First Division football and the goalkeeper won the first of his two player-of-the-year awards.

"It went unbelievably well for me," he said. "Sometimes when you get that success early, you don't fully enjoy it or let it really sink in. It goes too quickly, and that's probably what happened in my case. Of course I enjoyed it at the time, we all enjoyed it, but sometimes you don't *savour* it. Seasons like that don't come around every year but I got two in the first two years when I was at United and Leicester will always be one of the highlights of my career. Not just because of the end result, which gave us promotion, but the support we got that day. It was unbelievable."

The early faith in his own abilities, to turn down the Wimbledon contract offer, had certainly been vindicated and just two whirlwind years after leaving, Tracey was going to be going up against his former side in Division One – as an equal. "When you move from another club, there's something there, nagging away at you, like: 'I'll show you, I'll prove that.' When you're young enough, you know there are still opportunities out there for you and you've got to take them.

"It's about the character or the person. Are they hungry enough to want to go and better themselves, and improve themselves? And want to be a success? And that's what I think Harry did, very, very well. Look at Bob Booker. He thought his career was virtually over when he came in from Brentford but probably had the best time and best success of his career coming to Sheffield United. He had a hunger to want to still go on and still do better for himself, and that's what Harry did well. Knowing how to get that from the individuals he signed.

"On a shoestring budget, he got players that were either young and wanted to do well, or still had something to prove and still had a hunger about them. That's why the people who came into the building were genuine. There were no big time Charlies; everyone still had to prove themselves. Harry was, and still is, very easy to get on with. You always wanted to go into training and that's something that means a lot. If we were training at 10.30 in the morning, we'd be getting in at nine o'clock just to have the craic with everyone. That was the sort of atmosphere. We'd finish training some days at 12 o'clock and come two or three o'clock, lads were still in the social club at the ground having a bit of dinner and a laugh. Harry brought everybody together, from the players to the supporters and the staff. Even the non-playing staff. Everyone was in the same predicament; everyone was in the same boat. Everyone was on the same page and wanted success."

None more so than the manager himself who, sensing that Tracey was perhaps not being sufficiently challenged by his understudy Phil Kite, strengthened his goalkeeping department with the signings of first Mel Rees, and then Kelly. It was an embarrassment of riches, really, to have three stoppers of such quality on the books at one time, with many believing that the trio were good enough to represent England, Wales and the Republic of Ireland at the same time. At one point Bassett rated Tracey as the best homegrown goalkeeper in the domestic game, but England recognition somehow eluded him, while Welshman Rees could have followed Kelly's path to international honours had his life not been tragically cut short by cancer at just 26 years of age.

The Tracey/Kelly era began in 1992, the summer that saw the advent of the Premier League and another change that had a big effect on Tracey's career – the new back pass rule. Previously allowed to pick up passes from teammates, something the game's governing body was concerned was having a negative effect on the quality of their product, goalkeepers suddenly had to rely on their speed of mind as well as feet to deal with awkward situations. The game has undoubtedly benefited as a result and in modern football there are goalkeepers who could probably play in midfield, such is their composure on the ball, and not look out of place. Tracey himself regards it as one of the best rule changes ever made in football but back in 1992, it was not an adjustment that he made easily.

It was early September and the Premier League era was just over a fortnight old when United travelled to White Hart Lane to face Tottenham Hotspur. Things were already looking ominous when goals either side of the break from Teddy Sheringham and Gordon Durie put Spurs in control at 2-0, before John Gannon – potentially in autopilot mode and forgetting his goalkeeper couldn't pick the ball up – passed back to Tracey. There seemed little danger when he shifted it slightly onto his right foot but under pressure, decided to try and dribble his way out of trouble. His left-foot kicking was virtually non-existent so Tracey ended up running the ball out of play for a throw-in, trying to wrestle the ball from a ball-boy and then essentially rugby tackling Andy Gray to the ground to prevent a quick throw and an easy third goal for Spurs. The subsequent second yellow card equalled a red. "I thought there was mad cow's disease out there," said Bassett after the game. "He knows the rules, so he will miss one game and lose his place. It was an expensive mistake … unprofessional and naïve."

Bassett wasn't exaggerating for effect; Tracey made only five more appearances that season as Kelly seized his chance between the posts. A succession of injuries didn't help Tracey's cause and, in an era when squad rotation didn't really exist, only an injury or suspension could offer either man the chance to seize back his spot. It is testament to Kelly's abilities that he still made 255 appearances for United in the face of such a quality rival – if both men had played in separate eras, they would have comfortably cleared five or six hundred games apiece.

The two were friends, as well as rivals, and admit now that the competition simply spurred them both on to become even better goalkeepers. "Alan was another young player who had something to prove," Tracey said. "He was waiting for his opportunity and it came around when I dislocated my shoulder and was out for 18 months. He had done fantastically well and virtually cemented his place in the team. He probably could have got a move if he'd wanted to. That's how highly I thought of him. He took it by the scruff of the neck and he was outstanding. I wasn't fit but I knew I was going to be struggling to get back into that team, with the way he was playing. That's how quickly it can change for a goalkeeper.

"I came in for those six games of the promotion season, didn't miss a game the following season and then the first game back in the top flight, Ian Rush accidentally caught me with his knee and broke my cheekbone against Liverpool. I was out for nine games or so and it was probably the first of some horrible injuries that I had."

With full-time goalkeeper coaching still some way off being commonplace, United had enlisted the former England staff member Mike Kelly – no relation to Alan – to put Kelly and Tracey through their specialist paces, twice a week. "The training between us, and the competition between us, was fantastic," said Tracey. "Alan will agree, we wanted to be better than each other and it improved me massively. We both had serious competition and I thoroughly enjoyed it."

Some years later, after Bassett's departure, Tracey remembers he and Kelly being pulled to one side by new manager Howard Kendall and told: "One of you has got to go." United, Kendall felt, didn't need two goalkeepers of such comparable quality and one interested buyer in Tracey were Crystal Palace – by then managed by Bassett. The deal was at an advanced stage when Tracey became entangled in the middle of a political row between Bassett and owner Ron Noades, and the move broke down. The friendly rivalry between Kelly and Tracey continued until 1999, when the former moved to Blackburn Rovers, and Tracey remained at Bramall Lane until he hung up his gloves, signing off with a testimonial against Middlesbrough in 2003.

"It was a fantastic time to be involved in," he said of the Bassett era. "It was a place you wanted to go into, and there's no bigger compliment than that really! You wanted to go to work. You were excited about going to work. Harry was someone you wanted to play for. He got you to want to play for him, and I think that was his main strength. He was very easy to get along with. One minute he'd have the hump with you and the next, it was all gone. That was Harry. If we got beat, he'd sit at the front of the coach for the first hour of the journey back and for the last hour, he'd be fighting with someone and saying to players: 'You were shit today.'

"It was like a big family and it was a very good time. It was a good environment to work in and I can't imagine anyone saying anything different. I loved my time there. I'd love to have had the opportunity to play now. You've got better facilities, you've got better pay and because the game is quicker, you'd be fitter as well. But I wouldn't have had my time any different, to be fair. Because Sheffield United was a fantastic place to be."

Fifteen years, 383 games, a lifetime of memories. All sparked by one simple phone call.

7

THE STEAM TRAIN ROLLS ON

It was a sunny summer's morning, in the middle of nowhere, and Sheffield United's players were cosily tucked up in their beds when they were woken to the unnerving sight and sound of a tank barrel poking through the window of their dormitory. "It shit us right up," remembered midfielder Bob Booker. This was pre-season, Dave Bassett style.

The United manager was inspired by the armed forces' mentality of trust and camaraderie, of never leaving a man behind, and had begun taking his players to army camps in pre-season during his time at Wimbledon. The thinking was simple; the tough physical training would improve his players' fitness but also toughen them up mentally, and the experience could only aid the pursuit of team bonding. During their time with the Dons, Bassett, physio Derek French and players Wally Downes and Alan Cork got lost on one army excursion and ended up being shot at by an irate farmer, running for their lives.

United's players avoided that pleasure, but they were still severely tested. They were dumped miles from the camp and told to find their own way back. There were assault courses that included being thrown into a pit of water full of dead pigeons, deafening flash bangs set off outside the players' dormitories and cross-country runs with heavy backpacks that ended with 40-foot drops into the sea. On one camp, in Salisbury, they were sent on an all-night orienteering exercise and the final exhausted players to return collapsed into their camp beds soon after four o'clock in the morning. "Normally they are up at half past five," said assistant manager Geoff Taylor. "But as it was the last day, we relented."

"The instructors were jumping around like a load of nutters like the world had ended. It was to give us the full army treatment," Booker added. "There were a few moans and groans from those who didn't enjoy it, but I loved all that. You just had to get on with it."

Striker Peter Duffield laughed at the memory of five-a-side games being arranged against local squaddies and even at a local prison. "One of our lads kicked the ball over the wall," the striker said, "and three or four of the inmates volunteered to go and get it back!" Duffield, who would have joined the army if he didn't become a footballer, also remembered firing a rifle on one of the army camps and the kickback damaging his shoulder. "It still hurts sometimes, to this day," he admitted.

The thought of valuable professional footballers jumping off castles onto a zip-line and firing rifles and tanks would send heads spinning in modern-day football, but it was the perfect way to breed the mental toughness and resilience that Bassett demanded in his players. If they could handle this, he reasoned, then what else could possibly be thrown at them throughout a season?

"It served its purpose because it brought people together," said midfielder John Gannon. "People were challenged all the time, taken out of their comfort zones. If you didn't like heights, you had a problem. If you didn't like water, you had a problem. I remember there was a course where you had to go under a tunnel and you had to swim under water to the end. Someone then dragged you out. Harry did it on one occasion and he cut his head because he got up so quickly at the end and smashed his head open. There was blood everywhere, because he was panicking. You had to wait for someone to pull you out because it was all about trust. So I think that was a little bit challenging mentally for some."

Pre-seasons would be a mixture of the tough army camps and trips away, with Scandinavia a popular destination. One year, in Sweden, Bassett organised a boat ride for his players, with the added surprise that it turned into a white-water rapids trip that ended with them all dumped into the freezing river; in his autobiography, he remembered "at least two" of his squad getting acquainted with a recently-married local bride and one of her bridesmaids, who he described as "a couple of soccer groupies" who were "good for a laugh." "I've often wondered just how long that marriage lasted," he wrote.

The trips were not glamorous in terms of location or hotels – the Blades were there to work, after all – but the players were also treated like grown-ups and allowed to have a night out in the evenings. The only rule? They had to be up, ready and fit to run in the morning. The players appreciated the freedom and respected Bassett for affording it.

Perhaps the manager suspected that his players would put some of their new-found army navigation and endurance skills to the test and find a local pub anyway.

Promotion the previous season had begun to heal the wounds of Watford for Bassett and all talk of resignation, and that offer to Derek Dooley a year earlier, had been long forgotten. The revolution was well underway, and Bassett's experience of climbing the leagues with Wimbledon left him aware of the need for reinforcements to take on the likes of West Ham, Leeds United and Newcastle United in the second tier. With Brian Deane, Tony Agana, Jock Bryson and Co. all well established at the top end of the pitch, Bassett turned his attention to his backline and new faces on the pre-season assault courses included Colin Hill, David Barnes and Bassett's ex-Dons man Mark Morris.

Bassett agreed terms with Hill despite describing Colchester's £350,000 asking price as "a million miles away from what he is worth," with the £85,000 fee eventually decided by a tribunal after United's £50,000 opening offer. Wilf Rostron signed from city rivals Wednesday while former Owl Carl Bradshaw returned to the right side of Sheffield from Manchester City, taking Bassett's summer spend to a not-inconsiderable £360,000.

The purse-strings had not suddenly been loosened at Bramall Lane, though, with director Paul Woolhouse stumping up the cash to sign Bradshaw and around 75 per cent of that total transfer outlay recouped through the departures of Steve Thompson, Alan Roberts, John Francis, Martin Pike and Jim Gannon. Season ticket sales had also soared past the £200,000 mark by the time Bassett made defender David Barnes his first summer signing, with the manager admitting that "the amount of money brought in by season tickets will determine the sort of players we buy."

Bassett had expected to succeed at United but perhaps not quite as quickly, meaning his long-term plan had to be accelerated in terms of the upgrades needed in his side. He was a man playing constant mental chess, trying to make sure all his pieces were in the right order, while squeezing every last drop out of a budget more suited to pawns and the odd rook than kings and queens.

Pike had more than done a job for Bassett – no one had made more than his 68 appearances in all competitions in the 1988/89 promotion season – but the manager had identified his lack of pace as a potential weakness in the division above and he was moved on, spending time on loan at Tranmere and Bolton before making a permanent move to Fulham. Hill had also been brought in as a replacement for Chris Wilder on the right of defence but Wilder resolved to stick around at his boyhood club and ended up alternating with the Northern Ireland international, the two sharing a pitch together later in the season.

The evolution of the side meant that skipper Paul Stancliffe was the only surviving defender from the promotion campaign to line up on the opening day of the 1989/90 season at West Brom, while both Simon Tracey and John Gannon had cemented their places in Bassett's starting XI after following him up the M1. Not every signing paid off, though, and sometimes in the cruellest circumstances; midfielder Julian Winter came in from Huddersfield but didn't make a first-team appearance for United before a serious knee injury forced him to retire. Winter went on to work in behind-the-scenes football roles, becoming United's chief executive in 2011.

He was not the only player who disappeared almost without trace at Bramall Lane that summer. Bassett had taken a look at former England U21 winger Louie Donowa, who was looking for a return to England after an ill-fated spell with Dutch side Willem II, and the ex-Norwich man played in all three games of United's pre-season tour of Germany, scoring against TSV Havelse and then Skegness Town after returning to England. Donowa and his agent, Terry Densham, then shook hands with Bassett and agreed to join United, but the manager was left raging when Donowa reneged on his word and instead signed for Ipswich Town.

"They are welcome to him," a "fuming" Bassett said at the time. "I had my doubts about his character when we took him with us to Germany and I have been proved right. We spent several hours together on Monday and at the end of it all he had made a decision. But he did not have the decency or the guts to stand by it.

"We made him a good offer and promised to renew it at Christmas, and he gave me the firm impression that he would be coming. He gave me his word that he would be a Sheffield United player. I know this is not legal but it is the way I do business and it is the way I expect to be dealt with. Frankly, I am glad he has gone."

Bassett not only resolved to never work with Donowa again, but also blacklisted Densham and his firm. "They clearly could not control their client," Bassett added. "I know that agents have a part in the game but I have bombed them out, unless they remove this player from their books. I felt I could have done something with Donowa and I felt he needed us. We were offering him a new start in a new environment, in a big city club where football is a way of life. But he has gone for the cosy option, back in his own environment. He will never play for any team I manage."

Other players made a more indelible mark on Bramall Lane and any player or staff member from that era cannot help but smile at the mere mention of Barnes' name. A "Barnardo's Boy" who was born in London but grew up in Sussex in the care of the children's charity, Barnes arrived at Bramall Lane from Aldershot – who had finished rock bottom of Division Three the previous season as United went up the other way – and wasted little time making his mark. He had learned his football in the slightly more 'refined' environments of Coventry City, Ipswich Town and Wolves before moving to United, but would have fitted in perfectly with Bassett's Wimbledon Crazy Gang.

To describe Barnes as an interesting character would be a significant understatement. Nicknamed "Digger" by his teammates, a reference to a character in the American show *Dallas,* Barnes' party piece saw him strip off and wedge toilet roll up his backside before setting it on fire and dancing on tables in a restaurant, singing *Lord of the Dance.* Goalkeeper Alan Kelly remembers "a good player, full of energy, hard, determined but definitely with a touch of madness," who once sat up all night, playing the piano of the Moat House hotel on New Year's Eve, with no clothes on. In another hotel on another trip, Barnes spied a huge, life-size knight statue at the side of reception and decided to headbutt it; the statue subsequently crumbled, sending metal arms and legs and sword and shield all over the lobby.

Kitman John Greaves was tasked with packing Barnes' plug-in keyboard, which had a series of backing songs, in the kit skip for a trip to Plymouth. United's players had been given a rare curfew after a rowdy evening, but snuck out of the back exit of the hotel anyway for a second go. Barnes' room was just down the corridor from assistant manager Geoff Taylor's; to help the ruse, Barnes had left his keyboard playing *La Cucaracha* on repeat and Taylor thought he had been in there all evening. Barnes also took a particular shine to new signing Phil Kite and used lids from the tea urn in the canteen as cymbals to frighten him when he walked into the room. On other occasions he threw an empty ball bag over Kite and attacked him, in scenes midfielder Jamie Hoyland later described as akin to something "from Pink Panther with Peter Sellers ... just attacking him from somewhere and then running off."

Barnes' saved his most memorable prank for a Britannia Airways Boeing 767, waiting at Birmingham International Airport to fly United's players to Spain after promotion in 1990, when he imitated a Bassett team talk on the plane. But the pen Barnes used wouldn't wipe off the screen that he used as a makeshift tactics board, and a group of United players were subsequently escorted off the plane by police. Most of the charges were eventually dropped but Barnes and Billy Whitehurst had a day in court, with chairman Reg Brealey turning up to provide character references and the matter settled after talks between the airline and the Crown Prosecution Service, and upon payment from United for the £1,300 worth of damage. The plane incident even made *ITV's News at Ten* bulletin that evening.

There was rarely a dull day at Bramall Lane, which may have swung things in their favour when the *BBC* settled on a club to follow for a fly-on-the-wall documentary. The Blades, in their centenary season, were one of two clubs on the shortlist and were eventually chosen for a six-part *BBC Two* documentary, to air on Friday nights from April of that season and imaginatively titled *United!* The groundbreaking broadcast gave the *BBC* cameras unfettered access to the previously off-limits areas from boardroom to boot room, following United's progress throughout a season that would end in such dramatic fashion. In the modern era, access-all-areas shows are ten-a-penny but back then, *United!* was a typically forward-thinking move from Bassett, bringing in some much-needed revenue and also gaining some valuable exposure for the club at the same time.

"Harry was a trailblazer," remembered Wilder. "For him to agree to that would have maybe surprised quite a few of us at the time, but it's something that is there and on record. We were one of the early ones to go deep into that type of insight into a professional footballer and a professional football team, on and off the pitch."

Cameras were given behind-the-scenes access to all areas of the club with the spotlight on a different topic each week – players, wives, board, fans, manager and apprentices. Not everything in the documentary met with universal approval, though, including the incorrect portrayals of Bryson's wife Kirsty as a stay-at-home mum and Jill, the partner of Wilf Rostron, shown as having little interest in football. "We were not happy with that," Bryson said. "They tried to manipulate a lot of the stuff they did to a certain degree. They brought her to meet us in a nightclub in Sheffield. They were waiting for us to come back home. That would never happen. I think Paul Stancliffe's wife was there, and Simon Webster's. They went out and filmed them trying to have a meal. It wasn't real, but it's what they wanted the players' wives to be doing. A lot of it wasn't actually true and to a certain degree, it was forced."

But in his autobiography, Bassett described *United!* as the best football programme to have ever been shown on TV and as the months rolled on, United's players and staff didn't even notice the cameras filming them on coaches and in dressing rooms up and down the country. They even became close to some of the *BBC Bristol* staff. "They became part of the team in many ways," Bassett remembered.

And there was plenty of content as United attacked the new season as they had finished the last. A 10-game unbeaten start saw United score 20 goals and top the early table, their style continuing to upset the right people. Bassett remembered spending the previous summer in Magaluf and getting "earache" from Harry Redknapp, then manager of Bournemouth, and West Brom boss Brian Talbot about the way his side played. Most of it came from Talbot but Redknapp also nodded along, albeit he didn't agree strongly enough to prevent him betting Talbot £50 that the Blades would beat his Baggies side on the opening day of the new season. United returned from the Hawthorns with three goals and three points, and in a congratulatory letter to Bassett at the end of the season Talbot promised to keep his big mouth shut in future.

Bassett's well-oiled machine was clicking into gear quickly, despite the odd blip – including a 5-4 home victory against Brighton which saw United let a 3-0 lead slip before scoring a late winner. With no real household names in the team, clubs had not given United the respect they deserved when it came to doing their homework and a lot simply could not handle the ruthless effectiveness of the Blades' style.

"We were like a steam train, rolling with a group of players who were all believing in what they were doing," said Booker. "It was drummed into me that I was going to hook the ball on, when nine times out of 10 you might have wanted to take a touch and play a simple pass. Deane and Agana knew that I was going to do that every time, so they could make the appropriate run knowing I wasn't going to bring it down. Everybody had a role to play, whether that was me doing that or defenders putting it down the channel to win a throw-in.

"In the final quarter of an hour of a game you would see teams trying to play our way, but we were doing that for 90 minutes every week. That was the difference. We didn't change. It was set in stone. If any winger checked back and didn't cross the ball, they would get slaughtered at half-time because the strikers are expecting 10 crosses from each winger. For every 10 crosses, they were owed a goal. Harry would say to the likes of Bryson at half-time: 'If you don't get some crosses in in the first 10 minutes of this second half, you're coming off.' It was as simple as that."

It may have been simple, but it was also damned effective. "Football is all about scoring goals," said Bryson. "As Alex Ferguson used to say, it's all about what happens in the other box, rather than what happens in ours. The more times we got the ball into the 18-yard box, the more likely we were to score goals. From a winger's point of view, it was brilliant for me. My job was simple and all I wanted to do was get the ball and whip it in, either with my right or my left, with good players up front like Brian and Tony getting on the end of things.

"We were not hitting players; we were just hitting the ball into the box and these guys made the runs and scored the goals. It was direct football and I got my fair share of goals as well. We had to work hard on the defensive side, but everyone was quite happy to stick to the formula because it brought success. We trained and worked hard at it to make it work, and sometimes it didn't. But the majority of times, the percentages that Dave had worked out proved in the end that it was a way of winning football matches. And that's what it's all about ... winning football matches."

United did not taste defeat that season until the middle of October, a bizarre 2-0 loss to West Ham at Bramall Lane which saw the Hammers' defence hold strong in the face of an attacking onslaught from the hosts. A corner count of 28 to one, in United's favour, illustrated the flavour of the game. A good run to the quarter-finals of the FA Cup, United bowing out with credit after a 1-0 defeat at home to Manchester United, also brought in more money for the coffers and helped Bassett further strengthen his squad later in the season. Striker Whitehurst arrived from Hull City for £30,000, Paul Wood from Brighton for £90,000 and Mike Lake from Macclesfield for an initial fee of £400,000. Wood was a tricky winger who bolstered the supply chain after Roberts had departed to Lincoln, and caught Bassett's eye as part of the Brighton side from that remarkable 5-4 game.

"I scored two for Brighton that day," Wood said. "I got the first and the fourth goal to put us 4-3 up, before United came back to win it. When I signed, I remembered Jock and Barnesy coming over to me. They were both like: 'Fucking hell, you tortured us that day.' It was a blessing in disguise because Harry obviously saw something in me and signed me later that season. I played well, and everything came off for me. I had a good day.

"I was actually going to sign for Stoke City and Bassett found out I was available. He got in touch with me while I was in the manager's office, talking to Alan Ball. He got Gary Chivers, who was at Watford with him, to phone up the office and tell me that Bassett wanted to speak to me at United. So I had to stall on signing for Stoke so I could go and speak to Harry. I was literally talking to Alan Ball and I had to pretend I knew nothing about it.

"I had been in dressing rooms full of characters before. The Portsmouth one was full of nutters – people like Micky Kennedy, Noel Blake, Kevin Dillon, Micky Quinn, Micky Tait. The Sheffield United dressing room was full of characters as well. But what I found really comfortable at United was the fact that there were no superstars in it. No big names at the time when I joined it. They were all cheap buys, free transfers and rejects. Without any star players, everyone just knew what job they had to do. The way Bassett went about it, very direct, playing for corners and throw-ins … it didn't always work, but it worked a lot of the time."

On the opposite flank to Wood a young winger called Dane Whitehouse was beginning to emerge, the teenager scoring the opening goal in a 4-1 win at Bradford, and United answered another test of their promotion credentials with an impressive victory at Oldham to end the Latics' long unbeaten home record on their plastic pitch. But as Bassett's weary side embarked on the final stretch of their 57-game season, the toil began to show. A 5-0 defeat at West Ham in March was the first of four in the space of six games, with Bassett tearing a strip off every one of his players afterwards. Right-back Wilder was given a particularly torrid time by Stuart Slater and was told afterwards by Bassett that his own performance had probably helped the Hammers winger get an England call-up. Slater was named man-of-the-match, despite not scoring and Jimmy Quinn netting a hat-trick, and it was the only time Wilder tasted defeat that season. "I would have liked to see how anyone coped with Stuart Slater that night," he said at the time. Speaking in 2020, Slater remembered Wilder shaking his hand at full-time and saying: "Crikey, that's the closest I've got to you all night!"

United were second at the time, West Ham loitering in mid-table, and Booker was playing centre-half in Stancliffe's absence. "Me and Mark Morris got absolutely battered by Trevor Morley and Quinn," Booker said. "Harry made me feel three inches tall in the dressing room at half-time and after the game. He called me a donkey, spitting and shouting and pointing, telling me that milk turns quicker. There were times when you could have a row back, if you didn't agree with him, but this wasn't one of those.

"He would row with you and you would sort it out, whether in the dressing room or the next morning in training. But it was sorted out and we moved on. That's what he did, he never held any grudges. If you were unhappy, you would go and knock on his door and he would tell you how it was. 'If you do this, you'll get the rewards and if you don't, I'll put someone else in.' He was hard but fair. You couldn't have it any fairer than that and that was the beauty of him. His man-management was second to none."

Wood believes United could still be playing the West Ham game now and still wouldn't have had a shot on target. "We were absolutely dreadful," he said. "It didn't work that night, but the lads didn't even take it to heart. Because we knew we could turn it around pretty quickly."

Successive wins over Watford and Oxford saw United do just that, but they were still feeling the heat of Newcastle in third when they travelled to Elland Road to face Leeds. And it was another day to forget on and off the pitch, a 4-0 thumping compounded by unsavoury scenes in the stands as John Gannon's partner was hit by a bottle. It was a particularly uncomfortable afternoon for Booker, who had discovered his shirt in a knot so tight that the sleeves had to be cut off before the game and his shorts sabotaged with Deep Heat by his old pal, and Leeds midfielder, Vinnie Jones.

Newcastle's win at home to Stoke saw the Magpies push United out of the top two at the worst possible time. Only four games of the season remained and as United's players trudged off the pitch with heads down, jubilant home fans milling all around them, the same question was on the lips of many. Just how costly was that defeat going to be to the Blades' chances of automatic promotion?

Bassett had given his honest verdict at West Ham but didn't need to be as vocal this time round. "There were a lot of fucks flying about in the dressing room that day," Booker remembered. "Everybody was really disappointed. We didn't need Harry to tell us, we could sort that out. Everybody pointed fingers in the dressing room and we all had a say."

It was a tough result to take. "We had our arses kicked," Bassett remembered decades later. "It was a disgrace. There were a few people, even our fans, who thought: 'Fuck, we've blown it.' But we had another four games and it wasn't the cup final. The players were still up for it. We went: 'Come on, we've come this far. We're going to have reversals.' We recovered. But I could sense the nerves afterwards. *'Fuck me, we're going to miss out.'*

"The Leeds fans were out of order. But it happens, doesn't it? I've been to Oldham and Millwall and walked in with my back covered with spit. At West Ham, you got it there, and at Leeds you got plenty. It was part of the game. It's not nice but it ain't the end of the world. If someone gobbed on you in the street, you'd punch them. But you have to say that it's an emotional day out. People seem to forget that fans want to go to a match and have a hoot and a holler and a shout. People have been working all week, they want to go to the game with their mates and have a beer and call you a wanker. It's part and parcel. But the next minute you score a great goal and they love you. You become a hero."

After so long in the top two, and with Division One football seemingly in their grasp, United's fate was suddenly out of their hands. It was advantage Newcastle and Leeds, and all the Blades could do was take care of their own business and hope their rivals slipped up. Back-to-back wins over Port Vale and Bournemouth was exactly the response Bassett had demanded; Leeds wobbled again with a point at Brighton and a shock home defeat to Barnsley that almost saw the United manager crash his car in shock when he heard the result on the radio.

Newcastle also faltered, with draws against Plymouth and Swindon, and United had the first chance of all three to secure promotion with a game to spare with victory at Blackburn. A bizarre moment saw a linesman flag for a penalty for Rovers, for which none of their players actually appealed for, and the referee give a free-kick to United instead. The linesman put his flag down, United breathed a sigh of relief and in the dying minutes, Whitehurst was inches away from writing his name into United folklore with the winner. Instead, his header went just the wrong side of the post.

In a performance described by Tony Pritchett as one of "real character and endeavour," *The Star's* Blades writer wrote that the only thing that let United down was their finishing. A 0-0 draw set up a final-day date with destiny.

8

FOOTBALL'S HARDEST MAN

B y his own estimation, 99.9 per cent of the stories about Billy Whitehurst centre around him kicking, elbowing or biting people. Being a hard man. Everyone who has ever encountered him seems to have a Whitehurst tale, and some of them are even true. Many more are embellished, or more innocently mixed up.

There was a story told on a podcast about Whitehurst bringing his injured greyhound into Bramall Lane for Derek French, the United physio, to treat ahead of a big race. Whitehurst doesn't deny that it happened; just that he played for Oxford, rather than United, at the time. The bitch, called One Eye and co-owned with future Blade Dean Saunders, was in the semi-finals of the prestigious Television Trophy but, troubled by the groin issue, didn't make it through to the showpiece. "I remember walking with her and a kid asking me what I was doing with her. I said: 'I'm going to race her.' He replied: 'By the looks of it, you'll beat her.'"

Footballer, greyhound owner, bare-knuckle brawler, publican; stories of Whitehurst's escapades could fill a book of their own. Whitehurst was once branded a "maniac" by Harry Redknapp, who had warned his son Jamie to go nowhere near the striker on the pitch; he played one game with a hole in his face after 30 stitches, from a recent pub brawl, opened up. He also had a couple of bare-knuckle fights in his playing days, for £1,000 apiece. The first one ended quickly, but the second was not so easy. After returning to training with Oxford, Whitehurst lied to his manager Maurice Evans that his facial injuries had been caused by a car accident.

Whitehurst's Blades career amounted to 23 appearances after arriving in February 1990, an era when Brian Deane and Tony Agana were in their pomp up front, but he left the legacy of someone who played 10 times that number as one of the most iconic of Dave Bassett's Blades. After a couple of phone calls he agreed to meet for an interview at his local pub in Ackworth, a village somewhere between Pontefract, Barnsley and Doncaster.

Waiting for him offered just a taste of the apprehension that defenders must have faced coming up against him and as he swept through the doors of The Angel, it was impossible to miss him. He looked *hard*. Like a man chiselled out of the coal they used to ferry out of the mines in his home town of Thurnscoe. He had hands like shovels and a nose weathered, let's say, by countless battles on and off the pitch.

But sometimes appearances can be deceiving. It was a crisp winter day, but the welcome was warm; a hearty laugh at the interviewer's phone sending him trudging through a muddy farmer's field to reach The Angel, the insistence of a lift back to the local train station afterwards behind the wheel of a tiny Ford Ka, with his partner in the back seat. Sometime later there was a call from Whitehurst, offering to get in touch with more of his former teammates to discuss their Bramall Lane careers. One of them separately remembered struggling with their mental health later in life, and Whitehurst doggedly lobbying the PFA on their behalf for help. A big man with a bigger heart.

It gets lost a little amongst the tales of his extracurricular activities but Whitehurst could play, as well. A former bricklayer given a chance in football by Hull City, he never lost sight of his working-class grounding and squeezed every drop from his career, and then some. He was, at the time, Newcastle United's record signing, playing alongside Peter Beardsley and Paul Gascoigne (and later denying he had ever broken Gazza's jaw.)

One of his proudest moments was impressing World Cup winner Bobby Charlton after a game against Manchester United. Charlton came to watch Gascoigne and Beardsley but left, describing Whitehurst as the best player on the pitch, "by far."

It wasn't all plain sailing, though. Whitehurst looks back harshly on his performances early on at Hull – "I was shit" – and his time on Tyneside lasted just one year. Whitehurst moved to Oxford, Sunderland and Reading, with chaos and controversy inevitably following him. A return to Hull set in motion the chain of events that took him to Bramall Lane, with Bassett keen to recruit not just cover for Deane and Agana but the type of character to help United over the line in a tense race for promotion to the First Division.

Bassett watched Whitehurst in person in a reserve game at Hull, later sending coach Wally Downes to give a second opinion. "I only found out later that Wally, who had been with Harry at Wimbledon and Sheffield United, never made it," Whitehurst said. "He got pissed up the night before. So he had no idea if I had played or not. Wally later told me he rang up one of the lads I was up against and asked him about me. This lad – who might have been one of the centre-halves, I'm not sure – just said I was magnificent. So, that was the report Harry got back. 'Billy was magnificent.'" The rest was history. "To be fair," Whitehurst smiled, "I did play okay that day."

While Bassett and his coaching staff were dedicated to squeezing every marginal gain out of their players, with detailed tactical plans and clever routines, the manager's instructions for Whitehurst were a little bit more primitive. "Harry never really used to give me any other instructions when I came on, apart from: 'Go and cause some bollocks, son,'" Whitehurst said, with the grin of a man who didn't mind doing exactly that.

It didn't stop even after he left, either, to join Doncaster Rovers in 1991. Soon after Whitehurst returned to Bramall Lane with his son to watch United face Southampton, when a message came from coach Keith Mincher. Bassett wanted Whitehurst to have a quiet word with Neil Ruddock, the Saints centre-half, who was giving striker Deane a tough time. Whitehurst describes the incident now as "the most embarrassing thing I ever did, and I did some very embarrassing things." At the half-time whistle, Whitehurst made a beeline for Ruddock. "He said: 'Alright, Bill?'

"'Don't alright me,' I said to him. 'If you go near Deano in the second half and keep kicking him, I'm going to smash you.' That's embarrassing to remember, but I did it for Harry. And I wasn't even his player at the time! He made you want to go above and beyond for him. They were great times and I found Harry to be a good kid. He was great with the players and let the players be themselves. There was no pressure on people and that man-management is a massive thing in any walk of life, isn't it?

"Harry was great at that. He had a lot of players who were probably hard to handle, if you like, at other clubs. Other managers couldn't deal with them but he seemed to get the best out of them. His record spoke for itself, with the promotions, but I always found him fantastic."

Another of Whitehurst's best Bassett memories came after the striker had moved to Doncaster. "I was gambling quite a lot when I played. I gambled all my life, to be fair. One day I walked into his office and asked if I could borrow something, because I was skint. He gave me an advance on my wages and a couple of weeks later I hit him again for something else.

"I can't remember his exact words but it was something along the lines of changing my habits, or learning how to back horses that actually won races rather than lost them. He swore all the time and said: "I can't give you another fucking advance," but he put his hand in his pocket and lent me a few quid of his own money. I think that sums him up."

Whitehurst remembers the sum as £2,000. "It was a lot of money then. It's a lot of money now, to be fair. Well, £20 is a lot of money when you've not got anything, but back then it was a lot. For some reason I only gave him £1,900 back and still owed him £100. I'd gone to a PFA do in London with my good mate Iain Hesford. United's table was full, so Harry came and sat with us on ours and all the lads with us were so impressed that he was with us and telling his stories, having a good laugh. Every time I saw Harry he used to ask about the £100 I owed him and so I passed it to him.

"He said: 'Oh, thanks for that Bill, my son,' and put it in his pocket. About five minutes later he went up and went to the toilet, so the other lads asked what the £100 was for. I told them that I'd had to pay him to sit with us. They couldn't believe it. When he came back from the toilet Harry started talking to them again and they all started abusing him. 'Fuck off, you tosser.' Harry asked me what had gone off and I told him what I'd said. He called me a **** and we had a good laugh about it."

One of Whitehurst's more rudimentary pranks saw him defecate in a plastic cup and hide it in the corner of Derek French's treatment room. The former United physio didn't have a sense of smell, eroded over the years of inhaling Deep Heat while rubbing it into players' legs, but the stink gradually got worse over the course of a week or so before its source was discovered.

On another occasion United goalkeeper Graham Benstead, a former roommate of Whitehurst's, remembers his good pal decking a comedian who had dared to poke fun at his partner on stage. "He had skill but also brought intimidation for the opposition, which doesn't go amiss. He tried to get every bit of advantage he could.

"As a group we weren't the most skilful bunch of players in the world but we were effective in how we went about things, and a lot of that is down to management. I remember having a drink one night with Billy and asking about his scars. 'They're not from football,' he said. 'They're from the pubs and clubs.' I was like: 'Right, okay … cheers, Bill.' He told me I was safe with him. He is intimidating but he's a big pussycat, really. I dare say a big fucking pussycat, really."

Whitehurst is under no illusions about the fact that he would not last two minutes in modern football, and that VAR would have a field day with some of his antics that escaped the attention of the on-field officials. "Put me in a time machine and onto the pitch now and I'd probably get 12 years down the line," he admitted.

"But a lot of the older end of supporters wanted to watch a confrontation between a centre-forward and a centre-half. Referees would invariably let it go. Six and two-threes. You'd be smashing 10 bells of shit out of each other in the game and a lot of the older end probably prefer that. It is becoming a non-contact sport. It saddens me." The game that brought him to Redknapp's attention saw three Bournemouth players knocked out. Mike Tyson wouldn't have lasted two minutes with Whitehurst that day, Redknapp famously said. "I didn't even get booked," Whitehurst shrugged.

A burly physique was a big part of his game, leading to the nickname "Billy Tightshirt" and taunts from Leeds fans that Whitehurst answered by lifting up his jersey and sucking in his stomach. Bassett, Whitehurst believes, always thought he was overweight but didn't have the heart to tell him, so sent him to Lilleshall for some fitness testing.

"My fat count was the lowest at the club. I just needed extra tuition on how to pick a winner on the horses! Players nowadays say how fit they are. I see that as absolute shite. You couldn't get any fitter than we were. Obviously, the lifestyles are a lot better. The culture was to have a drink. I'd like to think that at my fittest back then, I'd be up there with the fittest players now.

"A lot of players nowadays have a dig as well but I can't imagine you'd find many of Harry's ex-players criticising him. It was a relationship where he was like your mate, although there was also a gap and a respect where you wouldn't cross that line. But when we went out for a drink it wouldn't be 'Gaffer this or that.' It would be: 'Come on Harry, are you getting a beer in or what?'

"But if you weren't performing, or doing what you needed to do, he would dig you out, in no uncertain terms, and smash you to bits in front of everyone. Whether you thought you were his mate or not. I had it a couple of times, for sure. I've been in dressing rooms where managers have given the same message whether you've won 5-0, lost 5-0 or drawn 5-5, and it loses its effect after a while. But Harry's post-match team-talks, or at half-time, were always interesting because you had no idea what was coming. Once he described us as playing like 'fucking carrot sellers on a market.'

"One memory always sticks out as an insight into Harry's mentality. We were in Sweden for pre-season and we'd just signed Paul Beesley. We were losing and I remember this Swedish kid knocking the ball past Bees and going round him like he was stuck to the floor. I could just picture Harry going: 'What have I done here?' Then, with about 20 minutes to go, he turned to me and went: 'Big man, go and cause some fucking bollocks.' It was only a friendly but he'd had enough. Their goalkeeper was coming to claim everything and there was a deep cross to me at the back stick. I had my eyes on the ball the whole way and the 'keeper came out as well. I could hear Harry from the sideline: 'Oh fuck me, no, big man ... oh no, fuck me.' *Bang.* I'd splattered the 'keeper. He was out for the count."

Later in life Whitehurst moved into the pub trade, taking over The Cricketers Arms on Bramall Lane. He also played for former teammate Chris Wilder's Sunday League side, Bradway FC, and hosted them regularly at the Cricketers. "It used to be like a nightclub, every Sunday night. All the Bradway lads had been up Ecclesall Road before coming down to the Cricks. This was while the John Street stand was being built and one night we decided to climb over the rickety fence, pissed as rats, and had a 12-a-side game at the Lane. It was great. A few years down the line, Chris was the United manager and took them into the Premier League. For me, that just summed up Chris as a Blade. He'd played there so many times before, but couldn't resist one more game on his pitch. From the top of his head to his toe nails, he is a Blade … through and through.

"It's testament to both Chris and Harry that they're still close all these years on. Chris has always kept in touch with Harry and always picked his brain, because he knows what he's on about. There are some similarities but they are completely different in the way they play football. Harry was more direct and as a manager, Chris is how he was as a player. He could play but he wasn't necessarily a Harry-type player. Chris wanted to play football whereas Harry wanted to play more direct, in the channels and in areas. But today's football suits how Chris wanted to play, because he was a good footballer.

"I do think the culture's changed in modern-day football. With the money and that foreign influx. When I played, we used to go into the Lane social club after games with all the fans. That wouldn't happen now. Not in a million years. Footballers nowadays are like the rockstars of our day because they're on that much money. You wouldn't bump into them over a beer. You'd have to make an appointment to see one of them. It would be like getting an audience with the Pope. Twenty or 30 years ago, that wouldn't happen. Times change, I guess."

But the cult of Billy Whitehurst remains. The big man who caused plenty of bollocks.

"One of the greatest managers in Sheffield United's history! Is that the accolade Bramall Lane fans will now bestow on Dave Bassett, after his remarkable feat of lifting the club from the Third Division to the First in consecutive seasons? In difficult circumstances reflected in club debts of over £3million, Bassett has competed against the big spenders — and won on a shoestring budget."

– Tony Pritchett

9

BASSETT'S FINEST HOUR (& HALF)

The sunlight was poking through the curtains on a warmer-than-average May morning as Adrian Starkes turned over and began to consider what the day ahead of him could bring. The talk the night before, at the Royal Oak pub on Mansfield Road, Intake, had been a mix of excitement and trepidation. It was May 5, 1990, *The Star's* photographer was outside The Stag at Woodhouse to capture the mood and soon, Starkes was one of thousands of Sheffield United fans bound for Leicester City.

Also heading down the M1 to Filbert Street were Batman and Robin – otherwise known as Unitedites Heath Castle and Grant Pirrie, who had squeezed alongside a group of friends from Chesterfield into a mini-van in an image reminiscent of the famous fancy-dress scene from *Only Fools and Horses*. It felt like a mass Sheffield exodus, the motorway awash with red and white from cars and flags heading south. For United's automatic promotion hopes, it was now or never. Do or die. The mood was tense. "I'm never full of confidence," Starkes said. "It's United we're talking about."

The apprehension was understandable. United have never been a club particularly adept at doing things the easy way and to those generations of Blades used to disappointment when it really mattered and push came to shove, the situation seemed eerily familiar. United were second in the table at kick-off, level on points with leaders Leeds and with the pair two points clear of third-place Newcastle. The top two would be going up automatically and places three to six condemned to the play-offs. United's shocking record in the end-of-season knockouts was still in its infancy then, but all connected to the club knew the importance of getting the job done.

Any two from the top three would be promoted, come full-time. Any one of those could win the title. Any one of those could miss out, and have to navigate the uncertainty of the play-offs. Manager Dave Bassett had long believed that the promotion race could go down to the final day, and it was completely in United's hands – a situation that predictably did little to calm the nerves of some of those fans en-route to Leicester.

But in reality, it felt like United's destiny. They had tasted the euphoria of promotion a year previous, the hangover of relegation banished as Bassett took the club by the scruff of the neck and set it on a different path. The 1989/90 season had been more of the same. They had players in, or approaching, the prime of their lives – Brian Deane, Tony Agana, Jock Bryson, Paul Wood. Simon Tracey at the other end was in the form that would see him crowned player of the year. They had one of the best defensive records in the division and boasted one of its most potent attacks.

Elsewhere, Leeds were facing Bournemouth, who desperately needed a win to have a chance of survival, on a Bank Holiday weekend that saw thousands of Leeds fans travel to the south coast and trash the town, causing £1million worth of damage in what has since been dubbed "The Battle of Bournemouth." Newcastle wouldn't have it all their own way, either, against north-east rivals Middlesbrough, who were also battling the drop. All the omens seemed to be favouring the Blades and to bolster their chances further, the game might as well have been at Bramall Lane. An exact figure has never been placed on the number of Blades fans in Filbert Street that day but 10,000 has been mentioned as the most conservative estimate. Unitedites were everywhere; packed into the away end but also popping up in home areas all around the stadium. The official attendance was recorded as 21,134 and some of those who were that day would be surprised if more than half that number didn't speak with a South Yorkshire twang.

One of them was Ian Parkes, who was just six years of age and, in a brilliant memory that sums up the era but would probably have modern-day parents riddled with anxiety, was passed to a stranger as he couldn't see through the crowd of supporters. "A random bloke put me on his shoulders and took me to the front," Parkes smiled. "My dad basically didn't see me all game until the end." Another Blade, Denis Ashford, found the soaring temperature in the Midlands too hot to handle and, during a drinking session that had started at 10 o'clock that morning in nearby Ashby-de-la-Zouch, decided to do away with his jeans. Without appropriate underwear, he popped into a nearby shop and came out with some Dennis the Menace boxer shorts. Wearing just those, his Adidas Sambas and the iconic luminous United away shirt that become synonymous with the day, he made it into the ground. Football, in so many ways, was different back then.

It was a sight to behold, the two-tiered stand at one end of the ground and another down the side packed with fans in fancy dress. Boyhood Blade Chris Wilder, in the side through skipper Paul Stancliffe's injury absence, can still recall taking throw-ins and seeing more and more of his pals in the end down one side of Filbert Street. Bob Booker caught sight of Donald Duck, Superman and Goofy in the stands, before spotting a giant cardboard cut-out of himself being thrown up in the air. "I wanted to get my hands on that and keep it," Booker said. The cut-out made it back to Sheffield and ended up in Josephine's nightclub that night, where Billy Whitehurst put his fist through it.

There were superheroes in the stands and, just yards away in the visiting dressing room, heroes of a different kind preparing for the biggest game of their careers. These were your more down-to-earth, grounded ones, plucked from relative obscurity to stand on the brink of greatness. They would be without their leader, Stancliffe, who missed the final few matches with injury and was trusted enough to decide himself if he was fit enough to face Leicester. In the end he watched from the sidelines at Filbert Street and that moment, on his 32nd birthday, was a tough one to take.

But one man's misfortune is another man's opportunity, and Stancliffe's absence meant that Booker was given the honour of leading the team out as skipper. "I was very proud to be captain that day," Booker said. "We had a strong dressing room with a lot of characters. And to be standing at the front of that tunnel with the armband on, looking across the pitch and seeing just how many supporters there were, with my family there … without being too blasé and arrogant about it, I was walking out onto that pitch, looking behind at those players, and knowing we were going to win."

There was a similar memory of total confidence from Whitehurst, who probably shouldn't have made the trip at all. His reward for throwing himself at a cross just days earlier against Blackburn, and being inches away from being the hero who scored the goal that took United to promotion, was a painful injury. Whitehurst still kids Blades fans that he dislocated his neck in three places; in reality, it wasn't that bad but still left him unable to move his head properly. Desperate to not miss out at Leicester, though, he hid it from Bassett and kept his place amongst the substitutes. "From the very minute we kicked off," Whitehurst said, "I could just sense that we were in total cruise control."

The iconic *United!* documentary has preserved an incredible behind-the-scenes look at that day for posterity and offers a brilliant insight into boss Bassett's own pre-match feelings. Attitude, commitment and character were the three elements of Bassett's focus, with his players reminded of the standards they had set on the opening day of the season against West Bromwich Albion nine months earlier. "If we get the rub of the green, we're on our way," said Bassett alongside his assistant Geoff Taylor, nicknamed 'Ballbag.' "And if you're shitting yourself, just imagine what me and Bag are doing." After sending his players out onto the pitch, Bassett took a moment in the dressing room. "Well, son," he said to an unknown figure off-camera as a tracksuited Stancliffe walked behind him. "It's either a loan from the HFS, or the bank manager's happy."

The manager will have missed what looked like a little hint at pre-match tension in the tunnel between Bryson and Tracey, with the goalkeeper sent packing by the Scotsman after an exchange of words. "I had a ball and he wanted it to warm up with," Bryson said. "I always liked a ball to take out. Players have a lot of superstitions, although I didn't have that many, to be honest. He wanted the ball but I wasn't giving it to him, so we had words. It was a silly thing."

And Bassett had barely made his way to his elevated position in the Filbert Street stands when Leicester took an early lead, Gary Mills rifling home after some hesitant defending. There had been signs of a nervy United start, Gary McAllister seeing a free-kick deflected inches wide with Tracey wrong-footed and Tony James putting a free header over the bar from a corner. Now, on their biggest day of the season, they were behind. That was not in the script.

Richard Windle had travelled to Leicester that day with his parents and brother, with their faces painted red and white and hair sprayed to match as well. "You're a United fan," he admitted, "so you're thinking:

'Oh no, here we go again!'" Mills' opening goal made for uncomfortable viewing for Batman and Robin, too. "My mate worked at a snooker club in Chesterfield and players would come in giving him tickets," Castle, who was dressed as Robin, said. "We managed to get tickets for the match, but the trouble was, they were in the home end. We spent the first half with the Leicester fans and at half-time we went down to the stewards. We said: 'We are Sheffield United supporters; can we go and stand with the rest of the United fans?' It turned out there were about 12 of us in that end and we got escorted round at half-time, with the United fans cheering, and we got let in."

There may have been panic on the terraces but on the turf, it was business as usual. "We got the ball out of the net, put it on the centre spot and gave each other that look," recalled Booker. "The one that just said: 'Come on.' We had too good a team. We were not going to be denied that day." And so it proved, United rattling in four goals without reply before the break – each met with jubilant pitch invasions by fancy dress-clad fans. Wood got United back level when he poked home Bryson's cross, before Deane rifled home from a yard out after a bizarre goalmouth scramble which saw the Leicester goal peppered with five shots, and goalkeeper Martin Hodge take a blow to the head that left him concussed, before the ball finally fell to the striker for sixth time lucky. Deane dropped to his knees after scoring. "It was that feeling of: 'We're on our way … nothing can stop us,' and that was testament to our determination to win the game. For me, it was just a continuation of the season that I was having, I was in the right place at the right time to score that goal."

Former Wednesday goalkeeper Hodge was unable to continue in the aftermath of Deane's goal, with forward Marc North taking over the gloves after initially starting the game in another unfamiliar position of centre-half. North was not a complete goalkeeping novice, having come through the ranks at Luton between the posts before deciding he fancied scoring goals more than saving them. But he was fortunate that a dropped catch from a corner didn't cost his side as Agana's shot was blocked on the line, and was soon back at centre-half after a dazed Hodge took back his gloves. Agana got himself on the scoresheet with a volleyed third, before Hodge failed to stop a bobbling effort from Wilf Rostron for 4-1.

"We were in the lower tier of the away end, behind Hodge's goal, and we were giving him some right shit because he used to play for Wednesday," Windle said. "He was getting a lot of pelters all that half. After being 1-0 down it seemed within no time at all that we were 4-1 up. I remember turning around to some random bloke with my arms out, as if to ask: 'What's going on?' He just hugged me.

"When we got home, I went to the shop with my grandad for a *Green 'Un* and saw the greatest headline in history. You're used to disappointment, being a Blade. I remember the first proper game I took my son to was Huddersfield in the play-off final in 2012. That was the start of his journey. I took him to Northampton in 2017 and we had that day together under Chris Wilder. Leicester was my day, and I am so glad that he had Northampton. Because those are the ones you remember forever."

Leicester pulled a goal back before the break, North volleying home clinically to continue his eventful day after the ball had dropped to him from a long throw, but United were in cruise control and 45 minutes away from a second successive promotion. But the half-time team-talk was dominated, to the players' amazement, by a disagreement between Bassett and Taylor on a set-piece tactic – and more specifically who was United's "zone man" when defending a corner.

Again captured by the cameras of the *BBC,* who must not have believed their luck at the rich trove of content they were being provided for their documentary, it was another iconic moment and has sparked one of the big debates in United's recent history. There are strong suspicions that Rostron should have been the "zone man", but no one seemed to really know for sure. "There are rumours," said physio Dere French. "I don't think we ever found out who it was."

While Bassett and Taylor thrashed it out, United's nonplussed players sat with cold towels over their heads on a boiling-hot day. "We were all buzzing but then Geoff and Harry decided to have a row," Booker said. "We were thinking: 'What the fuck are they doing that for?' Who should have been in the zone? Harry was saying Jock, and Geoff was saying it should be me. It was just chaos. They weren't even talking to us; they were going at it big time. We were 4-2 up and smoking, and they were just having a stand-up row in the middle of the team-talk.

"I remember saying to Mark Morris under my towel: 'What are they arguing for? We're cruising.' The team-talk went out the window at half-time. I don't think we even had one. By the time they finished rowing, the buzzer went and out we went."

For Booker, that short and bizarre clip said everything about the Bassett-Taylor relationship, and why it was so successful. "Geoff wasn't a yes man. He said it how it was and if he felt Harry was wrong, he would tell him. That was the beauty of it. I was assistant manager later in my career, working under seven different managers at Brighton, and I learned a lot from Geoff which stood me in good stead. I remember thinking: 'What would Geoff have done here?' and putting that mixture together, the pair of them, was quality. I went up to see Geoff on his 90th birthday and he was still in good spirits. Harry won't mind me saying this, but Geoff did a lot of the work and Harry picked the team. It was a nice relationship."

The result was put beyond any real doubt by Agana's second to make it 5-2, greeted by more pitch invasions from delirious Blades. "It was a bit surreal, really," said Bryson, whose all-important cross for Wood got United back into it. "The actual game itself, it was crazy. There were about 10,000 Blades fans there but they kept invading the pitch and we were worried about the game being abandoned and called off. It was an unbelievable mix of emotion during the game and then obviously we had the outcome at the end. I can still see my cross for Paul Wood now in my head; that just kick-started us and we were on our way. That first half was one of the craziest halves of football I have ever played in. That, coming back to win that game, summed up our season."

United had one foot in Division One for the first time since 1976 and rather fittingly, the next manager to take the Blades from the third tier to the first was on the pitch on that iconic day at Leicester. "We had that feeling that we were not going to be denied in this," said Wilder. "No matter what happened, and whether things went against us like the early goal, there was just a brilliant belief and an attitude that we weren't going to be denied. Those last 10 minutes were brilliant because we knew we were up and our fans were celebrating.

"With me being on the right, I was on that far side down by the fans. And every time the ball went into the crowd, I was seeing my pals. One of the fans who ran on to the pitch and was on the floor, lifting his arms up, was a pal of mine, Joe Irish, who I have known for years and years. The journey back was brilliant; it just wasn't long enough. When you have days like that, you wish you were playing at the furthest destination possible and it's the longest journey ever. It just flew, the whole weekend. And obviously, there was a little bit of icing on the cake when we came off the pitch, because of you know what."

"You know what" turned out to be confirmation that United's city rivals Wednesday had lost 3-0 at home to Nottingham Forest and had subsequently been relegated from the First Division. Fifty miles or so north from Leicester, *The Star's* designers were busily crafting the headline for that evening's *Green 'Un* edition which was due to hit the streets from their then-offices on York Street within half an hour of the final whistle. Capturing the mood of two very different fanbases in the Steel City could sometimes prove challenging but on other occasions, the beauty was in the simplicity and the eventual front page went down in Blades folklore almost as soon as the first bits of still-fresh newsprint rubbed off on eager fingers.

BLADES GLORY
— OWLS DOWN.

From a United perspective it didn't get much better and as the news filtered through to Filbert Street, Blade Paul Broadhead spared a thought for his then-wife – a Wednesdayite who had left for Hillsborough as Broadhead and his brother began the journey to Filbert Street. "She came to pick me up from Leicester services," he said. "There were loads of United fans there, and we had a great time. With no phones, it was just guesswork when we would both arrive. As it happened, I started to walk across the footbridge and my wife was coming the other way. I am not sure what she noticed first, my shirt or my huge grin. As soon as she saw me, she burst into tears. I did give her a hug, but I was still smiling from ear to ear."

Pirrie's uncle Jimmy, dressed as the bear from the Hofmeister beer adverts of the time and with a radio glued to his ear, jubilantly relayed news of Wednesday's demise after full-time at Leicester. "There were lots of hugs and jumping up and down," said Castle. "We got close to Bassett, who we knew anyway, and managed to get a wave. Outside the ground afterwards, we did the conga around all the coaches. That is one of the greatest days I have had. It was just ecstasy."

Up in the stands, journalist Tony Pritchett was punching out a match report that hailed Bassett for "achieving a football miracle … at least three years ahead of schedule," and in front of him, most of United's players had managed to squeeze themselves off the pitch in time to start their own celebrations in the changing rooms. Bassett, meanwhile, was held aloft on the shoulders of supporters; the coronation of their new king. As Bassett was carried around the pitch, police formed a semi-circle to get him safely back into the dressing room where his wife, Christine, was waiting. As Bassett planted a kiss on his wife's cheek in front of a bank of cameras, Christine was possibly still clutching the piece of "gipsy lace" that she had bought not long before as a lucky charm.

"I was in a dress shop in town on Saturday morning when a gipsy lady tried to tell me some lace," Christine said at the time. "I didn't want any lace, but I felt I should not turn her away on that day of all days, so I bought a little good luck charm. From that moment, I felt confident we would do it. I just knew we could not lose."

One of the first batch of fans on the pitch, Starkes managed to get Mark Morris' shorts as a souvenir; at least until they were stolen from his balcony on holiday in Portugal not long after. A better memento soon entered his possession, as he got round the back of the cordon and waited by the tunnel. "I said to Bassett: 'Give us your shirt, Dave,' and he replied: 'Fucking hell, I don't think I'll get it off.' It was wet through with sweat because of how hot it was and all the fans that had been with him. I said I would get it off him and you can see me at the end of the documentary, taking it off him. It was a really tight fit, figure hugging. A week later there was an open day at Bramall Lane, so I took it down and he signed it across the front.

"At the beginning of the season, I'd had a picture taken with my son sitting on Bassett's knee and he was wearing that white Umbro shirt. At the end of the season, we got promoted and I finished up having it. On the 30th anniversary of Leicester, which was during the Covid-19 lockdown, I took a picture of myself wearing it in my back garden and put it on Instagram. Bassett's daughter, Carly, messaged me to say she had seen it and loved it, so she showed it to her dad. He said he was glad I still had it."

If the scenes at Filbert Street were memorable for United's history makers, there was still the journey back to Bramall Lane to come – with thousands more supporters waiting to greet their heroes in scenes never really seen before. The team coach struggled to make its way through the crowd of people, who then mingled with players in the social club. It was not just about the players, or the staff; it was about everyone. The club had never felt as *united*. The fans handed the keys to Bramall Lane over to Bassett that night, and it was the start of a bond that endures to this day; this was his club now, every bit as much as theirs, and they would be behind him no matter what.

The scenes back at Bramall Lane were an eye-opener for Bryson. "I didn't realise how big a club Sheffield United was until then," he admitted. "And that's not meant with any disrespect. I just wasn't aware of how big they were, and what that success meant to the fans. When we arrived back from Leicester, it was unbelievable. I had never experienced anything like that before, and I never will again. It started to dawn on us. 'What have we actually done?' The success, to get back into the First Division … you didn't realise what it meant to the fans. They hadn't had success for a long while, and that night was just an unbelievable experience."

In The Vine pub in Mosborough, just down the road from the Royal Oak, a Blades fan left fellow punters stunned when he walked in and ordered a round of drinks completely naked, as part of a bet following United's win. And while the Blades players prolonged the festivities in the social club, one of the heroes of Filbert Street made an early exit with his wife and young son. "I was absolutely drained, physically and mentally," Wood said. "I used to live in Grindleford and I went into the local pub and asked for a couple of meals to take home. I just had a quiet night with my wife. I was shattered. I didn't go into town with the other lads. The season was done and it was time to turn off.

"You would be surprised just how many times Sheffield United fans have shown me a video of my goal that day. I was working in Dorchester not long ago and there was a lad working next to me in a van that had a great big Blades sign by the seat. We started chatting and I asked him: 'Were you at the Leicester game?' He looked at me a bit weird and said that he was. I said: 'I was there that day as well. I scored the Blades' first goal.' He thought I was kidding. He then got his phone out and there was a video of the game on it. 'I watch it all the time,' he said. 'It's my highlight of following the Blades. The best day in history.'

"It was a whirlwind period for me, because I joined halfway through the season. But to be a part of that Leicester game and play a big part in it was even better. You can talk to any Blade that day and they all know about it. I can still see the cross from Bryson for my goal. I just tried to get my head on it and I remember thinking the ref might give a foul on the 'keeper if we clashed. But when it came to me, it felt like the 'keeper just moved out of the way of it, as if he bottled it. And that kick-started us. I was involved in the next two and then in no time we were 4-1 up. It was just surreal.

"It summed up our season, that game. You could not have got a better strike force than Deane and Agana, who were best mates and two of the nicest blokes at the club. They just wanted to score goals and they could both play as well. All around the pitch you had nice lads; honest, hard-working. Good players on the bench, too. It was a great squad. For Bassett to have put that squad together with the money that he had was amazing. Bob Booker? Who would have signed Bob Booker at that time, with his knees and at his age? But he had three amazing seasons and became a legend at the Lane."

Victory at Leicester was almost two years to the day since United's last league game of the 1987/88 season, which saw them condemned to a relegation play-off despite beating Huddersfield. United went on to lose on aggregate to Bristol City and dropped into the Third Division. "When you think about where we were then, to being promoted to the top division two years later ... no one thought that was possible," Bassett said. "The way the boys responded to being a goal down at Leicester, and to come back and give a performance like that, was a credit to them. They dealt with the nerves. The fans had gone a long time without anything and when we got off the bus back at the ground ... it was a great feeling, what we'd achieved. It was one of those memorable days that you didn't want to end. I won't ever forget it."

There is a saying in the Steel City used by both sets of fans when one team wins and the other loses on the same day. "I had 200 badges made to celebrate that day at Leicester," Starkes said. On each one read: May 5, 1990 – the ultimate Sheffield double.

"I am very proud to have played for Sheffield United ... I had a lot of success in two and half seasons, more than I had in my career, and I would like to thank the fans for sticking with me and believing in me. I wasn't the world's greatest player but I had a big heart. If you have that and you are a half-decent player, you can do it. Fortunately for me, it fell at the right time. And I am so glad it happened."

– Bob Booker

10

BOOKER PRIZE

It would be a little unfair to characterise him as an *accidental footballer* but it's probably safer to say that Bob Booker was not exactly pre-destined for a career at the top of the game from a young age. That's not to say he didn't have talent; just that not many players these days are plucked from an apprenticeship upholstering furniture and eventually end up playing top-division football. But this was the late 1970s and Booker, by his own modest admission, was simply in the right place at the right time.

For Booker, that place was Hille – a renowned furniture factory where the stackable Polyprop, later to become the world's best-selling chair and sat on in school classrooms all over the globe, originated. Their head-quarters was a former brewery, an ugly, brown building in Watford, but offered Booker his first taste of work after leaving school at 16. Useful with his hands, Booker had sought an apprenticeship making cabinets but had to settle for a role in upholstery before the offer of a four-year course eventually arrived. His first pay packet was £60 a week, with £20 going to his mum, Brenda – renowned as an excellent baker whose wares Booker sold to his co-workers to top up his income. Top-flight football felt, at that stage, a world away.

As a youngster Booker didn't support a club religiously but Vicarage Road wasn't far from the family home and he and his dad, John, occasionally stood on the Hornets' terraces, the young man inspired by the veteran Watford striker Cliff Holton. Booker was 15 when John saw, and answered, an advert in the *Watford Observer* seeking young players for the Hornets – two weeks training under the watchful eye of the formidable youth coach Tom Walley followed, before the sessions were abruptly cancelled because of power cuts. As Booker remembered in *Ooh Aah,* his biography written with Brentford fan Greville Waterman:

"Football was fun, because I enjoyed running around but I was never serious about it. Making a career out of football was never even a consideration or on the radar."

Taller than most other kids his age, Booker excelled as a runner and once came third in an 800m race behind Steve Ovett, who went on to win Olympic gold in that distance at the 1980 Games in Moscow. His size and speed saw him initially utilised as a striker in his school and junior teams, once losing a number of teeth and having to eat through a straw after stooping to head a ball and taking a kick in the face from an opponent. The turning point came with an invite to play for Bedmond, in a local village, where his new teammates included a young Vinnie Jones and future Blades physio Derek French. It was the butterfly effect in motion. Booker scored 15 times in his first season in the first team and manager Dave Bromley, a landscape gardener, tended to the grounds of the playwright Willis Hall – who wrote episodes of the TV show *Minder* amongst other renowned projects. Hall was also a director of Brentford, and Bromley recommended Booker for a trial. The foreman at Hille agreed to give him the day off and Booker was handed his chance in a London Midweek Game against Brighton in March 1978.

In *Ooh Aah,* Booker remembers running around like a headless chicken and giving away a number of free-kicks in his eagerness to impress, but he also scored both Brentford's goals in a 3-2 defeat and Brentford liked what they saw. After a continued spell as a trialist he was offered a one-year deal – on £60 a week. His salary at Hille had increased to £200, but the chance to become a professional footballer meant more than any figure in his pay-packet. Booker signed, Bedmond reportedly received a set of new tracksuits as a transfer "fee" and his foreman at Hille promised to keep his tools handy, "just in case."

They wouldn't be needed again.

Booker went on to become a club legend at Griffin Park, making over 250 appearances for the Bees and notably playing in every outfield position available. He was their player of the year in 1982 and by the late 1980s, his salary had increased to £225 a week plus bonuses for appearances and results. Life was good. Then it all came crashing down. It was a League Cup tie against Southend, and an innocuous-seeming tackle with opponent Danny O'Shea. O'Shea's knee made contact with Booker's knee, destroying his anterior cruciate ligament – a seismic injury in the modern day, let alone in 1986. As he collapsed onto the wet Griffin Park turf, it crossed Booker's mind that he may be finished.

Two months at a rehabilitation centre that usually dealt with victims of car crashes saw Booker make good progress and also offered some sobering perspective, working alongside people who would never be able to speak or walk again. Physically, Booker's knee recovered but the mental scars lasted longer, a loss of confidence not helped by struggling to regain his place after returning to full fitness. It didn't help when Brentford signed Simon Ratcliffe, another midfielder, for £100,000 in 1989. Sheffield United manager David Bassett was also said to be interested in Ratcliffe but wouldn't pay more than £50,000. Booker was pushed further down the Brentford pecking order, and United were a midfielder light. The stars were continuing to align.

Out of favour with new Brentford boss Steve Perryman, with a dodgy knee and the wrong side of 30, Booker was approaching the football scrapheap. There seemed little prospect of an extension to his Bees deal and an investment in a friend's cleaning business looked the most likely avenue for his future, until his old pal French got in touch again.

"Me and Frenchy used to play up front for Bedmond. I was 16 or 17, he's a bit older than me, and we were like Toshack and Keegan. He was the little bald one and I was the big, tall one. We were not quite as good as those two, though! Simon Webster's misfortune, with his broken leg, was my opportunity. But I thought Frenchy was winding me up when he asked me to come up to United. I thought it might be a coaching gig, or kitman or something."

Not quite; Bassett had earmarked Booker as Webster's replacement in his midfield with the Blades chasing promotion from the Third Division. It was something of a footballing salvation, a chance to prove himself all over again. The *Sheffield Star* announced the move with the headline "Booker Prize for Bassett" but moving north brought what Booker described in his book as "a sense of abject terror." "I was worried about my knee," he said. "When it was straight I wanted to bend it and when it was bent, I wanted to straighten it. There was a lot of wear and tear after I snapped my cruciate. I had it lasered a few times and the gap was getting bigger between my joints. I was in a lot of pain and it was a case of managing it. Frenchy worked wonders on me.

"It was very difficult to start with, because Harry liked to do a lot of physical work. I would have a good running session and then the next day I would be in bits. It was a bit of TLC and a lot of hard work from Derek French. I would not have got through any of it without him. Harry's fitness regime was a lot different to what we were doing at Brentford, with little five-a-sides and things like that. Harry ran the bollocks off us because you had to be fit in that position, to get from one penalty area to the other."

Early in his United career Booker was going short to his full-backs and centre-halves, asking for the ball to feet; they would respond by knocking it 70 yards over his head up to strikers Brian Deane and Tony Agana. "Fuck off," Bassett would shout at Booker. "You're not having it there … go and get the knock-down."

Perhaps unsurprisingly, Booker struggled to initially adapt. "The crowd must have thought: 'Who have we signed here? Why has Bassett brought him in?' I had a lot of low moments to start with. But fair play to the manager; he didn't leave me out of that team. He said: 'No, you're going to keep playing, you're going to get there.' That was brilliant for me because I was getting a lot of stick. It's very difficult when you are driving home, listening to *Praise or Grumble* on the radio. I know I shouldn't have listened to it really, but the fans were saying: 'He can't run, he can't do this and he can't do that.'

"The same happened when I joined Brentford, with the crowd booing you and things like that. I didn't think I had made a mistake, because I knew the manager believed in me and the lads were as good as gold. They could see the effort I was putting in. I wasn't the greatest player but I was an honest player. I was trying, but it just wasn't happening. Because I'd had the same experience at Brentford, I knew what was coming. The only difference was that at Brentford there were 4,000 fans and at Sheffield United there were 24,000. The levels had gone up tenfold and that was a little bit difficult."

Booker was as low on confidence as he was on fitness and still winces at the thought of the cruel "Bobby Blunders" nickname that some sections of the United fanbase had bestowed upon him. With his then-partner remaining down south, Booker's regular post-match routine saw him pick up four cans of beer and a takeaway of fried chicken and devour them alone, with just those intrusive thoughts for company. But the experience of similar treatment early on at Brentford was something to fall back on, and Booker realised he had a choice: give in, or overcome it. Fight or flight. Sink or swim. A life raft appeared in the shape of Mick Rooker, the well-known figure behind the scenes at Bramall Lane who was the first person Booker saw when he arrived. At first Booker struggled to understand a word Rooker said but the two became close friends, with Booker confiding in his new pal about his tough start. Rooker's advice proved prophetic – along the lines of: "Give 100 per cent and don't hide, because you'll get sussed out by the fans. Show them that you're not intimidated."

Booker had been a United player for four and a half months by the time he walked out at a freezing Field Mill to face Mansfield on April 4, 1989 but that was the game in which his Blades career really began. Battling gale-force winds and a snowstorm Booker was colossal in the middle of the United midfield and won the penalty from which Peter Duffield scored the Blades winner. "It all changed that night," Booker said.

"I could see where I had to get to, but it was getting there without getting wrecked mentally. Even the press were not that kind to me, but that's football. You have to take that. It's alright taking the glory and everyone buying you a drink when everything's going well. It's the bad times, when you come through it, that really matters. The rewards are great when you are winning but when it's not happening, it's very difficult. Players have all been through it, and you have to go through it; otherwise you just fall by the wayside."

Close relationships with his United teammates certainly helped, with defender Chris Wilder and midfielder Mark Todd amongst the first to welcome him to Sheffield and offer a lift to United's training ground. For the first month or so Booker was alone in the Moat House hotel, almost 200 miles away from his family. "I had never experienced that before, because every day I had just travelled in from Watford to Brentford. All of a sudden, I couldn't just pop home after training and there was a lot of time on your own in the hotel. But as soon as I buddied up with Chrissy Wilder, it was a lot better.

"I had a time at Upperthorpe with Derek French and Geoff Taylor but Geoff, bless him, kept farting and shitting too much, so I had to get out of there. He stunk the place out. It was also haunted. I am telling you now. I am not a believer in all that stuff, but me and Frenchy jumped out of our skins when we saw an old lady sitting at the end of a bed. People will laugh at that, but it frightened the shit out of me and Derek."

Booker escaped to live with Wilder's mum and dad. "It all fell into place. They had a couple of labradors there and I loved walking dogs. I had my own annex at the end of their garden. You went upstairs and I had my own bedroom and kitchen, a little lounge area. It was like paradise, really, and I felt really comfortable. I still wasn't getting home a lot, which unfortunately took its toll on my marriage. We parted ways a little bit after Sheffield. Ideally my first wife should have come up to Sheffield straight away, but that didn't happen and we just drifted apart. I was very happy living in Sheffield. People said 'good morning' to you. It's just a nice city with nice people." Some years later, when Wilder signed for Brighton, Booker returned the favour by allowing his former teammate to stay at his house on the way down south.

Within 18 months of arriving at United, Booker was a top-flight player as the Blades stormed to back-to-back promotions. "It was something I had not experienced. I had never had a promotion at Brentford, and unfortunately I missed out on that night at Wolves because I had pulled my hamstring. I was standing on the sidelines that night but the celebrations in the dressing room were fantastic. Because of the fact it was late in my career and I thought those times were not going to happen, it was precious. It made it even more special.

"We trained hard, we played hard. When it was football time, it was football time and when it was social time, it was social time. Turning up in the social club for lunch after training every day, the wives getting involved… it was just one happy family. You won't ever repeat that team spirit these days. We took team spirit to another level back then."

Booker had made his Brentford debut against Watford, with a bit of bad blood existing between the two clubs, but moving to Sheffield gave him a taste of a *real* derby when United took on Wednesday – even in a pre-season friendly. "I had clocked on to that rivalry as soon as I entered the club. You could feel it, you could see it and you could hear it. Playing in the same position, you hear other players saying things like: 'Carlton Palmer thinks he's the dog's bollocks.' It was just one of those, a big wind-up. You try and get the word out there that we are going to do them and they are going to do us and that sort of thing. There's just a build-up of pressure leading up to the game.

"I wouldn't say I disliked Palmer as a person – it was just the fact it was Sheffield Wednesday. He was quite a big name, he had played for England, and he probably thought: 'Who is Bob Booker?' I had great respect for him, he was a good midfielder. But on that day, he was mixing with Sheffield United, and mixing with 'Ooh Aah.'

"He was running around and kicking me, but he wasn't getting very far. When someone gets kicked these days, the first thing they do is go down and put their arm in the air. I was taught not to go down unless I was hurt. We were having the tussles and the verbals and if I went over, I just got back up and ran off again. I could see the steam coming out of his ears. I said to him: 'Is that all you've got?' and that was like a red rag to a bull. He just ran and put his studs down the back of my leg. I went down and I could see all the other players getting into a ruck, and could hear the crowd. Frenchy came on and said: 'What have you done?' I asked him what was happening and he said: 'I think he might get sent off.' As soon as he said that I told him to get the sponge out and look busy while I stayed down. I milked it a little bit – call it professionalism or whatever – but he went off and that put paid to his start to the season.

"I don't think our paths have ever crossed since to talk about it. He probably can't even remember it. That was always a great battle against Sheffield Wednesday. I was lucky enough to score in the Zenith Data Systems Cup at Hillsborough but unfortunately John Sheridan ran from the halfway line and scored the winner. That was a nice moment, scoring one of our goals in front of 30,000. They were good derbies during that time and good for the city."

Booker was soon fully up to speed, and United were on a roll. "Definitely. Especially with 20-odd thousand at home and the following we used to take away from home – five or six thousand. It just showed the size and magnitude of the club. It was all happening very quickly under Dave Bassett. Getting him in was a masterclass. The train was rolling and nothing was going to stop it. To be part of that with the fans, and the players that we had at the time was unbelievable. Bringing Billy Whitehurst in was a quality move, to come off the bench and cause major chaos. John Gannon was on set pieces and was similar to me, coming from down south and having a bit of stick to start with. We had a good relationship in the middle and it was a nice blend of players. We had local lads and the two up front … with wide players supplying them 20-odd goals apiece, you are going to be there or thereabouts. It was great man-management."

The crowning glory came on that day at Leicester. United travelled to Filbert Street knowing that victory would see them reclaim their place in the top flight, with Booker wearing the armband in Paul Stancliffe's absence. "Harry pulled me on the Wednesday to tell me I was going to be skipper. I thought: 'Hang on a minute ... we've got Chrissy Wilder, a local lad ... Wilf Rostron, Mark Morris, Colin Hill ... years of experience.' But Harry said: 'No, you are going to take us out there.' It was a massive honour for me and something I will never forget. I remember going down the tunnel, looking back and seeing that lot behind me. It's easy to say in hindsight, but I knew there was never going to be any other result that day."

Another stand-out memory from Filbert Street is an on-field battle with Gary McAllister, in midfield for Leicester that day. "I remember it well because I really respected him. He could pass a ball, was quality on set-pieces and was one hell of a player. We had a bit of a tussle and I ended up on the deck, when he leant over me and said: 'Who the fuck are you?' As I looked up at him all the Unitedites started singing the 'Ooh Aah Bob Booker' song. So I just said: 'Do you hear that? That's who I am. I'm Ooh Aah, Bob Booker. Now fuck off.'"

The 'Ooh Aah' chant was later attached to Eric Cantona at Leeds and Manchester United, the iconic Frenchman following in the footsteps of Booker. "A lot of fans say it started with me before it got to Eric, which is quite nice. I'll stick with that. If I have had it before Eric then that's not a bad one to follow me, is it? A lot of things happen in football clubs but when you speak to United fans who were around at that time, it always comes back to Leicester. It is quite phenomenal, really, because it was such a rollercoaster time and that game won't ever be forgotten in United's history. All those of us who were involved will never forget it.

"We played a massive part in the history of Sheffield United and I am very, very privileged to have been involved in that. I have played at Wembley, scored hat-tricks and had promotions, but Leicester was the highlight of my football career. I was privileged enough to just play in that game, never mind being captain as well. I'm forever grateful for that to happen. I am very, very proud of it."

There are regrets, though. Booker was happy to give his iconic luminous green shirt from that famous day to his pal Rooker, as a thanks for his support, but he still laments the decision to let a fan who had invaded the pitch have his captain's armband. "When I come back to Sheffield there will be kids at 18 or 19 who will come up and ask for my autograph. I look at them and think: 'You weren't even born when I played,' and they say things like: 'My dad brought me up singing your name and I watch the DVDs.' I think that's amazing, that 30 years on people still remember. It touches a nice note. It means everything."

One supporter in particular has especially fond memories of Booker. As part of his initiation with Unitedites, Rooker took the midfielder to meet and greet them in local pubs and shops and sign autographs for hours on end. "I loved it," Booker said. "It would never happen today but I worked in a factory before I became a footballer so I knew what it was like to work in the real world. They were my people. That's the way I saw it. I was signing one day when one little lad, called Richard Flower, came up to me and said: 'Will you come and have dinner with me at my mum and dad's?' His mum said: 'Don't be silly, Richard, he can't do that.' I said: 'Yes, I can.' I took their address and went round there with a signed ball. He must have told his mates because there were about 30 kids outside his house when I got there. I went in and had meat and potato pie with Richard and his family, and we are still friends to this day. He has kids himself and it's been a nice journey. We have stayed in contact and he sent me the picture of us on the settee, with the ball. It's a nice moment. I am quite proud of little things like that. I think it goes a long way and should be more of that. But times have changed and players are protected."

Booker laughed at the memory of being told that Flower's dad usually ate tea from a tray on his lap in front of the television but when the United midfielder came round, he was at the dinner table wearing a suit and tie. Word soon spread and Booker was inundated with requests from United-mad kids keen for him to visit their house for tea. He wrote to each one to politely decline, blaming Bassett putting him on a strict diet that didn't leave much room for nightly meat and potato pie and including a signed photo to soften the blow. Booker once signed autographs for fans in the middle of a film at Crystal Peaks shopping centre and when United were relegated at Chelsea in 1994, long after he had moved on, a group of Blades fans gathered outside his house to sing his 'Ooh Aah' song. Booker invited them in, and they drank his house dry.

Booker's First Division debut had come four years earlier, when United welcomed the reigning English champions Liverpool to South

Yorkshire and just over 29,000 fans packed into Bramall Lane. Booker was 32 and could easily have been cleaning windows if life had taken a slightly different path – during a break in play, he sought out his dad in the crowd and just grinned at him, taking in the magnitude of the journey. The harsh realities of life in the top-flight soon kicked in when United went on a long winless run but when they recovered to achieve a remarkable 13th-place finish, it was Booker who fittingly secured safety with the winner away at Queens Park Rangers. To this day, Booker tears up at the memory of his dad in the upper tier at Loftus Road, looking down proudly on his son after he'd scored that memorable goal.

Just over six months later, Booker's Bramall Lane career came to an abrupt and surprising end. United were preparing for a long-awaited Sheffield derby against Wednesday at Bramall Lane when Booker was called into Bassett's office. "He said to me: 'I'm going to be upfront with you, but I don't know if you are going to like this. Brentford have come back in for you,'" Booker remembered. "I still had a year of my contract to go and he just said: 'Listen, you're 32 years old, coming up to 33. You have done the job I wanted you to do. You are quite welcome to stay, but you'll be on the bench. You've had back-to-back promotions and you are a legend here.' That 'legend' status didn't sit well with me, to be honest – that's your Brian Deanes and Tony Curries of this world, your Len Badgers and all those names.

"I said I didn't want to go but he told me that Brentford would match my wages on a contract until I was 35 and said: 'I think you should take it.' I was really reluctant but I spoke to the Brentford manager over the phone while Harry was there. It was strange because I had left there as a nobody and now, I was going back after back-to-back promotions and being skipper. They thought they were getting Ronaldinho! But I was going back on my terms now. They were getting the same Bob Booker; it was just that I had come up here and played in a brilliant team. Did what the manager had asked, and had some success.

"I decided reluctantly to go but the truth is that I only went because Harry thought it was the best for me at that stage of my career. He was looking out for me and telling me what he would do, telling me I should be looking after my family and signing a bit more security for a couple of years, which he couldn't guarantee. I think it was just as hard for him to tell me it as it was for me to accept it. He then told me that the club would announce it to the fans and that he wanted me to go on the pitch. He said I deserved to go out there and get the accolade from the fans. We'd not done that before.

"I was a bit dubious about it, with Wednesday fans being in the stadium, but I took the applause from three sides of the ground. I stood there with a lump in my throat and tears in my eyes. It was really tough but it felt good. The ovation I got really stuck with me. I had mixed emotions. Part of me wanted to stay because I'd had that success and that bond with the players and the fans. I went back and made my Brentford 'debut' the following week away at Bournemouth. I woke up the morning after and my knee was in bits. It more or less packed up. I managed to play a few games and got promotion with them but it wasn't the same, because I knew I had to call it a day. I didn't see the contract out; it came to an end with the injury. I saw the surgeon and he told me to jack it in."

The injury got him in the end but there is no denying that Booker squeezed every drop out of his career at Bramall Lane, playing 109 of the 127 league games for which he was eligible and leaving the Blades with a million memories. When he was granted a well-earned testimonial, there were only two clubs that could have faced off but only 1,531 fans turned up to Griffin Park – the £4,500 proceeds boosted by a healthy contingent from Sheffield. Bassett had encouraged Booker to switch the game to Bramall Lane but, as a measure of the man, Booker refused to inconvenience Brentford fans for the sake of a few more quid in his pocket.

"Harry was and always will be my mentor. He looked after me in different ways. I still had about 18 months to go on my contract when he pulled me in and topped my wages up a bit more. I had never experienced that at Brentford. It was year-to-year and you were thinking: 'Am I going to get signed again?' He gave me all that security and financially my life changed. Even at the level then, in the 1990s, I had done well out of it. It wasn't about that, but the success brought rewards and he did reward me, big time. He looked after me financially and he looked after me physically and mentally as well.

"I lost my dad but I still had a dad in Dave Bassett. I still speak to him on a weekly basis and I have so much time for him. We all did. Although we called him "Harry the Bastard," you would run through a brick wall for him. He could ridicule you and belittle you in his team talks, but then you knew he would have a drink with you when the work was done.

"That was man management. I remember on one occasion, I had not been home for a while and I asked him on the Friday if I could travel back after the game on the Saturday. We were going well at the time and he said: 'Get yourself off down south, you haven't been home for two months.' We drew the game and he went absolutely ballistic in the dressing room afterwards. He dug us all out. 'Bob you were shit today … you didn't head, you didn't tackle, you didn't do this, you didn't do that …' He absolutely slaughtered us and then said: 'You're all in in the morning. You didn't run around for 45 minutes so you can run around the pitch in the morning. You're all in at eight o'clock.'

"My first reaction was: 'Oh bollocks, I've got to tell the family I am not coming home now. What am I going to say to the family?' Then, I'll never forget him coming in for his shower and popping his head into my cubicle. 'Get yourself home, son,' he said. 'You haven't been home for ages.' I said: 'Harry, if the lads are running in the morning, then I'm in. Otherwise it looks like I am jumping ship, and I don't want any of that.' He said it was up to me, but I had his blessing. In the heat of the moment, when he was angry with us and slaughtering me, he remembered I had not been home and he told me to go home and see the family. That's not about coaching skills, that's just priceless. It will always stay with me. But I didn't go home, and I ran my bollocks off the next morning.

"It was such a short time, but United feels part of my family. My dad is not with us anymore, God bless him, but I know I could go to Dave Bassett for anything and he would be there for me. I am totally respectful to the man; not just for what he did for me, but what he did for that football club as well in that era. I think we should be forever grateful. I am very proud to have played for Sheffield United and it was so late in my career that I never thought it was going to happen. I had a lot of success in two and half seasons, more than I had in my career, and I would like to thank the fans for sticking with me and believing in me. And still having the relationship I have with them to this day. I wasn't the world's greatest player but I had a big heart. If you have that and you are a half-decent player, you can do it. Fortunately for me, it fell at the right time. And I am so glad it happened."

The right time, and without doubt the right place.

11

THE GREAT ESCAPE

As a youngster, Jamie Hoyland never wanted to play for Sheffield United. It seems like a strange position for a boyhood Blade to take, someone who had stood on the terraces as a youngster to cheer on his own heroes and then taken a step closer to them by becoming a Bramall Lane ball-boy. The young Hoyland was in the crowd when Tony Currie sat on the ball against Arsenal, to mock Alan Ball; he was there on that dark day at home to Walsall when United were relegated to the Fourth Division, joining the pitch invasion after the full-time whistle. He lived at one stage a decent goal-kick away from the Lane in his dad's pub, The Sheldon, on Hill Street. The Blades were in his blood.

Quite literally, too. Hoyland's father, Tommy, had been a United player of some distinction in the 1950s until 1961, playing alongside the great Jimmy Hagan and Joe Shaw. But Hoyland Jr. was determined not to be defined as the son of his father and so instead of taking his first footballing steps in his beloved red and white, they came just over 30 miles north-west of home in the sky blue of Manchester City. Life at Maine Road began well, with a debut goal, before a bad injury caused a troublesome succession of them. At 20 years of age, he was let go.

Football salvation came in the shape of Division Three side Bury, having impressed manager Martin Dobson at exit trials, and four years at Gigg Lane, free of the knee injuries that had stalled his progress at City, helped Hoyland to get his career up and running. A memorable goal at Old Trafford against Manchester United, in front of the TV cameras, brought him to the attention of plenty of clubs; a £250,000 offer from Ipswich was turned down by Terry Robinson, the Bury chairman and future United chief executive who players nicknamed "Greengrass" after the character from the TV drama *Heartbeat.*

Hoyland had started out as a centre-forward at City but by the time he landed on Dave Bassett's radar had dropped back to midfield, with Dobson – himself a cultured midfielder in his time with Burnley and Everton – sensing that Hoyland's physical ability and eye for goal would be better suited to the middle of the park. Hoyland was 24, out of contract at Gigg Lane and, despite an attractive offer on the table from Robinson to stay, was ready to fly the nest. It was a sign of the times that his next move was to write to dozens of clubs and ask if they would be interested in signing him. He even tried his luck with the Red Devils, with manager Alex Ferguson writing back personally to say thanks, but no thanks – adding, by way of encouragement, that he was convinced that Hoyland would get a club.

One that did show a fancy were Wolves – in Division Two at the time, and exactly the size of outfit that Hoyland hoped would take a fancy. They also offered the sort of money – scribbled down by manager Graeme Turner, on the back of a beer mat at the Great Barr Hotel near Birmingham – that made Hoyland, who readily admits that he has never had much of a poker face, gasp. Newly married and even without his own car at the time, Hoyland recognised quickly that the move would be life-changing and quickly scrambled to the phone in the hotel bar, to inform Bury boss Sam Ellis that he was off to the Midlands. "Before you sign anything," Ellis replied, "Dave Bassett at Sheffield United wants to speak to you. Today."

That initial promise he made as a youngster raced back to the front of his mind; how he had resolved not to follow in his father's footsteps, not to risk becoming merely *the son of Tommy.* But now, he sensed, it felt different. He was older and wiser, a fully-fledged professional in his own right and with almost 200 senior games under his belt to prove it. For a boyhood Blade, turning down Sheffield United was one thing in theory and quite another when a very real Bassett was on the other end of the phone and trying to bring Hoyland back to his literal and spiritual home. The lure proved just too great.

Only days earlier Hoyland had watched United's promotion to the First Division unfold on the TV in the players' lounge at Gigg Lane. On a memorable day United were promoted with victory at Leicester, their city rivals Wednesday were relegated and Bury had rubberstamped their play-off place with a 2-0 home win over Cardiff. Little wonder that Hoyland remembered "running around like a mad man in the bar. Everyone was looking at me and asking: 'What are you doing?' But they all knew I was a United fan and because we had got in the play-offs, and Wednesday had gone down … it was a triple whammy for me."

The offer from Wolves was put on ice as Hoyland raced over the Woodhead Pass back to Sheffield, with Turner's beermat in his back pocket and a flutter in his stomach. Those Wolves figures proved a valuable starting point in the wage negotiations with United, which weren't really negotiations at all and were concluded in a matter of minutes. The once-reluctant Blade was now a fully-fledged Sheffield United player.

Even then, Wolves weren't going away without a fight, offering to beat United's wage offer and even add another £10,000 to Hoyland's signing-on fee. It could have been 10 times that and the answer would have been the same. Hoyland was going home.

Keen to keep evolving a squad that had bounced from the third tier to the first in two glorious seasons, Bassett had identified a weakness in the middle of the park – and saw Hoyland's box-to-box running and goal contribution from midfield as the ideal way to address it. Hoyland was also as fit as a fiddle, as he demonstrated early on when he joined his new teammates at their pre-season army camp in Reading and breezed through the bleep-test. Bassett's relaxed methods were a far cry from the sergeant major approach of City legend Tony Book that had shaped the young Hoyland and as he adjusted, he even turned down the chance to join his new teammates at a nearby pub during the camp.

It was the summer that saw Bobby Robson's England side capture the nation's imagination at Italia '90 by reaching the last four, and Hoyland's world was certainly in motion. A promotion bid at Bury the previous season had ended in the Third Division play-offs and just weeks later, Hoyland was preparing for life at the top of the English pyramid. Like every other England fan that summer Hoyland had watched the likes of Paul Gascoigne, John Barnes and Gary Lineker on World Cup duty – and suddenly, they were not simply distant figures on a small TV screen but direct opponents. It was a prospect that aroused inspiration, but also insecurity; Hoyland fought, and still fights, imposter syndrome. The biggest battle he would face in Division One was not against anyone else on the pitch, but against himself in his own head.

"It held me back, massively," Hoyland admitted of what he calls the "devil on his shoulder" constantly telling him he wasn't good enough. "Coming to United was difficult, with my dad's name and being a United fan coming from Sheffield. The pressure was just constant. I lived at my dad's pub for a few months until I got my own place, and it was just United all the time. Everywhere you went. They were also a successful team as well when I joined. Players who had got United to this place were leaving and I had taken their place, so I felt that pressure as well. I would be sick before games. But people would say: 'You never looked nervous.' It was just everything building up, and the imposter syndrome. 'Am I good enough to play in this?' It was a nervous trait that I had. Other players had it, too."

Hoyland's nerves were not eased by a difficult adjustment to Bassett's methods, either. In his very first training session Hoyland took the ball under control and laid off a neat pass to his full-back; Bassett stopped the session immediately and asked Hoyland, in no uncertain and less polite terms, what he thought he was doing. Hoyland's job, he quickly learned, was not to play those sorts of passes and instead, get the ball forward. There were several occasions, in the first few months, when he wondered what he had let himself in for. "Just from a football point of view. If I had been at any other club, I would have said: 'I want to leave. This is not for me, because it's not going to help my career one bit.' But because I was a United fan, I thought: 'No, knuckle down and have a go at it.' I will never regret it because of the memories and adventures that I had. Even though the imposter syndrome was there and everything that went with playing for United, I was still so proud that I did it. And I think my family were proud as well."

The pressure of the £250,000 price tag, a club record at the time, also weighed heavily on his shoulders but was soon lifted when Paul Beesley joined for £375,000 from Leyton Orient, and fellow defender John Pemberton returned north from Crystal Palace for a fee of £300,000. Goalkeeper Phil Kite, a replacement for Brentford-bound Graeme Benstead, also arrived from Bournemouth in a £25,000 move – later forming a close bond with defender David Barnes, despite the constant ringing in his ears from those tea urn lids.

Bassett was keen to add some pace to his back-line ahead of United's First Division adventure, while Pemberton had appeared in the FA Cup final for Crystal Palace just weeks before his move and brought some valuable top-flight experience to Bramall Lane. He met his new team-mates for the first time before their pre-season trip to Sweden, walking into Heathrow airport with a huge suitcase and wearing a tweed jacket and cravat. Striker Billy Whitehurst took one look at the new man and made his feelings clear. "Who the fuck is this?" he cried.

"Pembo loved all that," said Hoyland. "He was from Oldham, so he was a northern lad. He'd played at Rochdale as a kid and it was his career that took him to Palace. Because of that, he got it straight away. Had he been a southerner, turning up like that, he would have been in for the biggest culture shock of his life. But he joined in straight away. He was fine with us."

With United around £3m in debt at the time, managing director Derek Dooley admitted that promotion had "changed the whole future of the club overnight" and the Blades' reward for getting back into the big-time was a mouth-watering opening-day clash at home to reigning champions Liverpool. Paul Stancliffe had found it hard to watch the scenes at Filbert Street from the sidelines with an injury, but leading United out onto the pitch, against the likes of Barnes, Ian Rush and Jan Mølby, was at least some consolation for the United captain. Ultimately, though, that day summed up United's first part of the season as they gave a good account of themselves but ultimately came up short. Goalkeeper Simon Tracey was stretchered off in the first half with a broken cheekbone and Pemberton marked a memorable debut by taking over the gloves. Despite the lack of a recognised 'keeper, the hosts held firm until Liverpool put the game to bed in the final 25 minutes.

It would soon become apparent that United were struggling with the step up. Bassett's ruthless streak saw him shuffle his pack once more and after seven years of fabulous service, captain Stancliffe's time was up. Bassett was clever and cute but he wasn't cruel and it was a decision that brought him no pleasure. In fact, it felt as painful for Bassett to deliver the news as it was for Stancliffe to hear it. But the manager backed his judgement and didn't allow sentiment to cloud it, with his former skipper moving to York – via a brief loan spell with Rotherham – and later captaining City to promotion in the play-off final at Wembley in 1993.

The armband that had for so long lived around Stancliffe's bicep was passed to Vinnie Jones, another former Wimbledon man who had arrived from Leeds. Derek Dooley, the late managing director, remembered handling the negotiation and offering Leeds a take-it-or-leave-it fee, with the Blades unable to go any higher. Leeds initially left it, before changing their mind and taking it. Jones had a certain reputation in the game from his days in the Wimbledon Crazy Gang but was also remembered by many former teammates as a better footballer than he was given credit for. He also had a softer side, taking a bulk load of toys up to the Sheffield Children's Hospital and declining any publicity about it, and took a wage-cut from Leeds to link up again with Bassett at Bramall Lane. "Only Harry could get me to do that," he admitted privately.

Born in Watford and a long-term friend of United men Derek French and Bob Booker, Jones' first proper job was as a gardener at a masonic school, with 80 acres of grounds to maintain. His football journey began in the local amateur leagues before being plucked by First Division Wimbledon from semi-pro side Wealdstone for a £10,000 fee. A £650,000 move then took him to Leeds and he helped them into the top-flight, alongside United, before his time at Elland Road came to a premature end when he returned for pre-season and found Gary McAllister's name on his peg in the changing room.

Jones, of course, made the post-football transition to become a Hollywood film star and in a scene more reminiscent of *Lock, Stock and Two Smoking Barrels*, he kept hold of a shotgun he had used to go shooting that morning. Exasperated at his lack of game-time, he pointed it up Leeds boss Howard Wilkinson's nostrils and sneered: "Am I playing now?" Jones recalled in his autobiography that Wilkinson initially looked understandably nervous, before cracking up laughing afterwards. The writing was on the wall at Elland Road, though, and Jones was soon making the short trip down the M1 to Sheffield, modestly likening his Leeds departure to "someone telling the Queen that she was on her way out of Buckingham Palace." Bassett lived almost next door to Wilkinson and despite Jones' dad strongly urging his son to reconsider, the deal was done quickly.

Jones' arrival was big news for United, with the legendary Bri and Irene's shop on the corner of Shoreham Street offering fans sweets named after the new midfielder, while one of his first acts as United skipper was to change the pre-match music in the dressing room to *Dangerous,* the reggae song by Conroy Smith that used to accompany boxer Nigel Benn to the ring before fights. "It was a mentality thing," Hoyland said. "That we were all going out to fight for three points. I remember at Norwich, they kept unplugging it but he kept putting it back on, just to piss them right off. That's what he used to do. He used to put it outside in the corridor and we would try and wait for the opposition so we could go out together. You didn't have to back then, you could go out when you wanted, but we'd wait to get into them. It was his way of trying to unsettle them and unnerve them, all of that. He added a bit more fear for the opposition because they'd look at the teamsheet and think: 'Oh shit, Vinnie Jones is playing.' He was a name, a ruthless hard man in football. And he played for Sheffield United."

Jones had helped harness the Crazy Gang spirit at Wimbledon and took little time to settle into things at Bramall Lane, with United not short on characters themselves at this stage. Winger Paul Wood remembers wiping his backside on Jones' shirt at an army camp. "The next day he came out laughing, saying: 'Those army lads, they've just shit in my armpits,'" Wood said. "He thought it was great because he thought it was the army lads. He had no idea it was me." Beesley, known to many as the "Mad Scouser," was holding his own; Barnes was continuing his torment of Phil Kite; Carl Bradshaw, Mitch Ward and Dane Whitehouse had also established their places on merit and were ready to wrestle anyone who came near their shirt. Then there was Whitehurst. Once, at a speaking event, Jones was asked what it was like to be the hardest man in football. Pointing to Whitehurst, sitting in the front row, Jones replied: "Ask him."

A dressing room containing Whitehurst and Jones was certainly not a place for shrinking violets. Jones has claimed that Whitehurst once called United's coach company and told them that their reserve game had been called off, and organised the driver to take a group of players to Cheltenham racecourse instead. Another time, Jones kidnapped French from his front room and drove him to Manchester in the boot of a car, with the physio's stunned family wondering what on earth had just happened.

With two huge characters in the same dressing room, the opportunity for conflict was obvious but instead there was a huge mutual respect between Jones and Whitehurst – who never came to blows themselves and, on one occasion, even joined forces. It was a midweek night and United's players were enjoying a beer in Henry's, a city centre bar which sat across the road from the famous Cole Brothers shop before it was demolished. Wednesday had been due to play at home but the weather had caused the game to be postponed, with some of the Owls' hooligan element subsequently wandering up the hill and into Sheffield city centre.

"We were alright, me and Vinnie," said Whitehurst. "He was a good craic, and was good company. Contrary to all the shit in the papers about me grabbing Vinnie one day at Sheffield United ... let me tell you, that didn't happen."

But the infamous night at Henry's certainly did and around a quarter of a century on, it is still remembered vividly by those who were there to witness it. "We were having a beer at a big round table and the Wednesday mob came in," Whitehurst said. "They shouldn't have been allowed in, really, because there were bouncers on the door. But they let them in and they'd all got bottles of beer.

"I had my back to them and they were having a go at Jonesy, giving him big lips. Then a glass went over my head and after it smashed, a piece of glass hit Barnesy. I turned around and one of them shouted: 'What are you looking at, you big ugly bastard?' I looked around because I thought: 'They must be talking about Vinnie; this can't be me.' I said: 'You're a hard man with 20 people behind you ... let's me and you go outside.'"

Whitehurst offered to settle the stand-off with two members of the Wednesday party, and all eyes were on who returned to the bar first. It was Whitehurst and Jones. Jones wrote in his book that Whitehurst hit the Wednesday lad with the hardest right hand he had ever seen, in or out of a boxing ring. He was not a man with whom to take liberties. The next morning, Whitehurst and his teammates were summoned to Bassett's office; the striker's stomach sinking when he walked in and saw CID officers already in there. "I thought the idiot had died," Whitehurst admitted. "I was frightened." Instead, Whitehurst remembered the players being told that the Owls group had gone on to cause more trouble that night, and were being sought after the landlord of another pub had apparently been attacked.

"You're a target to a certain element of the public, aren't you? Sheffield's a massive divide with football and wherever we were, we ran the gauntlet of crossing paths with different sets of supporters. It wouldn't have happened if their game hadn't been called off. I don't know whether they were actually looking for trouble but I bet it was like going into a sweet shop for them, with the rival team being in there. It went wrong for them, really, and it could have been worse. The kid could have died and it could have been disastrous for everyone concerned. I've had friends that have just gone down with one punch and gone 'bang.' It is scary. Having said that, I've had a few situations since then … and the penny doesn't seem to drop, you know?"

Jones later described his season at United as "a fairly depressing experience," but many players from that era describe his presence, on and off the pitch, as one of the reasons United stayed up in 1990/91, after a nightmare start which had seen them go 16 games without their first win back in the top league. "I suppose there was always going to be a bit of animosity about Vinnie Jones coming in," remembered Booker, "because he's a high-profile character. But he came in when we weren't getting results and Harry looked at him as a leader. He was made club captain straight away and to be fair, he took control in the dressing room.

"I thought it was a great signing. He was going to take my position and take my number four shirt, but I was quite happy to give it to him. He took it with open arms. It was the least I could do. He put his mark on the football club, and in the dressing room, and he got things done. He really bought into it and made a good impression. He had that nice balance, doing all the pranks against the northerners but also taking as good as he got. He took it too far at Man City, when Harry told him he wanted him to get in to Peter Reid and he got sent off. Harry wasn't too pleased with that. Harry had a go at him in the dressing room but Vinnie had a go back, saying: 'You told me to get stuck into him." Harry replied: 'Yeah, but not to get sent off!' Part of the reason we stopped up is through Vinnie Jones and his character in the dressing room, taking us out on to that pitch. He did a good job."

Another of Jones' former teammates at the time described him as "Marmite" in the dressing room – either loved or hated – but there were other classy touches alongside his generosity at the children's hospital. One time, Jones heard about a Blades-supporting builder who had suffered a broken leg and was unable to work as a result, and organised a karaoke night to support him and his family. "Those things don't get reported," Booker added. "He was good at getting us all together and out for meals with the wives, he took charge of all the fines. He was also one of the fittest players I had ever met. I could run, and so could Chrissy Wilder on the long-distance stuff, but Vinnie was another level. That boy could run and run. He was an animal. An animal on the pitch and a gentle giant off of it."

Jones' first game as captain was away to Southampton in September, acknowledging an away end in fine voice with a fist pump as he led his side out. But it was to no avail, as goals from Matt Le Tissier and Rod Wallace sealed a 2-0 win for Saints, and United's results got worse before they got better. A November defeat by the same scoreline at home to Sunderland saw defender Beesley make two huge errors for two goals from striker Marco Gabbiadini, with Bassett ordering his players in for extra training on the Sunday morning. Kitman John Greaves and physio French had been in Josephine's nightclub after the game and slept in the Bramall Lane kit room, before picking up a copy of the *News of the World* on the Sunday morning. The headline over the match report of United's defeat screamed "Beesley's Boobs," Greaves remembers, so he and French cut it out and stuck it on the dressing room wall, alongside a topless page three photo of Sam Fox from *The Sun*. Beesley was raging when he came in and saw it, while his teammates fell about laughing. Beesley was then summoned to Bassett's office and fully expected to be dropped for the midweek cup clash with Spurs. "Harry told him he'd be playing," Greaves said, "and he came back down looking like he'd won the Pools."

Goalkeeper Tracey returned from his broken cheekbone for United's October trip to White Hart Lane, where Gascoigne led the Blades' midfield a merry dance and they were thrashed 4-0 – a result compounded when Barnes kicked the ball against a linesman and was shown a second yellow card. But Tracey's display at White Hart Lane didn't dissuade clubs from showing transfer interest, with a £500,000 offer from Spurs – including Bobby Mimms coming the other way – and a £750,000 bid from Manchester United on the table for the 22-year-old stopper. That was serious money at the time and would have represented a near-10,000 per cent profit for the Blades on their £7,500 investment just a few years earlier. But he stayed put.

"I had opportunities to leave," Tracey said, "but I didn't want to leave Sheffield, or United. I was happy. I never once went into Harry's office and asked him about interest from elsewhere or what was in the newspapers about me. I was just happy playing my football, happy with the way my life was going. Maybe I should have pushed more when those opportunities came, but I was never ever really interested at that stage. It might have been a bigger club and more money, but I was just content. Was it a lack of ambition? I don't know. But I have fantastic memories of Sheffield United and I wouldn't change it for the world."

The winter of 1990 was beginning to draw in when Norwich put three goals past United without reply, to make it 11 league matches without a win, and Bassett was low. His spirits were lifted somewhat by a chant of his name from a still-supportive travelling contingent, at a time when other fanbases would have lost faith, and it gave him something of a second wind. But it was the start of a six-game stretch in which United failed to even find the net. They were rooted to the bottom of the table and roundly written off.

Towards the end of their long winless run, journalist Alan Biggs interviewed Bassett for a feature in the *Daily Express*. "He looked haggard, deadbeat ... he looked totally worn out," Biggs remembered. "He actually said: 'Life at the moment is like a living nightmare.' A recurring living nightmare. He kind of revealed a little bit there about what life was like then. After back-to-back promotions with United, the first half of that season in Division One was an ordeal.

"There was self-doubt. There were occasions when that would be reflected and things that showed that. He was notorious for picking his team on a Friday and then changing it on the Saturday. He genuinely wasn't being devious but he would give you an idea of his team on Friday and give the players a better idea. Then, on the Saturday, he would make a change because he'd been agonising over it overnight. He would do that regularly."

Or at least when he had the luxury of doing so. As the results continued to go against United, the injuries were also beginning to pile up. Wilf Rostron, Barnes, Mike Lake, Pemberton and new face Brian Marwood were all regular visitors to French's treatment room, which hardly helped calm the growing sense of frustration. An operation to correct Tony Agana's troublesome back issue had also interrupted his partnership with Deane, and Bassett was left wondering where the next goals were going to come from.

Then came a Zenith Data Systems Cup clash at home to Oldham Athletic. The much-maligned tournament was held between 1985 and 1992, as an additional competition for clubs in the top two divisions of English football after English sides were banned from European competition following the 1985 Heysel Stadium disaster. It was not a tournament that captured the imagination of the Sheffield public, and just 3,144 braved a chilly Tuesday evening in December to travel to Bramall Lane. When United went 2-0 down after just 11 minutes, they probably wondered why they had even bothered.

But instead, those hardy souls witnessed the turning point for the season as United bounced back and rattled in seven goals without reply, with Hoyland amongst the scorers with his first for his boyhood club. After netting seven times in their first 15 league games, United had rattled in the same number within an hour. Suddenly, some of the dark clouds developing over Bramall Lane had shown some signs of shifting.

Normal service was resumed in the next league game, when United travelled to Anfield and lost 2-0, and it was three days before Christmas when the present that every Blades fan desperately wanted was delivered. Brian Clough's Nottingham Forest were the visitors and Blades supporters making up the bulk of a crowd of just over 20,000 shuffled into Bramall Lane more in hope than expectation. Their hopes were lifted a little when Ian 'Jock' Bryson gave them the lead in front of the Kop before, in a passage of play that perhaps summed up their season to that point, Forest went up the other end and scored directly from kick-off, through an emerging midfield player by the name of Roy Keane.

Stuart Pearce then gave Forest the lead, and Unitedites resigned themselves to yet another defeat. But United, who full-back Chris Wilder remembered as "not getting the rub of the green" during that barren early-season spell, kept believing. A crazy nine-minute spell then saw Bryson equalise and go close to a hat-trick when his shot hit both posts and bounced to safety, before Brian Deane headed Carl Bradshaw's cross home for 3-2. At the final whistle there was a feeling of sheer relief amongst the players and supporters invaded the pitch as if their side had just sealed promotion, rather than their first league win at the 17th time of asking.

Bassett rightly celebrated, too, but in his own way, opening a bottle of whiskey in French's physio office and sending one of his players to face the waiting press in the Bramall Lane tunnel with the message: "Sorry lads, but he's got a bottle of whiskey and he's not coming out until it's gone." Besides, what could he possibly have said? There was a mixture of jubilation and relief, but the drink was certainly well-earned. United were not a million miles off their opponents in games but that represented its own issues, because the quick fixes which would normally be obvious if the shape wasn't functioning or the tactics didn't work were not apparent. Bassett would have experienced inevitable self-doubt and inward reflection during the tough spell, but did his best to keep it from his players.

"In that run before Christmas, we were getting beat week in, week out and he still believed in us," said Booker. "He probably softened a little bit because he couldn't just keep coming in every week and battering us. We were doing okay but losing by the odd goal and it wasn't quite coming off for us. But he still gave us the belief and encouragement that we would get out of it, which we did."

But there was one man watching on from the Bramall Lane stands who didn't join the on-field celebrations. Forward Glyn Hodges, with weekends clear after falling out of favour at Crystal Palace, had travelled up from London to watch his old manager's side and may have wondered how differently things could have panned out had he signed for the Blades the previous summer. Instead, he turned up to negotiate with Bassett with the help of an agent, and was promptly sent packing. "Harry refused to talk to me," Hodges said. "Gave me money for the train back to London, and told my agent that he could pay his own fare." Instead he signed for Palace.

A few years earlier, Hodges had watched on from the stands as United were relegated to the Third Division, travelling up with Brian Gayle, Mark Morris and Vinnie Jones to watch their play-off game against Bristol City. All four men had little idea that they would pull on the red and white shirt themselves years later but their first experience of Sheffield was a positive one, with the Josephine's nightclub a particular favourite. Their trip to the Steel City, which was supposed to last the one night, turned into a five-day bender. Now, six months or so after missing the boat at United, Hodges was available again on loan from Palace. Bassett, crucially, held no grudges and a deal was done – presumably without an agent involved.

And it proved to be an inspired one. Hodges had the craft and guile that could unlock a top-flight defence, and was also the sort of match-winner at that level that United ordinarily could not afford. A player who oozed class, with a left foot as good as any, Hodges is one of the most majestic players to have graced the Bramall Lane pitch in recent history and could, and probably should, have done even more in the game considering his mercurial talents. He also broke the mould when it came to Bassett signings; all incomings up to that point had to fit a certain profile, where hard work came first and individual ability followed. It had certainly worked, and United weren't being consistently blown away in the top-flight, but Bassett had recognised the need for a sprinkling of invention to add to his side's industry and granted Hodges more of a licence to roam. It was a potentially risky move, given what the United dressing room stood for, but Hodges was given a free pass by his teammates because he was able to deliver.

"We all worked hard, and we all did that," said Hoyland. "But when he came in, Hodgey didn't. He didn't really do it in training. He cheated everything in training. But he was one of those players you could accept because he would bring quality on a Saturday or that magic moment where he could do something, win you a game with a goal or a cross. Even though he might have been a little bit lazy with some of his stuff off the ball, his mentality was brilliant. He was a winner, an absolute winner and he wanted to win every week, no matter what it took. Whether it was a bit of skill or a bit of dark arts, he'd do it. He was brilliant and we all loved Hodgey. He was fantastic."

It wasn't all plain sailing, with Hodges banned for six games and missing the end of the 1990/91 season after headbutting Sunderland's Gordon Armstrong in a tunnel melee after a game at Roker Park. It was already a bad-tempered affair that had seen red cards for John Gannon and Sunderland's Kevin Ball, and Bassett remembered the melee starting when Armstrong kicked Hodges in probably the last place any man would like to be kicked. Jones responded by clumping Armstrong, so Ball joined in and kicked Jones. Gannon saw what had happened and struck Ball. A fuming Hodges, who had some previous with Armstrong, was subbed for his own good but clearly had not calmed down by the time the final whistle went. Bassett watched back the tape on the Monday morning, and concluded that all five players should really have seen red.

But Hodges' mid-January arrival was undeniably timely as United flipped their season on its head. Having gone almost half a season without a win, the juggernaut was rolling once again. United won eight games between January and March and climbed towards mid-table, well away from safety, with their fans responding with ironic chants declaring that United were going to win the league. But it was no fluke. It was the result of months of hard work, of keeping the faith in the face of doom and gloom. It was also vindication of Bassett's forward-thinking methods, which flew in the face of the critics who had wrongly branded him a dinosaur. Sport science, diets, video analysis and the use of psychologists are commonplace in the modern-day game, with the likes of Arsene Wenger credited with introducing them. Bassett's Blades were doing much of it before the Frenchman had even been approached by Arsenal. Bassett's video sessions, which he had started using VHS tapes at Wimbledon, were legendary; interspersed between clips of AC Milan defending and examples of how other teams play, were segments of blue movies or Tommy Cooper's stand-up. The plan was to stop players from losing concentration and keep their eyes on the screen, and it certainly worked. His men were offered the chance to undertake Dale Carnegie courses in leadership and personal development, taking place in a Sheffield hotel on Wednesday evenings, and goalkeeper Alan Kelly, who signed for United later in the Bassett era, remembered teammates travelling to York to see a hypnotist.

Bassett had brought in a psychologist towards the back end of 1990, working with the players around the December 15 trip to Liverpool before disappearing just before the Forest victory that kickstarted the great escape. Financially, Bassett's budget could not accommodate a consultant frequently travelling up from London to Bramall Lane, although the fact that some of United's squad had taken to calling the psychologist "Simon the Psycho" hardly helped his cause. A lack of football pedigree caused him to be treated with suspicion and reluctance by some players, but others responded well and Bassett carried on implementing some of his methods in training. One thing was for certain; the focus on players' minds, as well as their bodies, had become an increasingly important weapon in the arsenal. Dr. Ian Mitchell, a former Hereford United player, also spent a couple of seasons as a sports scientist at Bramall Lane under Bassett, and went on to work with Gareth Southgate and the England team before being appointed as Newcastle United's new head of psychology in 2023.

Andy Cale, a psychologist from Shrewsbury with a PhD in sports science from Loughborough University, was employed full-time under

Bassett and remembered much more fondly than Simon the Psycho. Cale joined United after following up undergraduate and master's degrees with a doctorate and has been credited as a big influence by a number of former United players, including Hoyland. Cale also helped one player develop a pre-match routine which saw the defender lay on a lilo in the Bramall Lane showers and repeat to himself, over and over: "I'm not fucking shit, I'm not fucking shit." It wouldn't have worked for everyone, but it worked for him and was another example of the shift away from the one-size-fits-all policy that had previously run throughout football. Importantly, Cale was also a football man and later achieved his UEFA Pro Licence qualification, winning five league titles in charge of Welsh side The New Saints alongside a role with the Football Association.

While Cale worked on United's minds, Ed Baranowski worked on their bodies. Born 30 miles from Sheffield in West Yorkshire, Baranowski was a wannabe footballer who had undergone an unsuccessful trial with Bradford City and instead followed a different path into the game via his passion for sports science. The field was, at the time, still very much a niche but Baranowski went on to become one of the most successful backroom staff members of the era, working at Blackburn Rovers as they won the Premier League title in 1995 and then moving with Kenny Dalglish to Newcastle as they finished second in the top-flight and reached an FA Cup final.

Amongst the innovations introduced by Baranowski were devices to monitor players' speeds and distances, which are commonplace in today's game but were practically unheard of in the 1990s. Early in his time at Blackburn, he remembers some players puffing on cigarettes in the dressing room just before going out to play. "Football was a working man's game," he told the *Otago Daily Times* in 2015, "so there wasn't much interjection on conditioning nutrition."

While things had evolved a little bit at Bramall Lane, United's players were still fuelling themselves on Friday nights with platefuls of steak, egg and chips and one of the biggest challenges was shifting that mindset. "All the hotels we stayed at hardly ever made pasta," French remembered. "It wasn't on the menus in those days. So all of a sudden, you had to try and convince them, when all they wanted was steak, egg and chips. They'd say: 'I've had it all my life and it's never affected me. Why change it?' But me and Eddie used to have to go into the hotel kitchens before games and discuss which pasta to cook. Sometimes it was okay, and sometimes it wasn't."

French recalls some players neglecting to eat the food laid out for them and instead ordering room service; usually, and predictably, steak, egg and chips. "It felt like a losing battle, but eventually they started to see the benefits. It's just an evolution of footballing life." The nutrition changes weren't universally welcomed – Baranowski once told First Division-winning striker Brian Marwood that he couldn't have a cup of tea at half-time, and was promptly asked how many league games he'd played and told where to go – but the impact was soon felt. Bassett's players often ran six miles or so on a Thursday afternoon before a Saturday game, following up their morning football sessions with afternoons on the weights and on the athletics track at Don Valley Stadium. Some even enlisted him for private one-to-one sessions; perhaps to escape the growls from the Sheffield Eagles rugby league players who were suddenly, and not altogether happily, sharing their gym with a group of footballers.

"We had this mentality that whoever we played, we were just going to run over the top of them," Hoyland said. "Teams couldn't cope with our fitness and we were finishing games strongly because we just kept going. Ed was massively influential in that. To be fair we hated it at first, thinking: 'What's all this shit?' Lifting weights? I'd never done any of that and all of a sudden, we were going to Don Valley. Initially we were thinking it was a load of bollocks, after training in the morning, but it made us fitter and it made us stronger. We ate the right food. We also had a bit of quality then, as well, with the likes of Deano and Hodges. And we could just pick teams off."

The changes and the fitness went hand-in-hand with the victories and the players eventually bought into Baranowski's vision. Most of them, anyway. Goalkeeper Simon Tracey was not regarded as a fitness lover and was perhaps the least enthusiastic about the sessions, while Brian Deane was much more on board – even turning up with his own spikes. "Deano used to eat up the track," Hodges recalled. "Then you had those like Trace. He would never do any running. Me, John Gannon and a few of the lads were on the track before the session started, before Ed had even got there. I was winding Tracey up, saying: 'Trace, you can't even do a lap. You couldn't even beat Johnny Gannon round the track.'

"Then it started. He was getting a bit rattled, insisting that he could.

The next thing we knew, they were on the starting line. We said it was a full lap, 400m, and they were off. Trace sprinted all the way round and beat Johnny Gannon, dipping over the line as he got to it. He was on his back. He'd only done one lap and he was on the floor. He couldn't breathe, couldn't talk. He eventually recovered, stood up and said: 'I've got to go home, I'm done,' and that was that. He went and got in his car and went home. He had to go and lay down. That was before the session had even started!"

A run of 13 victories and just six defeats starting from that Forest win tells its own story of how United recovered to pull off the greatest of great escapes. There were victories against Manchester United and Chelsea and Derby, when Hodges scored the winner and fell over the advertising hoardings while celebrating. There was also a 4-1 home hammering of Southampton, with Jones suspended and Chris Wilder handed the captain's armband against the club who had released him as a youngster. "We were 4-0 up at half-time, so it wasn't a bad start," Wilder smiled. "It was another example of Harry's man-management, knowing I'd been let go by Southampton. He was the master of little things like that. It was the one and only time I wore the armband under him, though, so I don't think he saw me as a potential captain in the Paul Stancliffe mould!"

The game was also midfielder Mark Todd's final league appearance for the Blades. "How can you win 4-1 and it be your last game?" he said. "Tony Pritchett gave me man-of-the-match in *The Star* and for the next game, I was out. I played a few friendlies and cup games and then I was gone. I never found out why. I was trying to rationalise it and didn't get it right. I had to leave.

"But I don't look back with any animosity. How could I? It was such a successful squad and a great dressing room to be in. If our mob turned up, not many were going to beat us. That lift we gave the club and the city, has lasted to this day. People keep in touch, players made life-long friends through the success. That ripples into fans. I go to Meadowhall and people stop and say hello, and my two kids get embarrassed.

"For the investment Harry made in Deano, Tony Agana, Simon Tracey... the output was worth millions. It's about the sum of the parts. How can I look back with anything other than pride? I was one of the chosen few, doing everything you dream of as a child. Playing at the top level, becoming an international while I was at United. Many people want to climb the mountain and I put the flag in. It maybe didn't stay in as long as I'd have wanted, but I put the flag in."

Just as losing games had become a habit, United had rediscovered the taste of winning – and remembered how much they liked it. "During that bad run, I was working hard with the players and their spirits were good," Bassett said. "We weren't getting hammered every week; there were games we deserved to win and didn't. There wasn't much more we could do. We just had to keep at it. The fans were with us. I think they realised we'd got to the top division when they didn't expect to be and thought: 'We're fucking lucky to be here … we could be at Rochdale or somewhere but here we are, at Villa Park or wherever.' They could see we were doing our best, I think, and that perhaps we weren't just good enough. The fans, I thought, were very good for us. The board were good with me and said I wasn't going to get the sack. The media were okay, I think. One or two slagged us off as not being good enough for the division but at the end of the season, they kept their gobs shut."

United's fortunes turned around so dramatically that Bassett even won the manager of the month award for March and their final game of the season, a 2-1 home success over Norwich, was cause for celebration indeed. United had finished 13th and Bassett celebrated – and annoyed his wife, Christine – by throwing all his clothing, apart from his underpants, into the crowd. Fans behind one of the goals were drenched in blazing sunshine after the Kop's roof was removed ahead of the construction of a new stand, and Jones led a group of players to the Sheaf pub to enjoy a few beers with supporters before the fun continued at Tommy Hoyland's Sheldon.

On the way the group of jubilant Blades gate-crashed a local resident's barbeque, eating and drinking the poor chap out of house and home and only further reinforcing the connection between supporters and their heroes. "How many Premier League players are doing that with the fans in the pub next to the ground these days?" said Hodges. "It was just brilliant. It was unbelievable. Everyone was singing. They were great times, and I'll never forget them."

"We all worked hard ... but when he came in, Hodgey didn't. He cheated everything in training. But he was one of those players you could accept because he would bring quality on a Saturday or that magic moment where he could do something, win you a game with a goal or a cross. Even though he might have been a little bit lazy with some of his stuff off the ball, his mentality was brilliant. He was a winner, an absolute winner and he wanted to win every week, no matter what it took."

– Jamie Hoyland

12

THE MAGICIAN OF BRAMALL LANE

Not many players over the years can say they had a stake in their own transfer fee, but then again Glyn Hodges was no ordinary footballer. The man described by *The Star's* Sheffield United correspondent Tony Pritchett at the time as "the magician of Bramall Lane" won 18 caps for Wales and played for Newcastle, Watford and Crystal Palace in his career. His manager, Dave Bassett, later described it in typically blunt fashion as "stupid for a player of [Hodges'] talent to have achieved so little" in the game and it was at Bramall Lane, almost 150 miles north of his native London, where Hodges really found a home.

Bassett had worked with the enigmatic forward before, during their successful time together at Wimbledon, and it was January 1991 when the two were reunited again in a loan deal that Palace had agreed that the Blades could make permanent if they stumped up a fee of just over £400,000. There was just one slight problem, though.

They couldn't.

Unitedites had fallen in love with the enigmatic forward, who had scored a late winner against Derby in just his second game and followed it up with key goals in victories against Everton and Luton Town to help the Blades' great escape act. As convinced as their manager that Hodges could be the missing part of the Bramall Lane jigsaw, Blades supporters raised money towards Hodges' fee with a Grand National sweepstake amongst the initiatives.

The concept of supporters raising funds to sign players was not as alien back then as it would seem in modern-day football – United's Blades Revival fund was set up back in the day to offer fans the chance to win prizes but also help boost United's transfer coffers – but this was an especially concerted effort, which paid off many times over.

"I joined in January and the Grand National was in April," Hodges recalled. "Every time I was out in Sheffield, I was collared by people trying to sell me these raffle tickets. If I said no, that would have seemed like an insult to those people trying to raise money to pay for me. It would make it look like I didn't want to be here. So I couldn't say no, could I? It didn't matter where I was ... there was always someone selling these raffle tickets, and I had to say yes every time. I was always buying books. I had loads of tickets, but didn't win anything. I must have been the only player to help pay for his own transfer fee!"

Seagram beat off the challenge of Cheltenham Gold Cup winner Garrison Savannah to claim a famous Grand National victory at Aintree, on the day that United, and Hodges, lost 2-0 at home to Arsenal. But it was a momentous afternoon for the Blades, who were able to push the button on Hodges soon after and make his move permanent. Hodges, Bassett felt, had something to prove after his move to Selhurst Park from Watford didn't work out. There were injuries and a cryptic reference to "lots of things going on at Palace" from Hodges, who was living in a mate's pub and quickly realising that a move up north may be worth exploring. Crucially, too, Bassett didn't hold a grudge, having rejected the chance to sign Hodges again earlier that summer.

"It was the summer of 1990, I was a free agent and I was leaving Watford," Hodges said. "I spoke to Jim Smith at QPR, Steve Coppell at Crystal Palace and Harry at Sheffield United. We didn't agree a deal. I had known Harry since I was 15 and used to play with him at Wimbledon, when he was player-manager of the reserves. I felt when I first came up to Sheffield to speak to Harry that it was an important deal. But I think he was quite upset that he couldn't speak to me. He knew me from way back when and I turned up with an agent who was making demands that he wasn't happy with. He basically refused to talk. That was that, so I signed for Palace. I didn't start great but I'd got myself in good shape and when the opportunity came to come on loan in January, I didn't hesitate. Because I wanted to play."

Linking up again with Bassett offered Hodges some welcome familiarity. Leaving Watford on a high after being named their player of the season, he walked into what he described as a "shambles" at Newcastle under their Northern Irish manager Willie McFaul. "I had Newcastle, QPR and [Bassett's] Watford all interested, but I just really fancied Newcastle. I remember playing up there and with the atmosphere and fans, thinking I fancied playing football there. So I turned Harry down at Watford to start with, but Newcastle turned into a shambles. I was used to Harry's work at Wimbledon, where we were so switched on and tactically aware of the strengths and weaknesses of the opposition.

"No disrespect to other managers but it was like chalk and cheese when I went to Newcastle. I was thinking: 'Jesus.' I had left that to go to someone who was winging it at the time. I signed for them in July and in September I was leaving and going to Watford. I wasn't as fit as I could have been and I had gone to a place where it just wasn't right. You sometimes have it where you go to a team and it's not quite right, and you go to another team and it's a great fit.

"Wimbledon and Sheffield United were the best fits I had and that's when I played my best football. You do go on other journeys. It was a three-year contract at Newcastle and I'm sure, if I had stuck it out, that things could have worked out. But there was an opportunity to come back to Harry, who I knew, and get myself back playing. I had got myself so fit that I was in good shape and ready to go. I hit the ground running at Sheffield United and had a big part to play in that season."

After the two previous approaches saw Hodges first turn him down and then incur his wrath with agent-gate, it was to Bassett's immense credit – and benefit – that he didn't let that stand in the way of a third, and ultimately successful, pursuit. Hodges agreed. "It's easy to get the hump and cut your nose off to spite your face, but he was big enough and strong enough to say: 'No, he's available.' He wanted me and it was an easy choice to make for me to come and enjoy my football."

It was something of a departure from the usual player profile of Bassett, who has openly described Hodges as "lazy" in the past, but there was an immense mutual respect and trust between the pair that had been cultivated during Wimbledon's remarkable rise through the leagues. Even if, at first, Hodges was not on board with Bassett's decision to alter the Dons' playing style. "I'd put a couple of transfer requests in at Wimbledon, but he refused to take them. I didn't like playing that way to begin with. I just wanted to get on the ball and it was something I had never known, playing Harry's way.

"But it became so slick. We just worked and worked and worked on it and we won the league the next year by a country mile. It just clicked into place. What people didn't realise was that every level you went up, you couldn't get away with playing that way. You had to have a little bit different. In the Fourth Division we could get away with it. In the third, we had to be a bit cute. Second, cuter again and then a couple of years later we were playing Liverpool and Man United and weren't going to get away with that style. We had a system, but we were much better footballers than people gave us credit for.

"I had a great relationship with Harry. I was a bit headstrong and thought I knew what I wanted, I would back my own ability, but under Dave you enjoyed going into work every day. We were like rough diamonds at the time but the work that he did in polishing us up paid off. We were a good outfit with homegrown players who went on to play as internationals off the back of the work that he did. I felt comfortable whenever I signed for him. When you go to new places you have to win over the manager and everyone else. It's a blank canvas and you're starting from scratch. But when I joined Sheffield United, I felt comfortable because I knew I had his backing. He liked me as a player and liked me as a person. And that's a big thing."

A big part of United's 1990/91 great escape season, Hodges was at Bramall Lane to see it kickstart with victory over Nottingham Forest – albeit in the stands rather than on the pitch. Out of favour at Palace and given Saturdays off, Hodges was in Sheffield to watch some of his wife's family on stage at a gig at Darnall Liberal Club and had earlier taken in that iconic 3-2 victory over Forest – United's first of the league season, at the 17th time of asking. "I knew from that day that I was coming to a good place and if I could make an impact, one of two things would happen. I would either get back into the Palace team, or get a move – either to Sheffield United or another club.

"I felt like I was in quite a powerful position. I am not being big headed here, but I would like to think my performances meant that United had to find the money to sign me. It was January and I had only played seven games for Palace, which just wasn't enough. I knew that the chips were down and I was at an age where I had to perform. Because I was playing so well, I could have probably gone elsewhere but I only wanted to come to Sheffield United. There was nowhere else I wanted to go.

"I enjoyed it that much. I enjoyed the fans and it was probably the thing that I was looking for at Newcastle. Wimbledon in Division One were getting 10-12,000, Watford in the 15s or 16s and then I came to Sheffield United and they were getting 25,000 or more. The away support was magnificent. It was the craving that I was looking for at Newcastle, that I didn't quite get. But I got it at Sheffield United. They were a magnificent crowd to play in front of."

That love from the terraces was reciprocated. Hodges was as capable of producing a moment of petulance as he was one of magic, and that uncertainty and unpredictability meant that life was rarely dull. When Hodges was preparing to move north to United, he bet his 50 per cent share of a speedboat with his mate over a winner-takes-all game of pool. "I lost, so it all went to him. I was devastated after. To be fair he was very good, and said I could use it whenever I wanted to."

A sublime chip over Peter Schmeichel against Manchester United in the FA Cup remains a fonder memory; a six-match ban and heavy fine for headbutting Gordon Armstrong at Sunderland less so. "I don't think I ever came home with a full month's money. Harry was always fining me for something. When I got sent off at Sunderland, I got a bollocking on the Saturday and then he got me in on the Monday morning because I think he thought we may get points deducted. I got done two weeks' wages with him and then a month's money from the FA. It was an expensive headbutt. I also got sent off at Hillsborough and I know he wasn't happy there. If you stepped over the line, he'd cut your legs off and bring you back down to earth very rapidly.

"He gave me my head. He gave me responsibility and let me do what I did. Obviously, it was within a structure in the game but I knew that he trusted me in positions. When we beat Forest away in the relegation battle, in Brian Clough's last season, he played me off the front and I scored. We went to Everton and I played off the front again, playing left-wing and then right-wing.

"When we beat Man United in the cup, I was marking Ince back-to-back and then running off the back of him. It was the licence to just go and play my football. He gave me good roles where he would trust me and I could do what I did best. He gave me free rein to do that.

"He knew when to push our buttons and when it was time to work. The difference between playing and working. He knew when it was time to work and work hard. No one ever overstepped the mark. There were never any really big fines. There were fines for things like getting sent off, unnecessary bookings and dissent, but no fines for behaviour. He loved it. He loved all the skullduggery, all the loons, and he would always turn a blind eye if anything happened that he could brush under the carpet. I should have kept a diary for Wimbledon and Sheffield United because it was that far-fetched that they would make a film out of it. If it got too serious, then he would have to act. But he had people he could trust in his changing rooms and we all looked after each other.

"That's one of the biggest things that sticks with me, with Dave Bassett, and you live your life to that. He would actively encourage rows and digging people out. I daren't pull out of a tackle. I daren't pull out of a header because I knew the dressing room would come for me. There was no hiding place and you were accountable. You fought your corner, but you got told in no uncertain terms. You could have the biggest row and need to get pulled apart. Then straight away it was gone and in the players' bar you're buying them a drink. 'Come on, come and have a drink. That's gone now.'

"It was like a life lesson in that dressing room. You're honest, you're truthful, you tell people how it is. It's not personal but if you want to get better and you want to improve, this is what we need to do. Get on with it, no sulking. That was his mantra and that was fantastic. No one has ever taken anything personal and no one ever held a grudge. That was normal to us.

"I remember coming up on the Wednesday before my first game at the weekend and Billy Whitehurst did me in training. I was limping about all over the place with a dead leg and thinking: 'Shit, I could be struggling to play here, he's proper done me.' In the end I was alright to play but you're thinking: 'What's going on here? We've got a game tomorrow!' There was no holding back. There was never a dull moment, always something happening, and everybody wanted to play, and was good enough to play. So you trained properly. You had Carl Bradshaw, Dane Whitehouse and Mitch Ward coming up and wanting to grab a shirt, and they weren't bothered whose shirt they got. They would have run through a brick wall to play for the club.

"That's what we always had. You can't flick a switch in the match and play at a pace that you don't practise. We practised everything, even set pieces. Players would be marked and balls would be flying in and you were sticking your heads in. There was no thought of saving yourself. Just a case of: 'This is what we do.'"

One routine in particular became something of a Hodges trademark, the forward coming short for a corner and then backheeling the ball into the path of the corner taker who had continued his run. Two defenders were usually naturally drawn to Hodges, invariably falling into the trap and leaving his teammate free. "There was an alternative to that corner, in the 6-0 win over Spurs. It was with Franz Carr and the option was that he would either do the backheel or take it with him. The Spurs defence were ready for the backheel so he turned inside instead and curled it into the top corner.

"It was hard to stop. We would practise that time and time again. The first one after half-time, we always did the backheel. Then there was the volley on the edge of the box ... we had loads. Now people are earning a good living coaching set-pieces. It seems managers don't want to do it today, they've washed their hands of that and delegate it to others. I find that hard to believe because it's a massive part of the game and you need to trust someone, because they can win you games. We had some great set-pieces and we scored lots of goals."

Every youngster playing football in the school dreams of being the one who delivers the moment of magic, the stunning strike and the big moment. The creator, rather than the enforcer. But being the main man can also bring a certain amount of responsibility as teammates, fans and even sometimes the manager look for something to be conjured out of nothing when times are tough. It was something that weighed heavily on Hodges' former teammate Brian Deane before his departure to Leeds in 1993. But for Hodges, it was something he relished.

"At Wimbledon I was a young boy, coming up and learning my trade. Yeah, I had that ability but when I got to Sheffield United, I felt that I was a big player, an important player. I could win games or turn games our way and I knew I had that in the bag. That was my best spell of football. I was experienced, I knew my body and I knew what I could do. I knew that at any stage, even if I was having a bad game, I could smash one in the top corner or pick out Deano. I was supremely confident; I was in a good place and I was happy off the pitch.

"Everything clicked and I relished it. I couldn't wait to play. That six-match ban at the end of that 1990-91 season absolutely gutted me. When we went to QPR and Bob Booker scored, it was a big celebration and I missed out on that. It was my own fault but I was at a good age, enjoying it and playing my best football at the time.

"It was just a brilliant time for me. It's right up there. Wimbledon is, to be fair, but I was young then, whereas at Sheffield United I was more experienced, a bit of a leader and I had more input and a bigger effect on some of the younger ones. It was the most enjoyable and I played some of my best football there. That was when I was in a really good spell. I was really proud of how I played and what I achieved there."

13

DERBY DELIGHT

English football was still basking in the post-Italia 90 World Cup glow when six men gathered around a large meeting table to completely reshape its future. Those present in London included television mogul Greg Dyke and representatives of the "big five" clubs, including Arsenal, Liverpool and Manchester United, and the main topic on the agenda was the formation of a new breakaway league; ostensibly designed to support the England team, but really with the aim of ensuring that clubs could keep a larger slice of the financial cake for themselves. The first steps towards the Premier League era had been taken.

Television revenue for football had grown exponentially since the early days when the *BBC* paid £5,000 for the rights for *Match of the Day* in the 1960s; the money was shared equally by the 92 professional clubs in the English pyramid, netting them around £54 apiece. By 1986, a two-year TV deal was worth just over £6m; just two years later, a four-year contract commanded as much as £44m and was again shared equally. Dyke, from his position of power with *ITV*, knew that those figures were only going to keep rising. And, more importantly, that owners would easily be seduced by the thought of keeping more of it for themselves.

Most clubs had no idea that a financial revolution was in the offing, least of all Sheffield United. The Blades were around 140 miles north of the discussions, but as a club relying on Grand National sweepstakes and loans from their manager to sign players, they were a million miles off those sitting around that table in the capital. A season in the top division had done little to improve United's financial situation and a failed takeover led by Middle Eastern businessman Sam Hashimi, who later had a sex change and resurfaced as a woman by the name Samantha Kane, had broken down, despite wild promises of huge investment that had seduced manager Dave Bassett. The new man at the helm instead was Sheffield-born Paul Woolhouse – for the time being at least – and in terms of spending power in the transfer market, it was very much business as usual for Bassett.

Had United been able to hang around long enough at that time, in what quickly became the richest league in the world, they could have forged themselves a very different path and altered the course of the club forever. Instead, Bassett had to continue his familiar trick of selling to buy, in the hope that those above him in the corridors of power could conjure up the sort of investment that the club desperately needed in order to push on to the next level.

The sales of Mark Morris, Vinnie Jones, Mark Todd and Paul Wood had raised the best part of £850,000, and Bassett was under the impression that the £575,000 paid by Chelsea for Jones would be put towards the £700,000 deal he had agreed for Brian Gayle, a centre-half he had previously worked with at Wimbledon. It was only after Jones was unveiled at Stamford Bridge that Bassett discovered that his transfer fee was instead going towards settling club debts, with United's bank starting to get a little twitchy about the Blades' financial state.

Rather embarrassingly – especially after Gayle had appeared, in his new United shirt and holding a club scarf, on the front cover of the United matchday programme for a game against Everton in which he was nowhere to be seen – the move was on hold and Bassett, after discussions with Woolhouse, saw that the only way forward was to lend United £100,000 from his own pocket.

"I wanted it to work as well," Bassett remembered. "I thought I had to put my neck on the line. My accountant helped me raise £50,000 from savings and he arranged with my bank to also lend me £50,000 on my house. It was alright in the end. I probably wouldn't do it now, but I did at the time." Bassett got his man, and eventually got his money back as well. But it was a remarkable situation that, despite back-to-back promotions, a season in the top flight and consistent attendance figures, only further highlighted United's perilous financial state.

The departures of Morris, Wood and Todd, three heroes of the Leicester promotion season, were further evidence of Bassett's ruthless decision-making but still rankled with some. "There were a lot of players, including myself, who were moved on pretty quickly after promotion," said Wood, who joined Bournemouth on loan before moving permanently. "Dave signed a lot of players who didn't really make much of an impact or make the team any better. I think he could have done just as well without those signings. Once we got promoted, I thought he panicked a little bit. He'd taken that team up two divisions without really making a big signing, and I think he felt he needed some big signings to survive in the top division.

"I understand his mentality there, but I think he should have given more of the team who got promoted a go, and a chance to prove themselves. I was playing in the reserves and Harry was good friends with Harry Redknapp, who was Bournemouth manager at the time. I went down there on loan and really enjoyed it. I had three months and then went back to Sheffield, but they came back in and signed me. For me it was a great move, I enjoyed my time there and still live in Bournemouth, but I didn't want to leave Sheffield United, to be honest.

"I still felt like I had a lot to give there. I only played a few games in the First Division. If you play 20 games in the top-flight and it doesn't work out, because you haven't fulfilled the potential you think you have got, then I get it. But I only played three games and it would have been nice to have found out for myself if I was capable. I got better as I got older. I matured quite late.

"I have seen Dave a few times since. I liked what he did and love the fact he has become a legend. He had a good idea of what he wanted and I did the job on the pitch. I don't think I was ever part of his Crazy Gang because I wasn't there long enough but he signed me, so he believed in me at one time and it paid off. He got it right and I got it right. He was one of the lads.

"I had never seen anyone ever fight with their own manager before. I've had a list of managers – Alan Ball, Redknapp, Terry Venables – and Dave is up there. Ball is head and shoulders above, because of the fact I was young and heavily influenced by him, but Dave runs him a close second. His character, his success, seven automatic promotions … and he has done that with teams that are not fancied. What he has done has been amazing. He is really proud of what he has done in Sheffield."

***

It was the summer of 1991 and as Doug Ellis' yacht set sail to Marbella, there was one goal in the Aston Villa chairman's mind – to bring back Dave Bassett as the club's new manager. An underwhelming 17th-place finish in 1991/92 was enough to convince Ellis – who never *really* needed too much convincing to pull the trigger on a manager – to part company with Czech boss Jozef Venglos. Bassett's great escape heroics with Sheffield United the previous season had captured the imagination, and Ellis was determined to get his man.

It was an attractive proposition. Villa had finished second in the top-flight the season before Venglos' appointment and the platform in the Midlands, at one of English football's grand old clubs, had earned Graham Taylor the England job. Villa's squad was packed with talent; the free-scoring David Platt, the legend that was Paul McGrath, future Blades in Kevin Gage and Gordon Cowans. Bassett would be paid handsomely, Ellis promised, as he made his case by the pool. More importantly, he would be backed in the transfer market. But Bassett said no.

He doesn't deny he was tempted. But he couldn't put the support he had been shown by Unitedites the previous season out of his mind, despite Ellis' best efforts. Deadly Doug – a nickname he actually earned from his ruthlessness when fishing, but which just as well suited his reputation for hiring and firing managers – instead moved for Ron Atkinson, who had just led United's city rivals Wednesday to promotion back to the First Division but didn't show the same loyalty to his employers as Bassett. Atkinson's departure from Hillsborough did not go down well with Owls fans and, as Bassett observed the fall-out from the other side of the Steel City, it only further cemented in his mind the belief that he had made the right decision.

Besides, he had plenty to focus on at Bramall Lane, and one of his main concerns centred around his star striker Brian Deane. The forward's performances in front of goal early in the decade had earned him a first call-up to the England senior squad, after his first top-flight season saw him return a very respectable 13 league goals – only two fewer than Gary Lineker and Ian Wright and, bizarrely, as many as Manchester United defender Steve Bruce, who scored seven penalties that campaign. Deane was in the form of his life and Taylor had seen enough to call him up for England's summer tour of Australasia.

With Lineker coming to the end of his international career, it was

Dave and Christine Bassett with pop superstar, and Watford chairman, Elton John during their brief time together at Vicarage Road before the axe fell
(Trinity Mirror/Mirrorpix/Alamy)

Billy McEwan's Bramall Lane departure had left Sheffield United looking for a new manager ... and Tony Pritchett in *The Star* wasn't shy in calling for Bassett to take over
(Sheffield Star)

with Tony Pritchett

BASSETT IS RIGHT SORT FOR BLADES

SHEFFIELD United, in all sorts of trouble, should send for the man from Bassett's!

Matthews

One of the conditions of Bassett's arrival at Bramall Lane was that he would work with the existing staff in place ... but it was an arrangement that didn't last long. Above right: Bassett pictured in the Lane car park after being appointed as McEwan's successor
(Sheffield Star)

Some captions just write themselves. Dave Bassett poses with Bertie Bassett in 1988, soon after taking charge of the Blades
(Sheffield Star)

Clockwise from above: Bassett receives a kiss from wife Christine after promotion at Leicester; Blades fans at Filbert Street with a giant Paul Stancliffe cut-out; celebrations back at Bramall Lane with Bassett hoisted on fans' shoulders; Adrian Starkes with Bassett's shirt from that historic day and Starkes' son, Spencer, on Bassett's knee, with the boss wearing the shirt

(Sheffield Star, Hazel Little, Adrian Starkes)

▲ Boyhood Blade Jamie Hoyland asked for a celebratory photo after United's 2-0 victory over Wednesday in 1991

▼ Bobby Davison wrote his name into Blades folklore with a historic derby double at Hillsborough in 1992, wearing this shirt *(Martyn Harrison)*

▲ Iconic striker Billy Whitehurst. Most former teammates have a story to tell about the formidable forward, either on or off the pitch *(PA Images/Alamy)*

A series of portraits commissioned by the *BBC* to promote the *United!* documentary and taken by photographer Bill Stephenson. Clockwise from left: Paul Stancliffe takes a breather after a game; managing director Derek Dooley, a key man for Bassett; and Dane Whitehouse leaves the Lane on a stretcher after a bad injury
(Bill Stephenson)

A young Unitedite watches his side in action through a metal fence. The fences were common in the era but United chairman Reg Brealey was determined to remove them from Bramall Lane and promote a more friendly atmosphere for supporters
(Bill Stephenson)

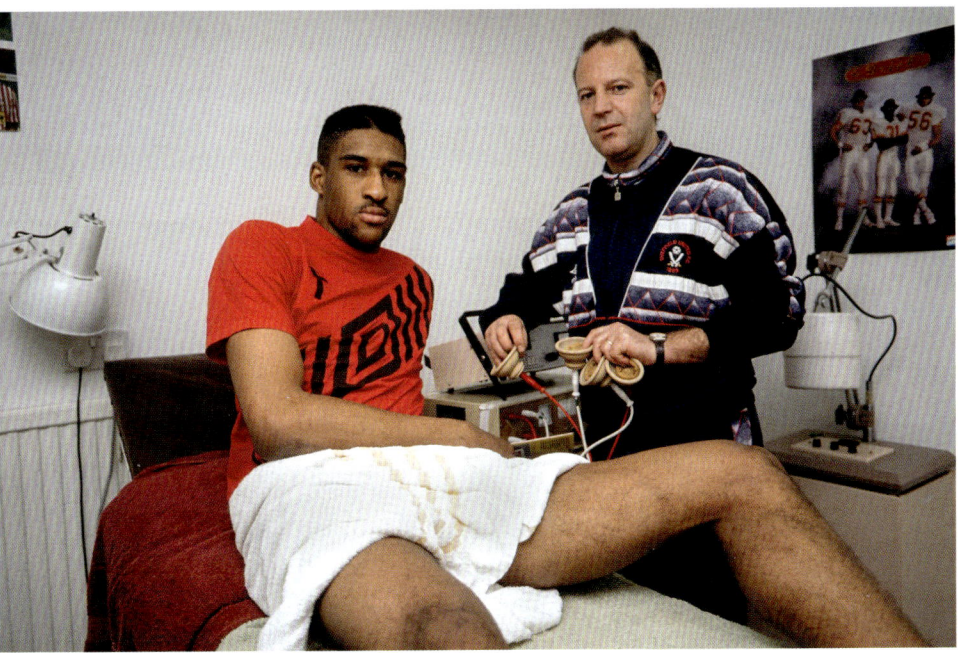

Another trusted Bassett ally was physio Derek French, pictured here attending to star striker Brian Deane on his trusty treatment table
(Bill Stephenson)

Tony Agana, another bargain Bassett buy who formed a iconic partnership with Deane, runs out ahead of an FA Cup clash against his former club Watford
(Bill Stephenson)

▲ Bassett gives instructions to Glyn Hodges during the 1993 FA Cup semi-final against Wednesday at Wembley, with kitman John Greaves and physio French also on hand while striker Deane takes on some fluids
(PA Images/ Alamy)

▶ Goalkeeper Alan Kelly's remarkable individual performance wasn't enough to prevent a painful defeat for the Blades
(PA Images/ Alamy)

A kiss for luck. Three girl fans wish their hero all the best as he prepares to leave

Goodbye Deano say tearful fans

▲ The headline says it all as striker Deane leaves Bramall Lane for the final time in the summer of 1993 after being sold to boyhood club Leeds, getting a farewell kiss from a female fan on his way out *(Sheffield Star)*

▲ Bassett welcomes popular defender Dougie Hodgson to United in 1994 *(PA Images/Alamy)*

▲ A moment of madness for Charlie Hartfield, who battled a gambling addiction throughout his career, as he is sent off for punching Manchester United's Eric Cantona *(PA Images/Alamy)*

▲ Bassett was named United's greatest-ever manager at their 125th anniversary celebrations in 2014 and is assured of a warm welcome whenever he returns to Bramall Lane (*Darren Staples/Sportimage*)

audition time for those strikers queuing up to pick up the mantle. And there was no shortage of quality for Taylor to choose from, with the likes of Wright and Alan Shearer around and a familiar face in Wednesday's David Hirst joining Deane on the plane. Deane's England debut came as a half-time substitute in a friendly against New Zealand at Mount Smart Stadium, Auckland, on 3 June 1991, the United man going on to earn two further caps that year and establishing himself as one of the country's leading strikers. "That year, the year before the Premier League, I knew no one wanted to play against me," Deane said. "I was difficult to play against and I was also scoring good goals. It was just a great era of pure football."

Buoyed by his international recognition, Deane continued his knack of scoring on the opening day as United let slip a two-goal lead with 14 minutes to go to draw 2-2 at Norwich, but he was in and out of the side for the early part of the season, playing the first two games before missing the next four. He returned, and scored, in a 2-1 defeat at Oldham, and was out again for the next two matches.

After a 2-1 win over Everton, Unitedites gathered in the Bramall Lane car park after rumours spread that an offer had been accepted for Deane from Leeds, and that Bassett had resigned in protest. The manager appeared in front of the supporters to reassure them that none of the speculation was true, but something was clearly not right with Deane. He returned once more for a trip to Arsenal, which saw United go 4-0 down after 34 minutes on their way to a 5-2 thrashing, but failed to reappear after half-time.

Bassett was convinced that Deane's head had been turned while on international duty; that he had been influenced by his new England teammates and wanted out. There was an offer on the table from Crystal Palace, who were in the process of selling Wright to Arsenal and saw Deane as his replacement, but Deane took great exception to Bassett's theory and was far from impressed at the accusation that he had come back from his England call-up a different person to the one that had left. The fact he was still driving the same sponsored car that he had been given when he arrived at Bramall Lane years earlier hardly suggested that he had been seduced by the trappings of fame.

"When I got substituted at Arsenal away, I was in a daze," Deane recalled. "I was sweating ferociously and on Monday morning, Harry pulled me. He said Palace had come in with a bid and asked me if I wanted to go. 'Deansy,' he said. 'I think you've been tapped up.' I said: 'What? I don't feel right, something's not right. But if you want me to leave, when I understand what's going on with me, I'll leave!'"

Deane kept his place for a League Cup trip to Wigan and scored both United goals in a 2-2 draw, but his health continued to deteriorate on the coach back to Sheffield. Unable to breathe properly, Deane ended up in his garden in the middle of the night to try and get some air and cool down. The striker had not felt himself for weeks and remembered being concerned for his health that evening as his condition deteriorated, with physio Derek French arranging a blood test the following day. The results confirmed that Deane was suffering from glandular fever and tonsillitis, and had been for some time. It went a long way towards explaining why he was a shadow of the player that Unitedites had been used to seeing.

"I think Harry was sorry," Deane said. "He rang me and sort of apologised, in his own way, without really apologising. But I didn't deserve that. I was in a fragile state. United was all I knew, and all I was interested in. But it was then that I started to think: 'This is too much for one person. If this is the pressure, what am I getting in return?' It was like someone whipping you all the time and trying to get blood out of a stone."

With Deane struggling, and long-time strike partner Tony Agana appearing to lose a little of the pace that had made him so deadly, United won just two of their opening 15 league matches – with Bassett describing their tumble down the division as "faster than a one-legged man in a bum kicking contest" and admitting that he wouldn't have blamed Unitedites for demanding refunds on their season tickets. Adrian Littlejohn arrived as the heir to Agana's throne, a raw 20-year-old with plenty to learn but who had caught the eye after breaking through at Walsall. He was also blessed with lightning pace and could stretch the opposition defence, chasing balls down the channel and helping his team up the pitch.

He was exactly the type of striker that Bassett liked and although nowhere near as effective or as prolific as Agana, Littlejohn caused plenty of teams problems. He was joined by the returning Clive Mendonca from Rotherham United, who was unable to make an impact, while Nathan Peel was injured in his first pre-season match after joining from Preston for £75,000 and made just one league appearance in his debut campaign at Bramall Lane. Bassett's pragmatism, a trait from his insurance salesman days, also saw him bring in extra left-back cover in Tom Cowan, spending £350,000 for the Rangers man with David Barnes in dispute over a new contract.

Charlie Hartfield also arrived from Arsenal following a recommendation to Bassett by former Wimbledon man Nigel Winterburn. Hartfield immediately warmed to his new manager, admitting: "It was like we had known each other for a long time." He had been brought in to add some steel to the midfield but there was a feeling at Bramall Lane that the former Gunner was a little too eager to impress in the early days, with Tony Pritchett in *The Star* noting that he had "established something of a 'Jack the Lad' character." Bassett can still remember Hartfield offering to look after his manager's koi carp pond while he was away, and nearly killing them all, while another time Hartfield noticed Bassett's wife, Christine, had stopped at traffic lights on Ecclesall Road and so opened her car door and pretended to steal her handbag.

But underneath that joker persona was a serious issue that would plague his career and eventually change his life for the worse. Hartfield suffered from a gambling addiction, which had started at Arsenal and continued throughout his playing career. He once gambled away just over £21,000 in the space of just three days, with his debts leading to his involvement in a drug trafficking gang and an eventual nine-year prison sentence.

Hartfield's addiction was ruining him. Football was no longer his number one priority; in fact, it never had been. From the moment he woke up to the moment he put his head back on the pillow at night, the thought of gambling consumed him. "It affected me, it affected my family, my playing career. It ruined everything," he said. "I hid it well. I knew early on that it was a problem, but I never admitted it to myself. Because I knew that if I admitted it to myself, then I would have had to stop. I was getting good money at that age and football took second place to gambling in the end.

"I was more focused on that than training and even when I did my cruciate ligament, I didn't do any rehabilitation. Because all I wanted to do was gamble and be at the bookies having a bet. I was gambling before games and then asking some of the youth team players for results while

I was actually playing. It took over my life. I lost houses, I lost relationships and got into so much debt it's unbelievable. The worst bit isn't even the money … it's the emotional side of it. What it does to your family and everyone else that you hurt. It's a devastating lonely road to be on, but it's the road I chose."

The prison sentence meant that he was finally able to accept defeat. "That was the last bit of the road, really," he added. "I had stopped gambling, but I hadn't stopped gambling with life. I knew the risk was there before I got arrested. But I was skint, and you're desperate for that lifestyle again." Hartfield turned his life around after being released and is now in recovery from gambling. He was later diagnosed with cancer, updating Blades fans in 2022 of his "successful" treatments of chemotherapy and radiotherapy.

United won just two of the eight games Deane missed after his illnesses and when he returned to action, his long-term strike partner and close friend Agana was not there to welcome him. The striker's successful association with the Blades ended when he joined Neil Warnock's Notts County for £750,000 – banking United a sizeable profit from his arrival back in 1988. It was a huge decision, considering Agana was United's leading scorer at the time and that the Blades had just two wins on the board, with Deane struggling with illness and Littlejohn still to find his feet. But the money on the table was too good to turn down, with United still losing £1.5m that year despite the sale of a prized asset that saw the iconic Deane and Agana partnership broken up. Agana's departure was confirmed just before November 17's Steel City derby against Wednesday at Bramall Lane, which was remarkably the first competitive meeting between the two old rivals since 1980.

He was not the only promotion-winner to miss out against the Owls, with Bob Booker informed just before kick-off that he was being allowed to rejoin Brentford before receiving the acclaim of a packed Bramall Lane. One player who had a closer view of the derby action was Kevin Gage, the full-back who was on the bench for the first time after joining from Aston Villa. Gage, another former Wimbledon man, was ready for a move after becoming frustrated by a lack of first-team opportunities at Villa Park and jumped at the chance to link up again with Bassett at Bramall Lane.

To this day Gage can still remember his first impressions of United, with Derek Dooley seeking him out personally to welcome him to Bramall Lane, and his first training session, just two days before a crucial match, left him gobsmacked.

"Derek said to me when he introduced himself that I will never have encountered a game like this one against Wednesday," Gage recalled. "It turned out he was spot on! Even in training in the days beforehand, it was a bit 'lively.' My new teammates were flying around, throwing themselves into tackles and no quarter was asked or given. I'd been part of the whole Crazy Gang phenomenon with Wimbledon and we could put ourselves about a bit when needed, but we rarely did it to our own teammates in training! The local Blades lads, Carl Bradshaw, Mitch Ward and Dane Whitehouse, were straining at the leash and Bassett was happy for them to set the tone for what was to come in two days' time."

With United rock bottom of the table on just nine points, and Wednesday going great guns at the other end, few people outside of the United dressing room realistically fancied a home win. The Owls had failed to score in just two of their 15 league matches and a win would take them into the top four. Only leaders Leeds and Arsenal had netted more than Wednesday at that stage of the season; only second-bottom Luton had shipped more goals than United. "They had a fantastic team," remembered goalkeeper Simon Tracey. "If you believe all the comments from the Sheffield Wednesday supporters or even the neutral, we shouldn't have even been on the same pitch as them. They were full of internationals."

It was the first time the sides had met in the top division since 1968 and all the talk before the game was about how many the Owls were going to win by. Midfielder Jamie Hoyland recalled hearing rumours that Wednesday were having bets in training, about how many goals ahead they were going to be by half-time. "So as you can imagine," he admitted, "that riled us a little."

Deane's return to the teamsheet gave the United dressing room another lift ahead of kick-off. The striker had been out for six weeks and was hesitant about playing, but Bassett had promised his star man he could come off if needed and Deane fed off the occasion. "I was running on adrenaline," he admitted. "And it worked out well in the end."

United's preparations for the derby didn't change too much but an hour before kick-off, there was tension in the air of the Blades dressing room. Not a nervous one, which would have been understandable given the form guide and size of the fixture, but a different type of feel. "It was more a kind of excitement, that they just wanted the game to start immediately and couldn't wait any longer," Gage said. "From being around it all and listening to it and seeing players gee each other up, you just got the feeling that these players here were going to tear into Wednesday and they were really, really up for it.

"I remember Brads … I've never seen anyone like it, just going mental and trying to headbutt fucking walls. He was quite a volatile character anyway but he was going around screaming his head off, and I mean really screaming his head off. Not at anything in particular and not at any one person. It was just a release of energy. We absolutely knew that the Wednesday players could hear all this, because their dressing room isn't too far from the home one. It's the rowdiest dressing room I have ever been in in my life. It was bouncing, absolutely bouncing."

United knew there would be only one way they could win. To try and play Wednesday at their own game would be foolish; the league table alone was proof of that. United had to not only operate to the very best of their capabilities but also outfight their opponents and, to put it simply, want it more. Early clashes saw Bradshaw square up to John Sheridan, with a number of players getting involved, and then Nigel Worthington lash out uncharacteristically and see yellow, and were just what United wanted. Hoyland knew, at this point, that the Blades had their rivals right where they wanted them.

"You saw the look in their eyes when a couple of incidents kicked off in that first half with a few melees," he explained. "We had myself, Dane Whitehouse, Brads … all Unitedites from Sheffield in the team. But it wasn't just us. Even the London lot, they all loved Sheffield and we were all in this. The Wednesday lads, they were better players than us. There was no question of that. But in terms of mentality and wanting to win the game, we were hyped so much for that it was untrue."

It was rather fitting then that one of those Unitedites enjoyed a moment he will never forget, Whitehouse slotting home the opener on the stroke of half-time in front of the Kop. Deane then marked his return by putting the ball through Chris Woods' legs to put the result beyond doubt 18 minutes from time. United fans duly revelled in the victory; bragging rights were theirs to enjoy. Bassett's men took the opportunity to celebrate, too, with John Gannon dancing on tables in the Big Tree pub in Woodseats long into the night. It wouldn't happen now, especially with another big game six days later, but this was a different era and drinking alcohol was a big part of English football culture.

Hoyland had taken on the responsibility of running the players' bar at Bramall Lane and took it as seriously as his on-field role to support the strikers from midfield. Having grown up in a pub as a youngster, Hoyland was seemingly the natural choice to man the bar, with his responsibilities including a trip to the Makro cash-and-carry the night before a home game to stock up on beer and then arriving an hour early on matchday to unload the goods and make sure that everything was in order.

Hoyland would also ensure a crate of lager was ready for the away team to take on their coach back with them – a gentleman's agreement that was reciprocated for the return fixture. "Everybody wanted to get in that players' bar," Hoyland said. "It was a hotter ticket than Josephine's at the time. It was unbelievable. I tell people and they say I'm lying. This would even be in the Premier League, playing the likes of Man United. Steve Bruce would give you a tap and say: 'We're off now, have you got anything?' and we'd give them their crate and then at Old Trafford they'd do the same for our coach going back to Sheffield. I took the role seriously. It was our bar and it had to be stocked right. Otherwise, the lads would have hammered me."

The aftermath of that famous derby day was soured a little when Tracey and Bradshaw were accused of taking their celebrations a little too far on the pitch and were charged by the FA for allegedly making gestures towards the away supporters. Both were fined a week's wages each but both refused to pay, with Bassett standing by his players' side. "The players and our club are incensed at the fines," he said at the time. "We can find no corroborating evidence on our own video of the match, nor on the police surveillance tapes."

The FA became involved after a report by police, who launched an investigation after Wednesday fans claimed the pair had gestured at them after both United goals. "Without independent back-up the players do not see how they can be disciplined in this way," Bassett added. "It opens the door to alarming problems. If enough of our fans at the return match with Sheffield Wednesday write in to say that one of the opposing players had been abusive towards them, what are the FA going to do?"

Despite that controversy, victory over Wednesday was a shot in the arm for United's season and was followed up by a 1-0 win at Tottenham, with Gage announcing his arrival in fine style with the only goal of the game. A 2-0 victory over Aston Villa soon after was a fine day for United's youth set-up, with academy products Whitehouse and Ward both on the scoresheet, and the upturn in results had suddenly breathed new life into their season.

But United, who kicked off 1992 having moved to 21 points and up to third bottom, still needed another strong finish to ensure they stayed up. A 4-0 FA Cup thumping of Luton in early January proved to be the first of six wins in seven in all competitions – including 4-2 and 5-2 successes at Southampton and Nottingham Forest respectively and a 4-2 home win over Manchester City. Michael Lake earned the nickname "Zico," after the Brazilian legend, with four special goals in those three matches, while Deane was back to his best with goals against Liverpool, Forest and City in the league, and two more against Charlton in the cup.

"It's probably the freest I've played," Deane said. "I just played off the cuff. I'd play in games like against Liverpool and think: 'Was that me?' It's very hard to put into words but if you've got talent and then get the opportunity to express yourself, it's great. And I have to give credit to the manager for that. He didn't put too much emphasis on me apart from attacking, going and causing the opposition problems. And when you're playing like that, it's very hard to counter what someone like me was bringing to the game.

"I was 6ft 3in and with all the attributes I had, it was difficult to know what I was going to do next. I think sometimes people were quite surprised at some of the things that I did. I remember playing Charlton in the FA Cup and the ball was heading out to the main stand. I had a defender on me and he was going: 'Go on, go on, what are you going to do?' Without thinking about it, I put my foot on the ball and spun, pirouetted and left him where he was. I didn't know I could even do that. I just did it. Afterwards, I could tell he thought: 'Okay, I should keep my mouth shut now.'"

***

It sounds like the plot of one of those far-fetched football stories, where ordinary people are catapulted into the professional game usually with the help of some magic boots or enchanted pair of gloves. But for Paul Rogers, swapping the commuter rat race in London for a starting berth in the English First Division was no fairytale.

For years, his daily routine was a little more mundane. The 6.42am train to London and his job in the City as a commodities trader, dealing in gold, platinum and other precious metals. The 8.42pm back home again, for three days a week. The rest was taken up with training and games with non-league Sutton United, turning out in front of a few hundred people in the Isthmian Premier League against the likes of Bognor Regis Town and Carshalton Athletic. "It was a little bit like living life on the treadmill," Rogers admitted.

Born in Portsmouth, Rogers began working in the City soon after leaving school and started as a messenger, collecting cheques and fetching sandwiches, before progressing to a broker and managing the money of his clients. "It was a great time to be in the City. People were making good money and it was the start of the computer revolution. It was a great place to work, with such a buzz and a good social life." Football was going well, too, with Rogers' Sutton dumping previous winners Coventry City out of the FA Cup in 1989.

Then one day, the phone in his office rang. On the other end of the line was Sheffield United manager Dave Bassett, with the offer of a two-and-a-half-year deal on the table and the opportunity to go up against the likes of Man United, Arsenal and Liverpool. "I didn't have an agent or anything like that," Rogers laughed. "I went in to see my managing director at work and luckily he was football-mad, so told me to go for it and see how it went. I always had the back-up option of going back there if things didn't go right, so it was a win/win scenario for me, really.

"Harry was quite clear with me, saying: 'You're not here to make up the numbers. I've got a small squad, and I'm looking for you to play.' So the decision took no time at all. I'd have signed for even less than he offered me for the chance to be a professional. Although I wouldn't have told Harry that at the time!" Rogers' realised the extent of his remarkable rise on his very first day at United, when there were brand-new goals at the training ground and 30 gleaming, matching footballs. "I'd been used to three Nikes, a couple of Mitres and a flat Adidas!" Rogers smiled.

Rogers was close to being reunited with his former Sutton teammate Efan Ekoku at Bramall Lane, with United launching a £50,000 deal for the then 22-year-old a few years earlier. But the attraction of joining First Division-bound United did not hold the same appeal as joining Bournemouth, freshly relegated to the third tier but still able to offer the promising striker a more lucrative contract. "I am sorry to lose the player," Bassett said at the time. "But if he really did not relish the challenge thrown up at our club, then perhaps it is for the best."

It was another transfer frustration for the United boss but the £35,000 he was able to invest in Rogers was more inspired Bassett business, repaid with just shy of 140 committed appearances in red and white. "You had to learn quickly," Rogers said. "At one point you're playing football for fun and then you're playing for your livelihood. I think that's a real change. Everything is: 'You have to win, you have to play well, you have to stay in the team.' The players I was playing against knew and understood the game so much better than I did at the time. I thought I had probably missed the chance of doing it, playing football for a living. But that's why I absolutely loved every day and tried to get the most out of it that I could."

Rogers' second competitive appearance in United colours came at Hillsborough in the return Steel City derby against Wednesday, with just over 40,000 fans in attendance – a far cry from the 400 crowds he was used to playing in front of just a month previously. An injury to Michael Lake brought him into the fold and it was a real pinch-yourself moment for Rogers as the United coach set off from Bramall Lane, with fans and flares in the car park cheering them on their way.

Rogers was going to be directly up against England international Carlton Palmer, but any nerves or doubts he had were quickly dismissed. "Harry was big on preparation," Rogers added. "He knew how they played and what they were trying to do. He was great at doing that, setting up teams for different oppositions but making sure we still kept our part of the game as well. That was the dream and as a game, it couldn't have gone any better."

Bassett prepared his players for the derby with one of his beloved bonding trips, this time north of the border to Scotland. It was an idea very much of-its-time, sending your players on a boozy jaunt just days before a local derby, but it was also smart, ensuring his players escaped the pressure and talk of facing Wednesday by staying in a city that would be dominated by talk of one thing. "He used to love a little two or three-day jaunt," defender Kevin Gage said. "It was just a piss up, basically. We went out for two days and I was just drinking." One of Bassett's other ideas was to send his players to Hillsborough to watch Wednesday in action, and sample the atmosphere they were going to be walking into. It wasn't his best idea. "We nearly got beat up by a load of Wednesday supporters," remembered midfielder John Gannon.

Rogers was not alone in sampling the fervour of a Sheffield derby for the first time, with Bassett signing Alan Cork from Wimbledon on a free transfer – Cork subsequently becoming the first player to play in all four English professional leagues for the same manager – and bringing in Bobby Davison on loan from Leeds.

Used to the disciplinarian methods of Howard Wilkinson at Elland Road, life under Wilkinson's big pal Bassett would be very different for Davison, who was given the option of joining the United party in Scotland or remaining in Yorkshire ahead of the derby against Wednesday. He chose the latter, meaning he only linked up with his new teammates in training on the eve of the midweek trip. As a packed team coach featuring squad players and even apprentices weaved its way from Bramall Lane to Hillsborough, Davison already knew what was expected of him.

"When I first turned professional," Davison said, "my manager said to me: 'If you turned up at Sheffield United and you had only 10 players, and you had to pluck a supporter out of that crowd, what would that supporter do? He or she would run until they dropped. And if you do that as a footballer, you'll have more good games than bad games.' And that stuck with me. So wherever I played, that's what I tried to do.

"On the bus going to the stadium, it was a nightmare. The dressing room was just as bad. At Leeds, with Howard, we didn't really have any music on and it was only the team that was starting and the subs that were allowed in the dressing room. An hour before the game, that was when the other lads could come in and wish you all the best. It was the opposite that night. Everyone was there.

"All the players who travelled on the bus, ones who weren't in the squad or picked to play were in the dressing room. The music was absolutely blaring. I wasn't used to it. I was just like: 'Where is my number, where is my shirt?' I was getting changed and sat there, just trying to switch off. Oh god, it was just totally different. The boys were shouting and bawling, and I just wanted to get out on the pitch and start the game."

It was also Davison's first meeting with Simon Tracey since the promotion season, when Leeds had battered United 4-0 and the United goalkeeper had given away a penalty after Davison had successfully got under his skin. "He's my mate now, we are good pals now, but not then!" Davison laughed. "When I first walked in the dressing room the boys straight away mentioned that. At the time there would have been swear words, no doubt, and I think I probably swore back with a big smile on my face.

"It was Simon being a bit hot-headed but I tell you what ... I didn't realise how good he was until I went on loan to United and worked with him. What a 'keeper, and what a great lad as well. We've since travelled around Europe together working for the FA. He was different from what you saw on the pitch. He was much calmer and took everything in his stride. A really good guy."

Now they were comrades, looking to secure a historic derby double over Wednesday. But just like the first encounter, the Owls – third in the table and out for revenge after the November beating – were huge favourites. Boyhood Blade Dane Whitehouse, though, set United on their way with the opening goal in a derby once again, after doing his homework on Owls right-back Roland Nilsson during their scouring mission, before Davison sent the away end into raptures when he pounced on Carl Bradshaw's ball and benefited from uncertainty from Chris Woods to slot home for 2-0.

Wednesday threatened a comeback in the second half, with a deflected effort from Phil King, before Davison marked one of the best-ever debuts in a United shirt by glancing home John Gannon's ball to put the result beyond doubt. Wednesday would be in the hunt for the title until the final stages that season – and how they could have done with those six points to help them. "I have supported United all my life and I've put a couple of goals in," Whitehouse said at the time. "Six points ... they could have won the league, but we stuffed them!"

Davison rightly joined Whitehouse in Blades folklore that night for his memorable double – a debut that still gets talked about to this day. "That dressing room after the match was just crazy," he added. "I just wanted to get a shower. I was just thinking: 'Just let me get a shower, get changed and go,' because that's the way I am. 'The job's done, let me get out of here. Let me go home and just sit and relax.' But the boys were buzzing. It *was* unbelievable, wasn't it? If you wrote it, people would say that doesn't happen. Loads of players have gone on and scored in those derby games but every time I bump into a Sheffield United fan they remember. I bumped into one in Disney World in Florida with the kids. Great memories."

Two more boyhood Blades in midfielder Jamie Hoyland and defender Chris Wilder watched on from the away end as their side completed a historic derby double. Hoyland was injured while Wilder had moved out on loan, but revelled in the victory by feigning ignorance and asking ashen Owls fans what the result was as he made his way jubilantly down Penistone Road.

It was a memorable evening, too, for new signing Glyn Hodges, who had missed the 2-0 November win due to injury and came on at Hillsborough as a sub. "I didn't have a particularly good start," Hodges said. "The next thing I knew, Corky came running over and said: 'Unless you liven up, Harry's taking you back off.' He was going to sub the sub, so I had to liven up a bit. It was phenomenal to win that 3-1. I will never forget the flags and the flares."

To this day Hoyland is still unsure if the line about Wednesday's players taking bets on how many goals they would score against the Blades was another psychological ploy from Bassett to further rev up his players. "They were really quiet before the game, and even quieter after," he added. "In those days you always went up to the players' bar after and had a quick pint. We made sure every one of us went up on this one just to rub their noses in it. It was a Wednesday night so it couldn't be too much of a big one because we had a game on the Saturday. But if that was a Saturday game, we would have been out that night and Sunday. 'And we'll see you on Tuesday, Harry!'

"They had a swagger and a few players who had a bit about themselves, but we just knew that physically they had to match us. It doesn't matter how good you are – we knew that, if they weren't physically competitive and weren't going to match our endeavour, then they were going to struggle. On top of that we got some good goals. We always knew that we could beat anybody at any time. We knew what we were doing and we had some good players. We had Deano up front and we knew we could score. We were always confident and the onus was on them, especially after beating them 2-0 at Bramall Lane. They were probably more nervous than we were. We were confident and it showed in the performance. It was a great night, and one that I will never forget."

It was a memorable one, too, for United's managing director Derek Dooley. A former Wednesday striker whose career was cruelly cut short by the loss of his right leg, Dooley was sacked as Owls manager on Christmas Eve in 1973. Deeply hurt by the decision, and feeling Wednesday should have had the decency to wait until after Christmas to wield the axe, Dooley did not return to Hillsborough to watch Wednesday for 19 years and only once in the interim, after being persuaded to attend the 1976 FA Cup semi-final between Manchester United and Derby County. But, encouraged by Bassett, he agreed to attend the Hillsborough leg of the derby, travelling there early in club secretary Dave Capper's car to avoid the crowds.

He was still recognised by Owls fans, with one stopping Dooley to tell him he was the finest centre-forward he had ever seen and sparking tears in the great man's eyes. Owls chairman Dave Richards persuaded him to walk onto the pitch before the game to soak up the acclaim from both sets of supporters and in his autobiography, Dooley admitted to making the transition to becoming a Unitedite. The way his heart leapt when United scored against Wednesday that night, he said, only further cemented his new affiliation with the red and white half of Sheffield.

The derby victory set United on their way to another fine end-of-season run, with six wins and two draws in their final 11 matches sealing their place in the top division for another season. Two of their defeats were to eventual champions Leeds, who put one hand on the title after a bizarre 3-2 victory at Bramall Lane, and runners-up Manchester United, highlighting the strength of United's season finish.

There was an impressive 2-0 win over Liverpool courtesy of a double from Brian Deane, including a remarkable 45-yard lob over a stranded Bruce Grobbelaar. It was the type of finish that few other United players could have envisioned, let alone executed. Deane then added a second for good measure, combining pace, power and poise to hold off the challenge of David Burrows and get onto David Barnes' ball over the top, before dropping the shoulder on Grobbelaar and rounding him to slot home.

"The first one, that was just instinctive," Deane recalled. "When you're so in-tune as a player, you just know. It was just a natural instinct. The second goal was a long ball where I pushed the defender and went round the 'keeper. But you work all week to get to know your body and your capabilities all the time, so those two goals stand out for me."

A clean sheet at the other end was also credit to Mel Rees, who had arrived as an emergency transfer from West Brom for £25,000 to cover for the injured Simon Tracey. Back-up Phil Kite was recovering from a hernia operation and Bassett had to act quickly. United's strong finish to the season was soured a little by news of Brian Smith's enforced retirement after a broken leg, but their form was so impressive that the Blades were in the top two, with Arsenal, for points picked up in 1992 when the Gunners visited Bramall Lane on April 18 for a 1-1 draw.

Bassett's men ended the campaign in ninth place and did not comprehend at the time the size of that achievement. At the time of writing, it is a feat that no United side has beaten since and only one has equalled it – fittingly managed by one of Bassett's promotion heroes in Wilder, who led the Blades to ninth in the Premier League in 2019/20.

The 1991/92 achievement was even more remarkable considering that Bassett ended that season having made a profit in the transfer market. He was not only playing the role of manager, but was also doing the job he felt others should have been doing above him in keeping the club afloat at the same time. As commendable as that was, the truth was that he was growing increasingly tired of fighting fires and watching a boardroom stumble from one issue to the next. After another season of consolidation, the chance was now there for United to kick on and back their manager to compete further up the top-flight table. The question was: could they take it?

"My dad always said to me: 'Whatever happens in life, go out there and earn it. It'll never come to you on a plate.' My mum and dad brought me up the right way. Some people are born into wealth, and good luck to them. But I wasn't. I've worked hard. I've worked hard, and I reaped the rewards."

– Dane Whitehouse

14

THE SLAPS

In Paul Newman's 1977 American cult comedy *Slap Shot,* the Charlestown Chiefs, the minor league ice hockey side, are struggling. The results are poor, the fans are angry, and the players don't care. The closure of a local steel mill threatens 10,000 jobs. Player-coach Reggie Dunlop lies to his side that they may be sold to Florida, in a bid to motivate them, but even that doesn't work. The turning point comes with the introduction of the "Slaps" – three Hanson brothers whose main approach, and ability, is brawling with opposition players. Slowly the more aggressive style catches on, exciting supporters and increasing crowds. It transforms the Chiefs to championship contenders, and they win the title after their top scorer begins an on-ice striptease and the opposition captain punches the referee in protest.

Exactly who first spotted the connection between the Hanson brothers and a trio of Sheffield United youngsters is unknown, but the term *Slaps* became a ubiquitous way to refer to Carl Bradshaw, Dane Whitehouse and Mitch Ward; usually relating to some sort of mischief. Whitehouse believes it was either Tony Agana or Brian Gayle who came up with the nickname, but isn't completely sure – either way, it stuck and even decades later, more than one player remembered "The Slaps" with a nostalgic glint in the eye. "We were part of the Sheffield mob," Whitehouse said. "Me, Brads, Wardy, Jamie Hoyland and Chris Wilder.

"We got the nickname because we were always together. They couldn't split us up. We were always by each other's side in training, we went out for meals together. And I think it helped the London lads because we showed them what it was like to be up here. They only knew London and we only knew Sheffield. But we knew what it meant to play for this club and so they had some great teachers in that respect."

Whitehouse hailed from Woodthorpe in Sheffield, not far from the

Manor estate where Bradshaw was raised, and despite an age difference of just over two years, the two were close from an early age. They played football together; they grew up together. Their families were tight. Whitehouse still regards Bradshaw as his best mate in football. Ward was slightly different, coming from Firth Park in the north of the city, but struck up a friendship with Whitehouse through their shared football abilities. All three were different characters but together, were thick as thieves – all sharing an ingrained love of United. The Blades' very own Slap Shots were born.

A former Junior Blade who had a steadfast resolve that he would make a career in the game, from a young age, Ward's introduction to the United first-team wasn't immediate and his versatility became more of a hindrance than a help later on. Once, his reward for two goals in a win over Watford was to be dropped for an Anglo Italian Cup clash with Udinese next up. But he was an important member of the Blades squad in Dave Bassett's era and later worked with the manager again at Barnsley after a big move to Everton prised him away from Bramall Lane. Even Ward's finest hour in a United shirt came from the bench, as an early substitute in the FA Cup quarter-final at home to Blackburn in 1993. He scored two goals in normal time in a 2-2 draw, firing home a penalty for good measure in the shoot-out as United booked their place in a semi-final at Wembley.

The trio were a big part of United's reputation as the Crazy Gang of the north under Bassett. "I wouldn't have thought they resented it," said midfielder Bob Booker. "It was a term of endearment. It's not an insult. The Slap Shots would have fitted right into the Wimbledon Crazy Gang. That's another feather in Harry's cap, to put together two teams like that and mix so many different personalities and ages. The Slapshots, I loved them. They were three quality players, too. Mitch went to Everton; Bradshaw had played for Man City and unfortunately Dane got a bad injury. They could use both feet, cross the ball and score. And in the modern game today, they would be worth millions."

Booker's first experience of the Slaps came soon after his move up from Brentford, when snow had cancelled training at Warminster Road and Bassett arranged a north-v-south snowball fight instead. "I got separated from the southern group and got pinned down by Brads, Dane and Billy Whitehurst. They stripped me, left me in my slip with just my boots on. I had to make my own way back to Bramall Lane. I started walking back, freezing my nuts off, and luckily David Barnes came back and picked me up." When a notorious joker like Barnes comes to the rescue, Booker knew he was in trouble.

Bradshaw was one of three brothers and two managed to forge a career in professional football, his older sibling Darren playing for Newcastle, Peterborough and Blackpool amongst others. His dad, who was the landlord of the Blue Bell pub after moving the family to Hackenthorpe, was also a player of some repute around Sheffield in his day. Football ability was clearly in the genes and both Darren and Carl quickly caught the attention of scouts, the latter electing to join United's city rivals Wednesday alongside his bigger brother.

Then a centre-forward, Bradshaw made a professional debut on loan at Barnsley and scored for good measure. He once netted a hat-trick in the intermediate league against United. Another debut goal followed for the Owls' first team and he gradually enjoyed more opportunities as a teenager in the top flight. But the departure of Howard Wilkinson to Leeds signalled the beginning of the end for him at Hillsborough and an unhappy move to Manchester City, a division below, followed. In Gary Armstrong's 1998 book *Blade Runners,* Bradshaw described his time at Maine Road as a "hell-hole" and remembered Bassett doing him a huge favour by taking him back home to Sheffield.

Overweight and disillusioned, Bradshaw fell back in love with football at his boyhood club as Bassett – who had paid City £50,000 up front – redefined his role, as a right-sided defender. Growing up in the Blue Bell had at times been enlightening and Bradshaw knew how to look after himself, once seeing red and headbutting former teammate Vinnie Jones at a corner after the ex-Blade had left for Chelsea.

His time at Wednesday had not dampened his love for United – as his Blades tattoo demonstrated – and before one Sheffield derby in United colours, Bradshaw was instructed by Bassett to get after Owls midfielder Carlton Palmer. Teammate Hoyland – who later had to restrain Bradshaw in an on-field spat with Palmer – remembers Bradshaw taking his orders a little too literally, getting in Palmer's face as the Owls team got off the bus at Bramall Lane.

Another to make himself known to Wednesday was Bradshaw's old pal Whitehouse, who scored the vital opening goal in United's 2-0 derby win over Wednesday in November 1991 – the first competitive meeting between the two rivals in more than 11 years. The Owls had a side packed with internationals but were no match for United that season, with Whitehouse living every boyhood Blade's fantasy by scoring against the old enemy, in front of the Bramall Lane Kop, after Jock Bryson's shot had been parried into his path by Owls goalkeeper Chris Woods. "I'm saying this as a United fan but they had a quality side, with the names on paper," Whitehouse said. "The build-up was immense. Playing Wednesday, for the first time in more than 10 years, was all people wanted to talk about. It's a good job we didn't have social media at the time because all we kept hearing was that they were going to put five past us and whatever.

"But I'll tell you now, we won that game before we even stepped out onto the pitch. We eyeballed every one of their players in the tunnel beforehand. We had some decent players at the time, don't get me wrong, but our strength was our team spirit and that day, we were pumped. We'd heard that they were going to do this and that and we looked into their eyes before the game, to see if they were up for it. Not one of them looked back at us. They probably just thought that their skill and their players would get them through the game, but it wasn't about that. It was putting in 90 minutes of solid graft, to a man.

"The way we played under Harry was basically get the ball forward as quickly as possible, and play in their half. His philosophy was that they couldn't score a goal in their own half. So the goal came from that. Two of their lads went for the same ball and Jock was free. I just wanted to get forward as quickly as possible and if Woods had parried it the other way, I think Brads would have had a tap-in. Whether you play in front of 500 people or 50,000 people, you don't really hear the fans because you're caught up in the game.

"All I did, as the ball fell to me, was concentrate on putting it in the back of the net and then afterwards I was thinking about jumping over the Kop railings, running up the steps and getting smothered by 10,000 fans. But at the time you don't think about it. It's weird. You're so focused. It's like you want to get in the ring and rip someone's head off, or go on the fastest ride at Alton Towers for the adrenaline rush."

For good measure Whitehouse scored in the return leg at Hillsborough – again right in front of his fellow Blades fans – as a 3-1 United win sealed a memorable derby double. Another close-range finish, another low-key celebration. Whitehouse actually began to wonder if he had been flagged offside, because of the lack of congratulations from his teammates before a little handshake from his fellow derby hero Bobby Davison.

It was some closure for the memory of 1979, when Whitehouse was in the away end at Hillsborough for a 4-0 Owls win that has since gone down in Wednesday folklore as the Boxing Day Massacre. Whitehouse's dad, Sid, was a bouncer and builder and with no buses running on Boxing Day, he took about 15 people – split between Blades and Owls – along to the game, and back to Woodthorpe after. "The result was rubbish but it was a good memory for that," Whitehouse said. "There were people sitting on each other's knees and we had a right laugh.

"I was an eight-year-old, Sheffield United-mad kid at Hillsborough, and 10 years later I was playing football for them. A few years later I was playing against Wednesday in front of 30,000 at Bramall Lane and 40,000 at Hillsborough. Then, hold on a minute, I've just scored in both derbies. It's a dream come true, and I've got all the memories. I had a load of Wednesday mates as well and all they wanted to see was a Woodthorpe lad do well. I remember one waiting outside the house when I got back after one of the games. 'Dane, I love you to bits,' he said. 'We've grown up together. But of all the people, it had to be thee, didn't it? It had to be you.'"

Growing up on Woodthorpe, by Whitehouse's own admission, wasn't easy. It was a rough estate, he recalled, and he lost close friends growing up "through stuff you don't want to talk about." Some went to prison. His dad, whose name he inherited as a nickname, did too. "He was an old-school bouncer, and some of the stuff I saw as a kid you don't want to see. It's not easy, but in one respect it opens your eyes. To say: 'I don't want to go down that way. I don't want to go down that route.'"

Whitehouse, however, firmly rejected the suggestion that football "saved" him. It was an upbringing that shaped him as a person. "My dad always said to me: 'Whatever happens in life, go out there and earn it. It'll never come to you on a plate.' My mum and dad brought me up the right way. Some people are born into wealth, and good luck to them. But I wasn't. I've worked hard. I've worked hard, and I reaped the rewards."

His early footballing abilities saw him scouted for Sheffield Boys before attracting interest from the local professional sides. He spent a week with Chesterfield and a few sessions with Wednesday but when United took a fancy, his mind was made up. He remembers around three quarters of his group of apprentices making the grade professionally, with a tough grounding seeing the YTA players scrub the toilets, paint the fences and clean boots, with the odd training session thrown in around the work. It was Bassett who gave Whitehouse his senior debut, away at Blackpool. When his name was read out over the PA system, Whitehouse can still remember seeing some fans looking at each other and asking: 'Who?'

They soon got to know as the young Whitehouse gradually established himself in Bassett's side, forming a close bond with his two fellow homegrown Blades. "The Slaps were a nightmare in the dressing room," laughed Davison. "The dressing room was massive and they had their little corner. They were murder. They came in one day, giggling, and all had little red marks on their chests. We never found out for sure but someone said they'd been playing darts and ended up messing about, dropping darts on each other's chests. It looked like they all had measles. They used to jump Harry and beat him up. Early on I thought: 'What are you diving on the manager for?' But it soon became normal. Absolutely mad."

In all, Whitehouse pulled on the United shirt more than 250 times, despite a career hampered – and then tragically curtailed – by injury. In the early days he damaged knee ligaments, keeping him out of the Leicester promotion game in 1990, and later broke his leg and missed a large chunk of the first Premier League season. He remained at United beyond Bassett's departure, despite frequent and lucrative offers to leave. "Leeds, around the time they signed Brian Deane, were interested in buying me. Whether they put an offer in or not, I don't know but Howard Wilkinson was definitely interested. Then Trevor Francis really liked me, too."

It was 1997, Francis was in charge at Birmingham City and United had not long lost the play-off final at Wembley to Crystal Palace. United were entertaining the offer but Whitehouse did not, after seeking assurances about his place in manager Nigel Spackman's plans. Birmingham were offering a long deal on big wages, a house in the second city and a new car. It would have set him up for life. But it wasn't United. Whitehouse instead shone in Spackman's superb side as they attacked Division One and were fifth in the table, three points off top spot, when they made the trip to Port Vale on November 22.

Just over 8,000 fans were present at Vale Park to watch a goalless draw completely overshadowed by a horror injury to United's No.11. A pass – ironically, Whitehouse remembered it being from his pal Ward – ran across him and his next feeling was the crunch of a challenge from Vale's Gareth Ainsworth. Whitehouse hadn't even seen him coming. "One minute I'm looking at the ball and the next I'm writhing in agony on the floor. I've broken my leg, I've broken ribs, I've broken my nose, I've broken my arm, but I've never been in pain like that. Ever. And I'm quite tough, I think. I never used to go down with a niggle and a lot of people said that if I stayed down, they knew I was hurt. The physio came on and I said my knee had gone pop, crack and snap. He basically told me not to look down. I'd broken my kneecap and done all my ligaments, so the bottom half of my leg was virtually hanging off."

Whitehouse underwent his first operation two days later, to recon-struct his knee, and when he came round, his first question to the sur-geon was whether he had a chance of getting back to playing. "Everyone has a chance," he replied. "It's all about hard work." That was one thing Whitehouse could guarantee. He was in the gym every day, admitting now that the mental toll affected his relationship with his family. The long rehabilitation process saw him play eight times for the reserves in 1999/2000 but his head, and his knee, were telling him that something wasn't right. "I'm not a cheat," Whitehouse admitted. One day in training he controlled a simple pass and his knee gave way. He took his boots off and reluctantly, heartbreakingly, conceded defeat. His last kick of a ball in a United shirt came at 29 years of age.

"I needed to be honest with myself. I tried and tried but I couldn't let the team down. I couldn't play a football game at 50 per cent, knowing full well that if someone came in and tackled me or whatever I could lose my leg. I needed to be 100 per cent, because that's who I am as a person."

All these years on, Ainsworth is still reviled at Bramall Lane, and Whitehouse will never forgive him. "If I ever saw him in the street, I wouldn't know what to do. I really wouldn't. Whether I'd lay into him and smash him all over the street. But I definitely would never shake his hand, and I'd definitely not accept an apology from him. It's far too late for that. It's far too late."

Whitehouse Sr. tried to take matters into his own hands when Vale next came to Bramall Lane later that season, attempting to board the visitors' team coach to confront Ainsworth. Only the presence of police and stewards prevented what could have been an ugly scene. "My dad could look after himself, and I think it took a lot of people to get him off that coach. I think he just did what any parent would do after an incident like that, though."

At that point Steve Thompson, a former senior pro at United while Whitehouse was an apprentice, was in caretaker charge of the Blades and called Whitehouse into his office on Monday morning. Whitehouse began to apologise on his dad's behalf when Thompson stopped him in his tracks. "Dane, you don't have to say a thing," he said. "I'd have done the same thing. Tell your dad he's more than welcome to come down to this football club, any day of the week."

While Whitehouse faced up to the realities of life after football, after being cut down before he potentially approached his prime, Ainsworth played until he was 39 before moving into management. There were few tears shed in South Yorkshire when he was sacked by QPR in 2023 after winning five of his 28 games in charge, and a hostile reception will await if he ever returns to Bramall Lane in the future. He was even jeered on managerial duty with Wycombe at Hillsborough stadium by some of Whitehouse's Wednesday-supporting mates.

"You know your career is going to come to an end one day but you don't expect it to end the way it did for me," Whitehouse added. "So you start questioning yourself then. If only this or that. You speak to people and they say things like: 'You know what Dane … if you'd have gone to Birmingham, you might have gone on to play at international level,' and so on. It's all if, buts and maybes, isn't it? I guess I'll never know. I prepared for the end like everyone does, with pensions and stuff, but with it ending with a click of the fingers, it was hard to adjust. One minute I was playing football on a Saturday afternoon and the next, I couldn't play anymore. I was fine one minute and the next minute … I wasn't."

Offered some coaching work by then-Blades boss Neil Warnock, Whitehouse discovered that the £25-a-session fee would barely cover his food bill, let alone his mortgage, and he instead threw himself into the big, wide world. A chance offer to deliver a package to London led to a spell as a courier, with a contract to deliver flowers, before he moved into working shifts at a steelworks close to his home in Rotherham.

"That was the way I was brought up. Fair enough, I played football but I had a mortgage and a family to provide for and so I had to get on with it. I was 29 years old and had the rest of my life to live. It wasn't all easy, because I'd been in the limelight for 10 years or so. A lot of the people I was working with were people who'd cheered us on a matchday. People used to ask me: 'How come you're working here?' but it wasn't like it is now, where one three-year contract can set you up for life. We were on decent money, but we weren't financially secure by any means and I think it's just ingrained in me to graft and graft and graft."

He still fits in visits to his beloved Bramall Lane, too, sitting in the south stand and enjoying a pre-match pint or two amongst star-struck supporters who used to idolise him. Whitehouse walked with kings, as the famous Rudyard Kipling poem goes, but has never lost the common touch. "I'll always have a chat. Because that's just who I am. That's me. My career ending as it did and when it did was tough at the time, but I think I just had to say to myself: 'Whatever's happened has happened. I can't change it. What I can control is how I live the rest of my life.'

"I don't think I let anyone down; I look back on my career and I think I did alright. Now it's the next step in my life. Football's gone, it's finished, and I am still absolutely gutted about that. But I'll give something back in any way I can, and that's why I love going to the games. I love chatting about football. Even with some of my Wednesday mates. It's all about memories now."

And there are many. Two iconic goals in a memorable derby double, representing his boyhood club on the biggest stages in English football. Euphoric highs and gut-wrenching lows. A boy from the Woodthorpe estate who lived the dream.

"Has it changed my life? While I was playing, I don't think it did. For me, it was just another goal. It was only when I finished playing. But I've learned to relax about the whole thing and the Premier League has really taken off, so I'm glad it was me rather than Shearer or Lineker or Ferdinand or Wright. It's me and something I'll always be remembered for, and so that's fantastic. But there wasn't just me on the pitch ... there were 10 others plus the subs, staff and fans. It was us who beat Man United, not just me."

– *Brian Deane*

15

A NEW DAWN

I t was August 1992, and the Steel City was baked in sunshine as football fans, on either side of the divide, looked eagerly forward to a new dawn in English football. Cheerleaders before kick-off, fireworks and the razzmatazz normally associated with American sports were winging its way over to these shores.

The way people consumed football, in this country and abroad, was about to change forever, thanks to an exclusive, and expensive, *Sky TV* rights deal. Five hours of broadcast around a live match on a Sunday; Richard Keys presenting from a different ground each week, with big name ex-pros as studio guests; players taking part in the build-up to their live matches each week as part of promotional material and games being shown to millions around the world.

The Premier League era had begun.

The split had been orchestrated years earlier between five top English clubs and by February 1992, 22 teams were all on board. All were guaranteed a bigger slice of the financial pie and although the clubs themselves were predictably ready for change, there was still opposition – including from the Professional Footballers Association, the players' union who felt that clubs and officials would be the ones to profit rather than their members. Their main complaint was that wages were not relative to the increased sums now pouring into club coffers – a scale that has certainly been evened out in recent years.

To this day fans remain divided on *Sky's* input, particularly when it comes to planning fixtures and changing kick-off times for the benefit of television viewers rather than match-going spectators, but they arrived at the right time and there can be no doubt that their involvement revolutionised the English game as we know it today. In late 2023, the latest Premier League TV rights deal was announced; a joint venture between

Sky and *TNT Sports* meaning that top-flight clubs will receive a share of £6.7billion in return for four seasons of coverage.

Sheffield United were one of the initial 22 clubs, having secured their top-flight status the previous campaign, but at the time of its inception, it was impossible to predict the behemoth that the Premier League would eventually become. "There's a big thing now, that every player in the Championship must have a clause in their contract that their wages go up a certain percentage if they go up," said defender Kevin Gage. "But ours didn't. We were playing in the First Division one year and then the next year it was the Premier League. You could have called it the Evo-Stik whatever league, it didn't make any difference to us. It was just a name at that time."

But a shiny new league necessitated a shiny advertising campaign and to launch the new era, one player from each of the 22 clubs was invited to a Sunday morning video and photoshoot at a warehouse near Wembley stadium. The result was the iconic Premier League promo video, set to the sounds of Simple Minds' *Alive and Kicking* and featuring, amongst others, Arsenal's Anders Limpar being woken up with breakfast in bed from his then-wife, Vinnie Jones of Chelsea in his first acting role and six or seven top-flight footballers together under makeshift showers. United's representative was Carl Bradshaw, with his main involvement the moment where he and Wednesday striker David Hirst pull on the other Sheffield club's shirt. Ordinarily, the prospect of wearing an Owls shirt would be horrifying for a boyhood Blade, but Bradshaw's time at Hillsborough before making his way to the right side of the Steel City probably helped soften the blow.

"I can still remember Brads putting the shirt on with Hirsty," said goal-keeper Alan Kelly. "At the time I was thinking: 'Whoa, we're here now.'" *Sky's* trailer ended with the proclamation that the Premier League was "a whole new ball game," and didn't prove too wide of the mark. The new TV deal meant that clubs were set to pocket more cash than they had ever tasted before – a huge financial boost for clubs like United, where money continued to be in short supply. Those in the Bramall Lane boardroom must have felt that Christmas had come early. For Dave Bassett and his Blades players, it actually did.

With Bassett searching for a way to ensure his side hit the ground running when the season began, after both the previous two campaigns started poorly and then kicked into gear after the new year, physio Derek French came up with the idea over a few pints at The Porter Cottage on Sharrow Vale Road, the regular haunt of United's coaching staff on the eve of a home game. United's players seemed to perform better after Christmas, he reasoned … so why not bring Christmas forward?

That is how a function room at Bramall Lane, in August, came to be decked out as a full-blown Christmas party – decorations, crackers, turkey and Bassett dressed in a full Santa suit. "It was fucking baking hot," Bassett said. "Derek Dooley, I remember, particularly loved it. We had a great old time." It started out well enough, with players in high spirits, but soon descended into a bread roll fight. "I've never seen so much bread flying about," said Kelly, United's main summer signing from Preston. "The directors were there, and Derek. But it just became a free-for-all."

The party worked to some extent, with United winning their first game of the season before reverting to type somewhat with a run of six more without victory. But what a win it was: at home, on the opening day of the new era, and against the mighty Manchester United – the eventual champions who only lost six times on their way to the title. The original United's 2-1 victory didn't attract too much attention at the time, but held incredible significance in the years and decades that followed.

The old clock on the Bramall Lane end had just ticked past 3:05pm when Brian Deane made a pre-rehearsed dash across Gary Pallister, into the space left by Alan Cork's run to the front post, which took Steve Bruce with him. Bradshaw's long throw was flicked into the path of Deane, and the striker nodded past a stranded Peter Schmeichel to continue his streak of scoring on the opening day of a season. What a start. He had no idea at the time, but Deane had just written himself, and United, into the history books with the first goal of the Premier League era.

"Has it changed my life? While I was playing, I don't think it did," Deane admitted. "For me, it was just another goal. It was only when I finished playing. I remember being really rude to someone once, when they asked me about the goal. They were trying to be nice but I was so shy and felt that if someone was trying to be nice to me, they were trying to be nasty. I didn't know how to take people. I felt I was always on my guard and I hated that side of it. But I've learned to relax about the whole thing and the Premier League has really taken off, so I'm glad it was me rather than Alan Shearer or Gary Lineker or Les Ferdinand or Ian Wright. It's me and something I'll always be remembered for, and so that's fantastic. But there wasn't just me on the pitch … there were 10 others plus the subs, staff and fans. It was us who beat Man United, not just me."

Deane, who slotted home a second-half penalty to secure victory, is regularly reminded of his place in history, and his magic moment is something he is able to enjoy a lot more now he has retired. Fans often ask for his signature on limited edition prints, and Deane likes to collect one of each for posterity. It's perhaps the most replayed goal in Premier League history, and continues to be talked about to this day; in 2023, the shirt Deane wore that day was auctioned at Sotheby's in New York and sold for $38,100, plus significant buyer's fees. "I still speak to Deano quite a lot and I said to him recently: 'If you'd have had copyright on that goal, you wouldn't be working again!'" said Kelly. "If you were a fan there on that opening day, full of optimism and belief, and then you beat Man Utd with the team they had … it was just a brilliant occasion. I always remember the razzamataz. There were always balloons, streamers and flags. There was always colour and always something happening in the crowd. I went back to Bramall Lane a while back and there was a light show pre-match, which really brought it back to me."

It may have been the start of a golden new era but not everything had changed. Goalkeeper Kelly was Bassett's only summer signing of note, for £150,000, while the only new face in the team to face Alex Ferguson's side was centre-half Alan McLeary, who had arrived on a short-term loan deal from Millwall and lined up alongside Paul Beesley in the heart of defence. While clubs around them cashed in their golden tickets, United continued their prudent approach in the transfer market – with the departures of Clive Mendonca (£85,000 to Grimsby), Colin Hill (£200,000 to Leicester) and Chris Wilder (£40,000 to Rotherham United) leaving the Blades in profit.

Elsewhere in the division Blackburn had spent more than £4m to bring in Alan Shearer and Stuart Ripley; Tottenham chucked £5m plus on Darren Anderton, Neil Ruddock, Teddy Sheringham and Jason Cundy, after selling Paul Gascoigne and Paul Stewart; Leeds brought David Rocastle to Elland Road for £2m; Aston Villa spent £3m on Dean Saunders and Ray Houghton. Even just down the road, Trevor Francis brought Mark

Bright and Chris Waddle to Wednesday, to the tune of £3m. Bassett could only look on in envy.

At least Kelly's arrival meant that, for the first time in a long time, No.1 goalkeeper Simon Tracey – the first name on the teamsheet for the previous three seasons – had genuine competition for his place. Bassett stuck with Tracey to begin the season, with Kelly taking his place in the makeshift dugouts that the players used to refer to as the "bus stop." The surroundings certainly did not reflect the glitz and glamour of their new league but confidence was high after that opening-day win. United pushed Liverpool all the way in game two at Anfield, with the hosts having to come from behind after Deane had given United the lead 10 minutes before the break.

The striker was again showing his importance with United's first three goals of the season, all against quality opposition, and constant transfer speculation linked him with a host of top-flight clubs. Bassett, rightly, feared that any genuine offer could see the board cash in but in the end, accepted that the situation was out of his hands and not worth losing too much sleep over. After all, he had enough to worry about in the here and now, with his team second bottom of the table and with just four points from their opening seven matches.

Included in that run was a 2-0 defeat at Tottenham, which saw Sheringham mark his home debut with the opener on the stroke of half-time before a second half to forget for Tracey saw him caught out of his goal for Spurs' second a minute after the restart, and then sent off after trying to dribble the ball out of play. Tracey had already been booked, after handling outside his area in the third minute of the game, and the referee had no choice but to send him off. To add to the calamity the referee who sent Tracey off was not the one who originally booked him; the first official was a replacement himself and then had to make way with illness, with one of his linesmen taking over the whistle with 17 minutes left to play. Tracey readily admits now that the whole remarkable episode was solely down to his lack of technique with the ball at his feet; Bassett memorably described his goalkeeper after the game as having "the brains of a rocking horse."

"My mum didn't like that one," Tracey admitted. "But mums are not going to when you are talking about their son like that, are they? Harry was as honest as the day was long and I think that's why he was so well-liked by the players. He used to come out and tell you. When I look back, I think: 'What was I doing there?' I can't explain that and I can't defend that. If I was coaching someone I'd be saying: 'Why are you putting yourself in that position? It's ridiculous.' So I completely understand that I let the team down, and I let the manager down."

Tracey began to make amends with a clean sheet in United's home win over Liverpool – his final match before his suspension – and Kelly geared up for his Premier League debut by joining his teammates at a nearby go-karting track. Bassett had sensed that his players could use a change of scenery amid another poor start to a campaign and it certainly raised spirits amongst the squad, with Bradshaw spraying Champagne from the top of the podium and Charlie Hartfield spending more time ploughing through tyres than he did on the track. United were five minutes away from victory over Arsenal, before Wright earned the Gunners a point, but four points against two stellar opponents – plus a goalless draw at Ipswich and 2-0 win over Southampton – moved United up to 16th. The day out go-karting had put United back on track, but only for a brief moment and they were soon back in the pit lane, with only two more wins before the end of the year ensuring United kicked off 1993 third-bottom.

Bassett turned to the transfer market for some fresh impetus, signing Chris Kamara on a three-month loan deal from Luton and Franz Carr – a player Bassett had long admired and felt should have enjoyed a more successful career – in a £120,000 move from Newcastle United. Despite operating now at the very top of the pyramid, Bassett retained an eye for an unpolished diamond and returned to Sutton United, from whom he had signed Paul Rogers previously, to tie up a £50,000 deal for young striker Andy Scott. A year later Bassett plucked Scott's defender brother Rob – who was working in the prison service at the time – from seventh-tier Sutton.

With United's league form floundering, the FA Cup came at a good time to breathe new life into their season. However, it almost didn't. It needed an almighty half-time Bassett bollocking for United to turn around their third-round clash at home to Burnley, who were two divisions below the Blades but 2-0 to the good at half-time courtesy of a brace from future United boss Adrian Heath. Two Blades goals in the last nine minutes forced a replay, and avoided the embarrassment of an early exit in front of one of the highest gates of the season at that point.

A Deane hat-trick at Turf Moor then saved United's blushes and set up a home clash with Hartlepool in round four. Deane followed that treble with another four days later, giving the Ipswich defence a torrid time in a game that saw Carr make his debut. Back-to-back hat-tricks duly strengthened Deane's appeal and it was becoming blatantly obvious at this stage that United were now going to have a real fight on their hands to keep hold of their talisman – with clubs circling and United's bleak financial picture meaning they were always vulnerable to offers.

Six goals in the space of four days ended a rare, 14-game goal drought for Deane and he can still remember the feeling vividly, albeit not for the reasons one might expect. "I'd got a knock to the front of my mouth early on against Burnley, and it made me really angry," he said. "I thought to myself: 'If I'm going to lose one of my front teeth, it is going to be worthwhile.' And I went nuts. I scored the hat-trick angrily. I was pissed off." After no goals in 14 games – 15 if you include a 3-1 testimonial defeat away at Worksop in mid-December – Deane rediscovered the scoring touch with seven in four.

Victory in round four against a Hartlepool side that had just been served with a winding-up petition landed United a plum tie against the Red Devils at Bramall Lane, in a repeat of the opening-day game. The draw was music to the ears of veteran striker Alan Cork, who had secured victory over Hartlepool and had vowed not to shave his beard until the Blades' FA Cup run that season was over. "Thank god for that," he joked after the draw. "I'll be able to shave it off now." But before the visit of Ferguson's stars was a clash at home to Queens Park Rangers, which Bassett had identified as a winnable one in their pursuit of survival. A 2-1 defeat kept United in relegation danger and Bassett made his feelings clear in the dressing room afterwards, leaving his players in no doubt as to what he thought of the performance.

Victory over Middlesbrough in the next home game – after defeat at Old Trafford – was the response Bassett had been looking for, with Carr and Deane linking up well and both inking their names on the scoresheet. The result set United up nicely for the visit of the Red Devils, who were top of the Premier League and favourites to lift the FA Cup for good measure. More than 27,000 packed into Bramall Lane on Valentine's Day, with Des Lynam on *BBC* duty as well hoping for some more famous cup romance. It would be a tough ask, against a star-studded side containing the likes of Ryan Giggs, Paul Ince, Mark Hughes, Andrei Kanchelskis and Lee Sharpe, and it looked even tougher when Giggs put the visitors ahead on the half-hour mark. But United turned the tie on its head within 10 minutes courtesy of goals from Jamie Hoyland and Glyn Hodges, whose beautiful lob over Schmeichel proved to be the memorable winner.

"That's the one which gets the most airplay and the one talked about the most," Hodges remembers of his 22 goals in a red and white shirt. "It was back in the days when the FA Cup was live on a Sunday and millions of people tuned in. We were the underdog and everyone loves the underdog. As soon as I saw Brian Gayle go up for the header I was thinking: 'He's flicking this on, and I'm in here.' So I was on the move, he did win the flick and when it came on the bounce I was thinking: 'I'm blasting this.'

"But then I thought Schmeichel was going to do that windmill with his arms and he was bound to get some part of his body on to it, so at the last second I decided to lob him. He didn't even go for it. He couldn't, could he? If I blasted it, he could have got any piece of his body on it but once that sat up nicely, I thought: 'Nah, he ain't getting this.'"

Liverpool legend Alan Hansen was alongside Jimmy Hill in the *BBC* studio and his summation perfectly represented United's group of players under Bassett. "You have got to give Sheffield United a lot of credit," Hansen said, "because a lot of teams would have packed up. But they came right back into it and it could have easily been 3-1 at half-time." It was a team that was never about individuals, more about the sum of its parts and one that was capable of beating anyone on its day – as victories over the league and FA Cup winners showed. And for all the wheeling and dealing Bassett was forced into, and the financial competition he was up against, he was not short on quality players.

Kelly had not been there long before he found that out for himself. "You look at Dane Whitehouse ... bar his injury he would have played for England," Kelly said. "You look at the energy of Bradshaw and the modern-day full-back getting forward ... there was no better left foot around at that time than Hodges. That goal against Man United was absolute quality. We had the personnel to suit the way we played and we were more energetic and fitter than most. But we knew we could play, too."

The win sent United into the last eight of the famous old cup competition but they were still deep in relegation trouble and could not afford to take their eye off their league form. The silver lining was that Bassett and so many of his players had been in the same boat before, with the manager refusing to panic and continuing to stick to the beliefs that had served him and the team so well the previous seasons. He asked to strengthen the team for the final push ahead of the transfer deadline but his squad ended up being weaker, with Michael Lake leaving to join Wrexham for £60,000. It was another season where Bassett had brought in more than he had spent, and the message for the remainder of the campaign was clear. If United were going to reach the cup final or avoid relegation, they would have to do it themselves without any help.

They certainly made a statement with a 6-0 hammering of Tottenham, who had arrived at Bramall Lane for a rearranged match on the back of six wins on the spin, scoring 16 goals in the process, and knowing that a seventh would take them into fourth spot. But the run came to an end in spectacular fashion as a devastating United attack of Carr, Deane and Ian Bryson ran riot. Four goals in the space of 16 first-half minutes, including a cleverly worked corner for Carr's opener, had United cruising at the break. Not that Bassett would allow his players to think that way.

"Mr. Bassett wasn't the best at handing out compliments," laughed Bryson. "The game was only half done. He sat us down and gave us his usual, laid into us for some aspects, because you can always do better. The idea was to get our feet back on the ground, which is right, and it worked. I remember a game against Brighton a few years before which we won 5-4 in the end, but we were 3-0 up and then 4-1 and before we knew it, we were drawing 4-4.

"We had been through similar games in the past, so he was calming us down and ensuring that we didn't take our focus off the task in hand. We had an experienced team that night. We had players who could handle the situation, we believed in ourselves and Bassett was brilliant in giving us that self-belief. We were 4-0 up, he knocked us down a peg, and we started again, telling ourselves: 'It is 0-0 and the job is to win the second half.' We did that ... it was job done, and a great night for the club."

Two more goals followed in the second half from Deane and Paul Rogers, with one of many inspired performances at the other end from Kelly keeping a well-deserved clean sheet – much to Sheringham's dismay. "The ball got crossed to the far post and he absolutely smashed one,"

Kelly said. "I just flashed a hand out and deflected it over. Sometimes you had those days – it looks like a worldie of a save, but at the time you just whip a hand out, it hits it and goes over and the gods are with you.

"I remember Sheringham looking at me and just going: 'How the hell did you save that?' We just annihilated them and I would have thought that was one of Harry's, one of mine and one of Sheffield United's most complete performances. We just took them apart. They get one chance, the 'keeper makes a world-class save and they must have looked at it and thought: 'Let's just pack up and go home.' How do you go from being bottom of the league in February, to demolishing Tottenham three weeks later? Harry built a team full of characters that never said die and never gave up. Put confidence and character together, and they can be dangerous."

The game also stands out in Gage's mind, but for different reasons. His parents lived down south, in Surrey, and did not get the chance to see their son play in too many live matches – but they were up for the Spurs game, and he couldn't wait to see their reaction to such a memorable victory. But when he got changed and headed for a drink, they were nowhere to be seen. Later he discovered his dad had been hit by a car in Trowell services and had been taken by ambulance to the nearest hospital in Nottingham. "He had crushed his knee, broken his leg and never went back to work," Gage said. "He still walks with a limp now. So that game stands out as a weird one for me … for all the right and wrong reasons."

For Spurs, it was their heaviest defeat in 15 years; United were up from second-bottom to 17th and, more importantly, now in possession of the best goal difference of the bottom six. And all just in time for a mouthwatering FA Cup quarter-final against Kenny Dalglish's big-spending Blackburn Rovers, who were in the top five of the league and pushing for Europe. A creditable goalless draw at Ewood Park led to one of the most memorable nights of that era in the replay, with Sheffield-born Mitch Ward fittingly scoring both goals as United twice came from behind to force penalties. It was by fortune that Ward was on the pitch, Ian Bryson coming off injured at half-time, but was this Lady Luck finally turning up for a change? The substitute forced extra-time, when he poked home beyond Bobby Mimms eight minutes from the end, and then did the same again from Cork's pull-back to take the tie to penalties.

"We had the belief that we were good enough to beat anybody," said Hodges. "Our run that year showed that. I don't think anyone expected us to get anything in the first game at their ground, so to knock them out after a replay was typical of Sheffield United at that time." Hodges was one of the successful penalty takers while Hoyland's nerves got the better of him and prevented him from watching the shootout. Instead he sat with his back to the action, looking at the Kop's reaction to tell him whether or not each spot kick had gone in. Ward showed what an inspired change it proved to be in the end by coolly dispatching the first spot-kick, before Kelly endeared himself further to the United faithful by saving Jason Wilcox's penalty low to his right.

"I seemed to save penalties better in cup games than in league games," Kelly admitted. "I took my cue from how he stood and what angle he was thinking about, knowing he was left-footed. I don't think he caught it right and once you go the right way, you always give yourself a chance of saving it. I have seen Jason plenty of times since and I always remind him of that save! We were in a relegation battle at the time, so we were used to scrapping and fighting for each other and showing that character and it all came to the fore on that night."

Hartfield then made no mistake, low and hard into the bottom corner to give United the advantage and also stick two fingers up at Dalglish, who was far from impressed with the midfielder that night. The Rovers manager felt he should have been sent off after a scuffle with Mike Newell with the score at 1-0. "Newell ended up with a bleeding nose," said Hartfield, "and at the end of the game Dalglish walked past me telling me I was lucky to be on the pitch and things like that. That walk for the penalty is a daunting walk, but I had a bit of confidence because Kelly's save made it easier. Cup nights were special at Bramall Lane, but that Blackburn win was off the scale."

Cork made it 3-1, meaning the beard had more growth left in it yet, and Hodges' heart then skipped a beat when he stuck the fourth into the top corner. It looked as good a penalty as you will see, but it went higher than he intended and although the taker can laugh about it now, he breathed a huge sigh of relief when it hit the back of the net. With boss Bassett admitting he was almost going into the Kop for penalty takers, it set up defender John Pemberton for the unlikeliest of winning kicks. Pemberton had already played in one FA Cup semi-final with Crystal

Palace, and secured his second with a rasping drive more befitting a seasoned striker. As Pemberton spoke to the TV cameras amid the chaos, Hodges planted a kiss on his teammate before United's players dragged themselves off the Bramall Lane pitch, got quickly changed and headed to one of their usual haunts, of Berlins nightclub on Eyre Street. The celebrations could begin. United were off to Wembley.

***

Reaching a first FA Cup semi-final since 1961 was a special enough achievement for Sheffield United, but the magnitude of the occasion was only increased when it sank in who would be lying in wait for them in the final four. Their bitter city rivals Wednesday had already booked their place in the semi-finals, by beating Derby in a quarter-final replay, and the first all-Sheffield clash at that stage of the famous old competition caused a logistical challenge.

The previous season's last-four clashes had been held at Highbury, Hillsborough and Villa Park but with two other rivals also meeting in the other semi-final, in Arsenal and Spurs, three stadia with a similar 40,000 or so capacity were not going to be sufficient. United v Wednesday could have been played at Elland Road or Villa Park, a short trek either just up or down the M1 for both sides, but a campaign saw the FA relent and agree for the biggest Sheffield derby of all time to be played at the national stadium.

Initially United boss Dave Bassett welcomed the change, feeling it would be a perfect chance to put Sheffield football on the map. He and so many others of a Blades persuasion now realise that, in hindsight, the change played right into Wednesday's hands. United goalkeepers Alan Kelly and Simon Tracey discovered the news while training at Warminster Road, from a fan who stopped his car and shouted from the road: "It's at Wembley, it's at Wembley. They've changed their minds."

"There was a real debate about it," Kelly recalled. "There's no doubt it added to the occasion, an all-Sheffield FA Cup semi-final at Wembley. But there are a few things. The pitch was obviously fantastic, and Bramall Lane's, at the time, wasn't. You might say that Wednesday had the better ball players, with people like Chris Waddle. It was also a much bigger stadium and less enclosed, whereas somewhere like Elland Road or Villa Park may have suited us more, in terms of bringing that Bramall

Lane experience to the game. All those little levellers could have played a part."

Instead, the city of Sheffield prepared to decamp down to Wembley and Bassett and Owls boss Trevor Francis, enemies on the touchline but good friends away from the pitch, travelled to Italy to watch the Genoese derby between Genoa and Sampdoria in the lead up to their own cross-city clash. United's players went down to London early in the week, staying at the luxury Sopwell House hotel in St. Albans – which was also being used by Arsenal – and taking in *Blood Brothers* on the West End in a bid to take their minds off the weekend derby.

"Imagine taking the three slaps, Bradshaw, Whitehouse and Ward, to a West End musical," Kelly laughed. "They were sitting there with a choc ice and a bag of crisps. It doesn't get any better than that, does it?" Bassett's men then enjoyed a tour of Wembley and picked out where their families would be sitting. Mitch Ward's Wednesday-supporting grandad travelled down on a bus full of friends and family, the Blades man joking that he may find himself walking back up to Sheffield if the Owls won.

The day of the all-Sheffield semi-final was also the 147th Grand National horse race at Aintree and on the coach to Wembley, United's players and staff drew their horses out of a hat for the Blades sweepstake. There were allegations of a fix when physio Derek French pulled out one of the favourites but in the end there was to be no winner, with the race declared void after a false start. Thirty of the 39 runners began the race and seven went on to complete it, but the decision was taken not to re-run and for the first and only time to date, the Grand National was voided.

Bassett delayed the naming of his team until later in the week and in the only change from the previous league game, Glyn Hodges came in for Tom Cowan. It meant Dane Whitehouse would play at left-back, and there was no room in the side for Carl Bradshaw. The Sheffield-born, Blades-supporting former Owl was desperate to be in the team; after finding out he wasn't, he responded by throwing his boots into a bush at the training ground and, in the heat of the moment, threatening to never play for United again. He did, of course, pull on the red and white shirt again but admits that the pain of missing out at Wembley still hurts to this day.

Bassett openly admits he made mistakes that day; he played Franz Carr from the start because he was one of the few Blades who had experienced Wembley before, but the winger had a quiet game. In hindsight Bassett believes he should have started Bradshaw wide right and Paul Beesley at left-back, freeing up Whitehouse offensively. Paul Rogers should have started in midfield, he admits, with Glyn Hodges just off Brian Deane and Alan Cork on the bench. "The occasion got to them," Bassett said. "It was just a bit too much for them." One Owls player later confided in Bassett that Wednesday's players were delighted that the game had been switched to Wembley, admitting: "We wouldn't have fancied it against you lot at Elland Road."

Another to miss out was winger Jock Bryson, whose injury against Blackburn in the quarter-final turned out to be a serious one. That game, as it happened, was his last start in a United shirt, the popular Scot only making one further competitive appearance off the bench before moving on. "It was a real shame because as a kid growing up all I wanted to do was play at Wembley," he said.

"It was the first time they got to a semi-final while I was there, and I wasn't fit. I had a groin operation during the season and a double hernia. At the end of the season Bassett decided I was no longer required, so I moved on." Hartfield was just as gutted to not be in the side. "I was having a good run in the team but, can you believe it? I was suspended. I cannot tell you how devastated I was. Honestly, it really hit me. I had never played at Wembley, and that absolutely floored me."

If those disappointed Blades needed any perspective over missing out, however, they didn't have to look far. Teammate Mel Rees, the former West Bromwich Albion goalkeeper, had made an impressive start to life at Bramall Lane but was floored by a bowel cancer diagnosis in the summer of 1992, just months after he had arrived at United and made such an accomplished debut against Liverpool.

Surgery was performed to hopefully correct the issue and Rees was well enough to return to the United bench for an away game at Aston Villa, but the cancer returned in 1993. Fellow goalkeeper Alan Kelly remembers being told that Rees was ill, when United returned for preseason in 1992. "He had a deep purple sports jacket on, which was the fashion at the time, and stuck his hand out for a handshake, saying: 'It's alright, I'm not contagious.'"

United had hoped to have Rees lead them out at Wembley amid his brave battle; when that idea was vetoed by the powers-that-be, Rees was accompanied on an emotional pre-match lap of honour by assistant manager Geoff Taylor, physios Derek French and Denis Circuit and kitman John Greaves. Wearing a red tie and a red jacket which hung loose over his thin frame, the Welshman looked pale and gaunt; to Wednesday fans' credit, they gave Rees the reception he deserved as he passed in front of them. For those short minutes, on the hallowed turf of Wembley, football paled into insignificance.

"Seeing him at Wembley put it all into perspective," said Kelly. "You've got someone there who's hanging on to life. Football is important, but not that important. When I went to the hospice to visit him, seeing an athlete like Mel, who was a big lad, ravaged by the illness … it was heartbreaking. I didn't know him that long but I felt like I had known him a lifetime, because he had that character. He had that wit and repartee, and he was the life and soul of the party. I think the best way to sum it up is that it was like losing one of your family. Because we were a family."

Less than two months later, Rees passed away. He was 26 years old.

Rees' first indication that something was wrong came when he suddenly found himself unable to walk 100 yards or so without having to sit down. He took his concerns to physio French, who arranged for some scans. The initial suspicion was that Rees had Crohn's disease. "I can still remember Dr. Green phoning me, and telling me he had some bad news about Mel," French said. "He was so fit, and lively. I'll never forget going to see him in the hospice. He was walking along the corridor, with his drip, and he looked so gaunt. He knew he was dying, but he said to me: 'I feel better today. I'm up and about.' I've never experienced anything like that. It was horrible.

"It was my idea to take him around the pitch at Wembley and in hindsight, I'm not sure it was such a good one. But I thought: 'You can't just leave him like this.' I asked if he wanted to go and I asked Harry if he had any problems with it. But walking round the pitch, he was really struggling. I think someone had to take him back home, if I remember right, because he was getting really bad debilitating headaches. You wonder if it would've helped him that day, having everyone cheer for him. Jesus, it was tough. It's one of the things of life, I guess, but Mel was a big part of the story. He was fantastic towards the end. He didn't play much but he made a massive impact and he is still revered by fans to this day.

"I went with Mel to see the surgeon, who was a lovely man, and he explained to me that he was absolutely riddled with cancer and that he wouldn't last long. What do you say to that? We tried to look after him as best we could after that. And then his dad, Ron, called me that summer and said Mel had passed away." Rees was determined to spend his last days at home, rather than in a hospital. He died in Derby, at the home of his girlfriend Louise, on May 30, 1993, and United players and staff filled a minibus to his funeral. On the way home, the bus ran out of petrol on the motorway. "Brian Gayle nearly ripped my head off," recalled French. "I'd never even thought about the fuel. It was one of the worst days of my life."

In the end it was Gayle, not Rees, who ended up leading out United at Wembley, with the Blades skipper looking to exorcise some of his own personal demons of the national stadium. Five years earlier, he was part of the Wimbledon set-up preparing for the FA Cup final against Liverpool; having featured in every previous round, Gayle was told on the day that he would not be in the matchday squad for the final. It was the most disappointing moment of his career and given what a return to Wembley meant, as his chance for redemption, it said everything about Gayle's personality and character that he was keen for Rees to take his place at the front of the queue as United came out of the Wembley tunnel to a crescendo of noise.

Commentator Barry Davies wondered aloud whether the famous old stadium had ever seen so many balloons, relaying that one Sheffield man had ordered 100,000 on his own. The mixture of excitement, anticipation and nerves was almost tangible at kick-off, and United fans will have feared the worst within seconds of the kick-off when Chris Waddle nonchalantly netted a free-kick from long distance. United's goal lived a charmed life after that, with a combination of the woodwork and Kelly keeping the scoreline 1-0, and the Blades were back in the game on the stroke of half-time when Cork was sent clear on goal, with just Chris Woods to beat.

It was not the cleanest of strikes from the veteran but it was enough to beat Woods and the chasing Waddle, who was unable to reach the ball and clear off the line. Bassett was incensed in the second half, feeling United should have had a penalty for handball, and more heroics from Kelly, surely his finest performance in a United shirt, kept Wednesday at bay. Then, after the game had gone into half an hour of extra-time on an energy-sapping afternoon, Mark Bright's simple header from a corner broke tens of thousands of Blades hearts. "We were hanging on," Bassett reflected decades later. "You just knew it was coming."

Deane looks back at the Wembley woe with honest reflection. "It was a crap game from my point of view. I didn't play very well and that performance from us ... we didn't do ourselves justice. If you're a Sheffield Wednesday fan you can say this and that, but I'm not someone who's bothered about stuff like that. They were the better team on the day, and they lost in the final. It would have been nice to get to the final but we didn't deserve it on that performance.

"We were punching above our weight, massively. There was a lot on my shoulders, if you look at the teams. They had the midfield they had and kept the ball; they had the players who could create problems and chances. We weren't as creative; we worked hard and everything was a 50/50. It was a source of frustration for me but at the end of the day it's just what we were about. I don't see many people complaining. You certainly didn't get players throwing their toys out of the pram. You just got on with it."

There was little time for United to lick their wounds, with Bassett opting against keeping his side at Wembley for Sunday's semi-final and instead taking them back up north to prepare for a second huge game in the space of four days. The Blades, third bottom of the Premier League table, faced Yorkshire rivals Leeds knowing that victory would move them above Oldham and out of the relegation zone. It was a big psychological test for United, to pick themselves up after the body blow of Wembley, and it is to their immense credit that they passed it with flying colours.

Bassett played the side he realised he should have picked against Wednesday, with Bradshaw back in the side alongside Beesley and Rogers, and Rogers justified the call with the opening goal in a seismic 2-1 win. Three draws and a defeat in the next four games, including a 1-1 stalemate with Wednesday at Hillsborough, followed, meaning United were not out of the relegation woods just yet. Three games in the space of eight days would decide their fate.

The first was away at Nottingham Forest, in what was the legendary Brian Clough's final game in charge of Forest at the City Ground. Clough was a legendary figure in the Midlands, after leading Forest to two European Cups and a First Division title, but he was plagued by alcohol-related issues towards the end of his career and although he was only 58, he wore the appearance of a man at least 10 years older.

Dressed in his trademark green jumper and red polo shirt, Clough sent his Forest side out against United knowing that defeat would see his iconic career sign off with relegation. United were scrapping for their own lives, too, and goals from Hodges and Gayle sentenced Forest to the drop. At full-time, when Bassett shook hands with Clough before he left the City Ground touchline for the final time, he looked into the eyes of a man whose race had long been run.

Victory at Everton, thanks to goals from Bradshaw and Hodges, meant United were practically safe going into their final match of the season at home to Chelsea, winning 4-2 and the game all but over at half-time as Andy Scott scored his first league goal. Alongside Scott on the scoresheet was another Sutton United old boy in Rogers, which perhaps summed up the cards that Bassett was playing with at the time.

He had pulled off another relative miracle, leading United to a 14th-place finish and securing another season of Premier League football. And as he was chaired aloft by jubilant supporters on the Bramall Lane pitch in the searing Sheffield sun, Bassett had no idea that his biggest challenge was yet to come.

16

WHEN IRISH EYES ARE SMILING

There was a slight touch to deflect Paul Warhurst's shot onto the crossbar. A double save down to his right to deny David Hirst. A curling effort from John Sheridan pushed around the post. A strong hand to John Harkes' cross/shot from a narrow angle. A close-range block to stop Hirst scoring an easy tap-in. And arguably the best of the lot, diving low down to his left to push away Mark Bright's effort that had squirmed through a crowd of defenders.

Alan Kelly's individual display in Sheffield United's 1993 FA Cup semi-final defeat to rivals Wednesday deserved its own highlights reel. But as he faced the *BBC* cameras in its aftermath, his face as pale as the suit he was wearing, Kelly bore the look of a man who had produced one of the great United performances on one of their most disappointing days. He had won the individual battle but, on English football's greatest stage, and against their greatest enemy, United had lost the collective war. "It felt like having the heart ripped out of you," a stony-faced Kelly admitted after the game.

It was a day that saw the Steel City take over the capital, with more than 75,000 fans packing into Wembley and at least twice as many red and blue balloons floating into the North London sky. With red flares going off around the stadium, Kelly remembered it being like something from the *Football Italia* highlights show. His dad Alan Sr. had graced the Wembley turf himself in the 1964 FA Cup final for Preston North End, and Kelly was determined to ensure that the moment didn't pass him by. "I remember walking out of the tunnel, with the atmosphere and the balloons and the flares, and smiling to myself. Thinking: 'Oh yeah, I'm going to enjoy this.' Then, after about 90 seconds, you think: 'Oh well, that's gone out of the window, hasn't it?'"

Chris Waddle's thunderous long-range free-kick was past Kelly before he had even settled into the game and his first touch of the semi-final was to pick the ball out of the back of his net. Boss Dave Bassett had discussed the set-up of defensive walls before the game, Kelly recalled, and for all the talk of whether United should have been better prepared, he readily admits that it was a "cracking strike" from the England international. "I knew straight away that I was in trouble. Truthfully, as soon as he hit it, I thought: 'I'm in trouble here.' But it was done, I couldn't turn the clock back and now it was about how I reacted and recovered from the early goal conceded."

United were down but not out and as he made his way to the edge of his area, with one half of Wembley in jubilation, Kelly's chin was up. "I'd obviously got a stony look on my face, but I'd got my head up. I look at it now and I think there was a defiance in my expression, saying: 'Okay, right … I can't change what's just happened, but I can affect what happens for the rest of the game.' There was no shaking of the head or any dramatics. It was just like: 'Alright, shit's happened. Now I have to do everything in my power to not let it happen again.' And that's what I tried to do.

"My dad always said to me: 'Don't show the opposition players any emotion, don't give them any encouragement. Control your emotions, control your next action in the game. Because it could be in the next 30 seconds.' I think probably one of the biggest compliments I had in my career was from fans, players, coaches and managers: that I always looked like I was in control of my emotions, or I was calm. Whether it was after a save in an FA Cup semi-final at Wembley or if I'd made a mistake. And that's the biggest thing I take from that goal – my ability to recover and perform."

The game became a test of composure and character amongst the chaos, with Wednesday hitting the woodwork three times either side of Alan Cork's equaliser just before half-time. Kelly then came into his own, a one-man wall of defiance keeping Warhurst and Hirst and Sheriden and Harkes and Bright and Hirst again at bay. Wednesday fans gloated afterwards that the scoreline could have been 10-1.

After one of the saves Hirst stared at Kelly in disbelief before mimicking a camera action, suggesting the United goalkeeper was somehow posturing. It was nonsense. He was simply having the game of his life. And then he was beaten by the simplest of set-play moves; a Harkes corner, a mistimed Brian Deane jump, a Bright header that broke United hearts and sent Wednesday to Wembley.

"I look back now and think about how the character of the team kept us in the game. To go 1-0 down after 90 seconds in an FA Cup semi-final, against our fiercest rivals, at Wembley, could have been a killer blow. But to come back and take it to extra-time, you have to dig deep and show you have a bit of grit and a bit of resilience. And there was no better man to get us back into it than Alan Cork. He went through one-on-one; his beard went one way, the ball went the other and poor old Chrissy Woods and Chris Waddle couldn't do anything to keep it out. Then you think: 'Anything is possible here.' Unfortunately, I think we'd invested so much to get back in the game that, come extra-time, we just run out of steam. But we gave it a hell of a go and I don't think the team gets enough credit for that."

Kelly was understandably crestfallen as he dragged himself off the Wembley pitch but the truth was that he had done more than any United player to give his side a shot of reaching a first FA Cup final since 1936. "Fucking hell, Ned," boss Bassett told his goalkeeper afterwards. "You made some saves today, son, well done." And after a few words from skipper Brian Gayle, and a few beers in Wembley's giant baths, the Blades were on the road back north with Premier League survival on their minds. "We had to use that resilience and ability to move on quickly, and get ready for another game a few days later," Kelly said. "I imagine it would have been easy to think: 'Oh, we were a few minutes away from an FA Cup final.' But we couldn't. We had Leeds at Bramall Lane in midweek, and we had to win to survive in the Premier League. And we did."

Kelly has always had a sense of perspective. Growing up in Preston, as the son of a North End legend who made 513 appearances across 13 years and whose face features on seats at one end of Deepdale, would bring its own pressures and when Kelly Jr. began his own journey as a schoolboy with Preston's academy, it was as an outfield player. Then one of the goalkeepers got injured, there was no replacement and Kelly stuck his hand up to have a go. Simon Tracey, Kelly's great friend and future rival, did exactly the same as a youngster. The fickle finger of fate conspired to provide United with two of their greatest-ever goalkeepers, at the same time, when either, or both, could have been lost to the game for good.

If his life had taken a slightly different turn, Kelly may not even have made it that far. It was 1988 and by that point Kelly had signed professional forms at Preston, as a goalkeeper. He was a headstrong teenager who had turned his back on a four-year electrician apprenticeship at British Leyland – much to his dad's displeasure – to chance his hand with a Preston side freshly relegated to the fourth tier. It was a gamble that looked to have paid off and on the eve of Preston's Sherpa Van Trophy semi-final against Blackburn, Kelly went to buy some new gloves. His mum worked as a florist on Meadow Street, close to the city centre, and Kelly used to pick her up from work. He decided to get the gloves first, but didn't make it across the road.

To this day he doesn't remember what happened but has been told since that a Kawasaki 750 motorbike had ploughed into him at 30mph, leaving him in the middle of the road, covered in blood and unconscious for three or four hours. He was left with 40 stitches in a head wound, a broken leg and a cauliflower ear but knows it could have been much worse. "I came round in hospital four hours later, and the first thing I saw was the hazy outline of my mum. Then I heard her calm Irish voice, God rest her soul, as she dropped an apple into my hand and told me I'd be grand. 'An apple a day keeps the doctor away,' she told me ... as my right leg was hanging over my shoulder!

"It was life-defining. I could easily have been in a coffin and I feel very, very lucky to have even been able to play again. It puts a lot of things into perspective. The break wasn't pinned and during my recovery the bones slipped down. I ended up losing about 13mm of height in my right leg and walked around, unbalanced, for seven years. I look back now and know that imbalance led to me picking up little injuries, and probably my subsequent knee replacements. Nowadays you'd be monitored 24/7, your leg would be pinned and all the modern technology would be there to help you make a full recovery. But it just wasn't that way in the late 1980s. My first game back was a memorial match for a good friend of mine and ex-Preston player called Mick Baxter, who had died far too young. I came out for a ball and Alex Bruce, the retired Preston striker, tried to nick it before me. His knee went straight into my same leg and I broke it again. Out for another six months. Maybe that's where my resilience and determination was forged."

Kelly used to be terribly superstitious, with habits including walking around and saluting magpies; after his accident and second leg break, he was not superstitious anymore. More injury woe followed as training and playing on Preston's plastic pitch took its toll on his knees and after taking the decision to move on, for the good of his health as much as his career, a trial at Neil Warnock's Notts County was organised.

In one training game Kelly once again took control of a situation, calling and coming out to clear a ball. His teammate that day, and a future one at Blackburn, was defender Craig Short, who also thought it was his ball. Kelly cleared the danger but collided with the strapping centre-half. Short was knocked unconscious, Kelly left semi-dazed on the grass. "Shorty was their star player so training was immediately cancelled and he got carried off," Kelly smiled. The trialist was left in a heap on the turf, head spinning and no one around to see if he was okay. "I thought that maybe it wasn't going to work here, and so I went back to Preston."

Kelly's wife Sara can still recall seeing the landline answer machine flashing, with a message from United boss Bassett. Kelly called the United boss back immediately and the call changed the course of his life. It was remarkably simple.

"We'd like to sign you," Bassett said. "What do you think?"

"Yes please, Mr. Bassett," Kelly replied.

"Well, what do you want?"

"Whatever you think, Mr. Bassett."

"Right, what about £25 more than you were getting at Preston?"

"Yeah, that's fine."

And with that, Kelly was a United player. It was the summer of 1992, with the advent of the new Premier League on the horizon, and Preston had just finished 17th in the Third Division. Kelly just wanted a chance to prove himself and felt this was it, hanging up the phone and telling Sara: "Right, we're off to Sheffield." Then the phone rang again. It was Bassett.

"Is it true you've just got married?" he asked. Kelly confirmed he had. "Right, make it £50 more. See you soon. Oh, and by the way, it's Harry."

The Kellys had been married for about a month and were still finding their feet in a new home that they had spent two years renovating, with Kelly getting stuck in and demolishing walls. The newlyweds had gone on honeymoon, just about unpacked into their new home and were suddenly on the move to the Steel City. Kelly had never been to Sheffield before and ended up driving towards Chatsworth House, discovering a house to rent nearby and calling his wife on the landline in Preston, telling her to pack the car and head to Baslow. It would be a difficult enough task for anyone new to the area, in 1992, and without the help of a specific address. But Sara set off, Kelly waited by the side of the road in Baslow until he saw her two and a half hours later, and flagged her down and directed her to their new home.

It was a whirlwind start to life at Bramall Lane. Kelly had a bit of an insight into life at the Blades from watching the *United!* documentary, which charted their iconic 1989/90 promotion season, and recognised Jock Bryson and his wife Kirsty from it. Paul Beesley was another familiar face from when the defender was at Wigan but other than that, the United group was totally alien as Kelly reported to Bramall Lane at 4am ahead of their pre-season tour to Sweden. Derek Dooley, the managing director who Kelly remembered as "wonderful," was not entirely sure who United's new goalkeeper was before he introduced himself and after putting pen to paper on his contract in the dark – "I could have been signing anything!" Kelly laughed – he was on the bus.

As the new boy, Kelly kept his head down while the bus thundered down the M1 towards Heathrow airport but he could sense something wasn't right. Suddenly Carl Bradshaw appeared from nowhere, said: "Nah then, who are you?" and began the first part of his new teammate's initiation by wrestling with him. Left-back David Barnes then joined in, grabbing Kelly in a headlock. "I'm thinking: 'What's going on here?'" Kelly laughed. "My new Sheffield United polo shirt had been ripped off, I was naked on the top half and my head was spinning. I managed to get hold of Brads – I don't know how, possibly through sheer desperation – and throw him over his seat.

"Then I stood up and Barnesy was standing there, saying: 'Come on then, come on then … let's see what you've got.' I'd had enough of it by that point and thumped him. He fell backwards down the stairs towards the toilet and it dawned on me in that moment that I'd been a United player for about an hour. In that time I'd lost my brand-new polo shirt, been in a full-on wrestling match with one of my teammates and then floored another. What had I signed up for? But Barnesy quickly got back to his feet, grabbed my arm aloft and announced to the rest of the bus: 'He's got a decent right hook, this lad … he'll do for us. Welcome to Shef-

field United, Ned.' That was how I got my nickname at Sheffield United."
Ned Kelly was a famous Australian outlaw in the 1800s, and the moniker
has stuck with Kelly to this day.

In his first training session with his new teammates in Sweden, Kelly
could barely turn his head after the coach antics. "I could see Harry wondering if he'd signed a wrong 'un because I couldn't move. He asked me
what was up with me and I told him I'd slept funny on the bus and my
neck was stiff. He knew what had happened! It was another little test of
Harry's, to see how you reacted to the initiation and if you just got on
with it, or you crumbled. I didn't crumble! 'Don't worry,' Harry said. 'Just
tip them over, son ... or should I call you Ned?' I told him that Ned was
fine, and we went from there."

Kelly's second memory of the inner workings of the United dressing
room came after the team's return from Sweden, when he walked into
Bramall Lane and Brian Gayle, the skipper, picked him up and bench-
pressed the new goalkeeper above his head. "It was amazing strength,"
Kelly recalled. "He put me down, shook my hand and then we all went to
training. Harry was across all of it. He wanted to see what I was made of
and how I reacted to stressful situations. So it was a case of: 'Let's go and
give him a rattle, see what he's about.'

"There were some mad moments but as I listened to some of the Crazy
Gang stories that Harry talked about, along with his current United side
that had won promotion to the top flight and stayed there, I knew he had
to have a certain type of player in his dressing room. A player that had
spirit, character and resilience. But most importantly, they had to have a
sense of togetherness to survive in the top league.

"Don't get me wrong, we could fall out. We could demand more from
each other. But it was almost like an army. As a team we believed in each
other. We could get on the front foot, ready for a battle, but we could
also be resilient and deal with disappointment. Because we were probably going to have more disappointment than successes. Look at where
we all came from. Bees from Leyton Orient, my brother-in-law Jamie
Hoyland from Bury. Me from Preston to name a few. We were all given
that opportunity at a higher level so if you think about it, it was like a
belief system.

"Harry was saying: 'I believe in you, now you repay me. I've given you
the chance, it's up to you if you take it.' He was very cute like that. To do

it once might be lucky but to do it multiple times was great recruitment, psychology and instinct. We all had the ability but many of us hadn't had the chance to prove it at the highest level. Harry had so many good hunches but he also did his homework on all his players. Ability, character, temperament, both in a game situation and in the dressing room. You could see the make-up of a player and a person that Harry wanted. And I suppose, as goalkeepers, he especially wanted that in Trace, Mel Rees, Phil Kite and me."

Kelly's initial £150,000 fee proved to be superb value for a total of 255 appearances, at a time when the Republic of Ireland international was competing with Tracey for the No.1 shirt. Kelly also followed in the footsteps of his father, a 47-cap Irish international and hall of fame goalkeeper who also coached and managed his country, by representing the Ireland national team, his 34 caps won in an era when the Irish were blessed with the likes of Packie Bonner and later Shay Given between the posts.

His full Irish debut came under Jack Charlton against a mighty German side who held the World Cup, had the likes of Jürgen Klinsmann, Lothar Matthäus and Rudi Völler in their squad and hadn't lost on home soil in six years. Charlton told his young goalkeeper not only that he would be playing, but that it was his responsibility to sort out set-pieces – and if Germany scored one, it was on his head. "So the night before I was knocking on the hotel doors of the likes of Denis Irwin, Steve Staunton, Paul McGrath, Roy Keane, Andy Townsend, Tony Cascarino, and telling them where to be for free-kicks and corners." It was a dream debut for Kelly. Ireland won 2-0.

Kelly subsequently kept his place in the squad for the 1994 World Cup in the USA, soon after United's relegation from the Premier League, and also travelled to Japan and South Korea for the 2002 World Cup, which saw Ireland's preparations disrupted by an infamous pre-tournament bust-up between manager Mick McCarthy and captain Keane. Kelly is a proud Irishman and one of his most iconic moments in a United shirt, saving three penalties in the 1998 FA Cup quarter-final shootout win over Coventry City at Bramall Lane, was fittingly played on St. Patrick's Day.

He would have liked nothing more than to toast reaching another semi-final with a pint of Guinness – but by the time he was chaired off the pitch by jubilant supporters, all the local pubs had shut and he had to make do with a cup of tea before bed.

Kelly's time at United came to an end in 1999 with a sale to Blackburn Rovers, to ease the club's financial position, but he maintains a close connection with the Blades to this day, working with a number of United players in the Ireland set-up before stepping down from his role as goalkeeping coach in 2021. "When I've been back to Bramall Lane with my wife and son, Bertie, it's amazing how many old faces I still see there. It's just that sort of club. The people I was sat with 25 years ago are still there and we still have the same conversations about all things Sheffield United. And they rip into me about Chris Waddle's goal. It's magic. It's brilliant. It's unique, really.

"Even on Twitter and social media, the reception is brilliant. It was great to see my son's reaction when I took him back at 14 years old. I was retired by the time he was born and then well retired by the time he was old enough to understand football and my connection to Sheffield United. But kids learn off their parents' actions and words. They absorb your passions and your views, and he's always said that he only ever heard Sara and I say good things about United and the fantastic seven years we had there. When I went back a few years ago I was belting out the words to the Greasy Chip Butty song and a fan next to me was gazing at me with a surprised look, that I knew the words. 'I did play 250 games,' I smiled at them, 'so I've heard it a few times!'

"I've got a lot to thank Harry for, looking back. He plucked me out of the Third Division, and after I'd had a lot of big injuries especially. Being run over, two broken legs, torn cruciate ligaments. He obviously saw something in me, something he could mould, and I'm so thankful for the chance to prove people wrong and prove him right. The courses he used to send us on have helped me enormously in my coaching career and when I see any of the lads from that era, it's like we've never been apart.

"But the biggest thing Harry gave me was allowing me to play for Sheffield United and to be there for seven years. To be able to play more than 250 games for the Blades and have the connection I did with the club and fans back then, which I feel is still there to this day, means so much to me. But that, or indeed my Ireland experiences, wouldn't have happened if Dave Bassett hadn't brought me to Sheffield United."

One of the most memorable experiences in an Irish jersey came in

February 1993 when he made his full Republic of Ireland debut against Wales, as a half-time substitute for Bonner and with the legendary Neville Southall in the opposition goal. One of the darkest moments was playing in a so-called friendly against England at Lansdowne Road which was turned into a riot by visiting English fans, later found to have been orchestrated by a far-right group known as Combat 18.

After the game, a number of British-based Ireland players were targeted by the neo-Nazi terrorist organisation, with Kelly receiving a letter through the post threatening, amongst other things, to drive him and his family into the Irish Sea for good. Special Branch deemed the threat to be real and present, with officers visiting Bramall Lane and advising Kelly to vary his route when driving.

"The Combat 18 stuff didn't bother me too much, because I couldn't do anything about it," Kelly said. "It sounds weird, but if that's what they wanted to do then of course we had to be aware. But we knew we just had to get on with our lives. When I was sold to Blackburn, some of my new teammates got the same threats. Jason McAteer got it, Lee Carsley got it, and other Irish teammates like Alan McGloughlan got it. So there were a lot of these letters going out. It's just another situation that people don't really hear about. I understand the pressures that players are under now, and the scrutiny they get. But when someone's threatening to chop your head off, it's a little bit different, isn't it? I think the early experiences, with the bike and with the injuries, gave me that perspective again. Be careful, be aware, but don't be worried."

It was another extraordinary chapter in a life less ordinary; forged by a little luck of the Irish and some Sheffield steel.

17

THE CHELSEA BLUES

When Sheffield United's crestfallen players felt the reality of their cruel, cruel relegation from the Premier League at Chelsea on May 7, 1994, it felt like the eyes of the footballing world were intruding on their grief. Twice in the lead, United had just had their top-flight status snatched away from them by two late goals and a series of freak results elsewhere. It seemed like the day had conspired against them.

But in reality, the club had taken the first steps on the path to relegation some months earlier, their fate effectively sealed by those in the boardroom rather than the dressing room. The final blow may have been landed in front of almost 22,000 people at Stamford Bridge, but it was in a nondescript hotel meeting room the summer previous that three men delivered the first.

United had not long sealed their place in the Premier League for another season and although not quite a repeat of the previous great escape acts, it had not been straightforward either. United had returned from their Wembley disappointment against city rivals Wednesday mired in relegation trouble, before a spirited late run including just one defeat in their last eight games secured a relatively comfortable 14th-place finish, albeit just three points above the relegation zone.

They had an undeniable spirit, and an underappreciated level of skill too. They had, in Dave Bassett, a manager who could get, in Sheffield speak, a pint out of a half-pint pot. They also had Brian Deane.

The England international had scored 15 goals in the first season of the Premier League era, plus five more for good measure in the cups, and was a man in demand. No one scores that number of goals in the top-flight, for a struggling team, on the quiet – Deane's 15 equalling the efforts of Arsenal's Ian Wright and Eric Cantona, for Leeds United and

Manchester United, and just one fewer than Blackburn's Alan Shearer – and suddenly, the extra *Sky* cash was burning holes in the pockets of some of the more powerful clubs in the league.

"You can't have it both ways … you can't have me scoring goals and not be linked with loads of teams," said Deane, looking back to that summer. "Did they want to keep me a secret? For what? I had dreams and desires as well and I needed fulfilment. I'd made up my mind that I couldn't carry on how things had developed, and I think it was a case of needing to understand what was happening. It was nothing against the club, I just felt undervalued.

"Not financially or anything like that – that's another story. But in terms of what I wanted to do at Sheffield United. How could I keep trying to become one of the top scorers in the league every year if I didn't have the service? If I got a chance and missed it, everyone was talking about it. You've got to remember I was in the England squads, competing with Ian Wright and Les Ferdinand and Alan Shearer and Teddy Sheringham … I was up there and wanted to be able to compete."

It would be unfair to categorise United as a one-man team but at the same time, there is little doubt about who was their talisman. Deane scored almost twice the number of league goals as his nearest challenger for the Blades' golden boot, Adrian Littlejohn, and his 15 goals – if you include a deflected strike off Chris Whyte against Leeds, which was attributed as an own goal in United's official complete record – earned United 11 points in 1992/93. The Blades would not have played with 10 men if Deane had not been in the team, of course, but they were undeniably stronger with him in the team than without him.

Deane had carried that weight of expectation throughout his time at Bramall Lane and occasionally it was something that did get to him. He can still remember scoring in a 1-1 draw against Manchester City in April 1993, instinctively smashing the ball into the top corner after it had crossed his path on the edge of the City box. Deane had begun to suspect that his moments of magic had become more expected than celebrated, and he found it hard to hide his feelings with his celebration – or lack of one. It was a sublime finish that any other top striker in the country would have been proud of scoring, but Deane's immediate reaction was the first hint that something was not quite right; a heavy sigh, with shoulders sunk, before a wry smile eventually crossed his face.

"The reason I didn't celebrate it was because there'd been some things said about me in the newspapers that weren't true," Deane said. "About me not being committed to the club, and that was about the time I thought: 'I need to move now.' I gave everything and there were things in the paper saying: 'He's looking to get away,' or 'So and so is coming in for him,' and people were thinking I was orchestrating it. Then the fans started believing it and having a go at me for no reason. We were struggling a bit at the time and everyone seemed to think it was my fault, that we weren't winning games. So I thought: 'I've had enough of this. It's time to leave.'

"Around the time of that City game, I was getting all kinds of stick and at the time, the journalists weren't interested in my side of the story. So there wasn't a balanced view and everything was on me. I've had it out with some people. It doesn't matter to me now; I am what I am and I've done what I've done. No one can tell me any different. I never wanted to leave. I felt like I knew every blade of grass on that pitch. But a lot of things started happening. I felt like the crowd got to the point where they sort of thought I was becoming over-familiar for them, and it was best to have a change. I'd got to the point where I felt like if we didn't score, it was my fault. If we lost, it was my fault."

While Deane was considering his future, the board were fretting about that of United as a club. Their extra slice of the *Sky* cash had been welcome, but not the golden ticket it later become – for context, their 14th-place finish in 1992/93 earned then £333,495 in prize money, compared to £129m 30 years on – while revenue from record season ticket sales was also being rapidly swallowed up to satisfy the club's mounting debts. United's financial picture was bleak, to say the least, and when chairman Reg Brealey returned rather unwillingly to the club after the shares saga with Paul Woolhouse, he estimated they would be in their overdraft again within three months if dramatic action was not taken.

Short of selling Bramall Lane, or suggesting a merger with Wednesday, there was no more drastic action at the time than contemplating the loss of Deane. He was one of the best forwards in the country, never mind just at United, and was their main man. That meant he was also their most valuable asset, and his sale could wipe out many of the Blades' money troubles in a stroke. It was a classic boardroom conundrum; a decision that made some sense financially, and absolutely none from a footballing sense.

The prospect of selling Deane had been tentatively raised earlier in the summer, over a breakfast board meeting at Sheffield's Moat House hotel, and raised its head again following Brealey's return to the club. Leeds initially offered £2m for Deane, which Bassett advised his directors to flatly decline, while there was also interest from Chelsea and a dream link with the reigning English champions, Manchester United.

There was even a sensational late attempt to hijack the deal by Wednesday, whose boss Trevor Francis launched a £3m bid to persuade Deane to stay in the Steel City. It was a mouthwatering proposition for the then 25-year-old, with a lucrative contract on the table and the prospect of a strike partnership with David Hirst, with the likes of Chris Waddle supplying the ammunition. From a football point of view, there was nothing to dislike.

But Deane simply couldn't contemplate sticking two fingers up at the club he had served so well, and the fanbase that worshipped him. He treated Wednesday's interest with respect, but it was never going to be an option. When he first heard of it, Deane actually considered the possibility that it was a prank from the TV show *Beadle's About.*

But the striker still had plenty to consider and turned to his friend and teammate Kevin Gage for advice on whether to stay at United or leave for pastures new. "I just said: 'To be honest, for your football career, it's probably best if you went,'" Gage remembered. "Perhaps that's the wrong thing to say but he asked me as a teammate and friend and I just gave him a bit of football career advice. Nothing I said was going to change his mind, because he was destined for better things."

Slowly, the mood began to shift at Bramall Lane and Unitedites probably sensed that the writing was on the wall when Deane submitted a written transfer request, outlining his reasons in an interview with local newspaper *The Star* under the headline: "It's time to go."

United resolved to stick to their guns and hold out for their valuation of Deane – which was never made public, but revealed by Tony Pritchett in *The Star* to be £3.5m – and the journalist later reported that Bassett had come round to the idea of losing his star striker, but only for a fee of £3.7m. Around a similar time, Bassett reasoned, Liverpool had spent £2.5m on defender Neil Ruddock and Nottingham Forest had paid a similar fee for Stan Collymore, who the United manager argued was an inferior player to Deane. But the Blades' hand had hardly been strengthened by Deane's public desire to leave, and also what he claimed was a gentleman's agreement with then chairman Woolhouse a year earlier when he put pen to paper on a two-year contract.

Woolhouse, said Deane, had agreed to sell the striker in a year's time if he so wished and despite Woolhouse being out of the picture, Deane still wanted the promise to be honoured. Bassett responded by publicly wondering why Deane had signed a two-year deal 12 months earlier, instead of a one-year contract on higher wages, if he was going to want out at the end of the season anyway.

The situation was becoming increasingly murky and *The Star* even cashed in by setting up two phone numbers to allow fans to have their say on whether Deane should stay or go by calling one of them. When the results were published, there was no surprise to see that supporters had voted overwhelmingly to keep Deane at Bramall Lane. The only real shock was that as many as 30 per cent of Unitedites were comfortable with the thought of Deane leaving.

The majority were enthused a little when boss Bassett reassured them that Deane would be going nowhere that summer. "Brian is part of our plans and there is no pressure on me to sell him," he said. "My objective for Brian is to increase his goals tally and get him back in the England team." But the picture changed quickly and after Leeds pulled out of a deal to sign young Scottish striker Duncan Ferguson from Dundee United, there was no doubt about their next move.

"I believe they will not take a penny less," said Pritchett in *The Star* as he reported Deane's £3.5m price-tag, which proved rather ominous. Director Bernard Proctor warned Brealey that it "economically made no sense" to sell Deane for the fee mooted. But things came to a head at that fateful board meeting, with the Blades' six-man board split right down the middle over whether to keep Deane or sell. Cash in, or roll the dice. Stick or twist. Derek Dooley, Alan Laver and Proctor voted to keep Deane; chairman Brealey, his brother Len and John Plant voted to sell. Brealey, as the chairman, had the casting vote and pushed it through; Dooley promptly got up from his seat and walked out, with Proctor and Laver following. All three resolved to resign in protest at the decision, but the damage had been done. Deane was on his way.

Bassett interrupted his holiday in Italy to persuade Dooley to remain in post, but the manager was in no doubt how damaging the decision would prove to be. "You have just relegated this football club," was his blunt message to Brealey. In the end United accepted quite a few pennies less than their £3.5m price tag, doing business at £2.7m – although the fee was later reported as £200,000 higher in some outlets. It was scant consolation to supporters, many of whom had previously seen heroes of yesteryear including Mick Jones and Alex Sabella and Tony Currie tread the well-worn path up the M1 to Leeds. As Deane left Bramall Lane for the final time this summer, a female fan planted a goodbye kiss on the striker's cheek; another supporter reacted rather differently by ripping up his season ticket in the car park.

In the pre-message board age, the letters page in *The Star* offered frustrated Unitedites an outlet to vent their spleens. The headlines rather summed up the mood, including: *Sick and tired of all this ... We will be relegated ... The Brealeys must go now! ... Where's the cash?* and the even simpler and more direct question: "What is going on?" The truth is that almost every penny of the £1.5m season ticket cash that had been banked by that point of the summer had been used to clear club debts; £600,000 was swallowed up by the 'new' south stand, with £340,000 in VAT payments and fines for late payments to the FA and a similar figure in interest and other loans owed.

"He was the only goalscorer at the club and we shouldn't have sold him," Brealey later admitted, in Gary Armstrong's book *Blade Runners*. "But unless we did, we were bust. The first tranche of the transfer ... was 50 per cent plus VAT: £1.6m. From that we paid all the bills and reduced our number of creditors from 400 to 50. Ninety per cent of the telephone calls to Bramall Lane stopped; the morale of the office staff trebled."

That may have been the case but in the United dressing room, the sale had the opposite effect. "Deano was top class," goalkeeper Alan Kelly reflected. "If you look at some of his goals, like the one against Liverpool when he chipped Bruce Grobbelaar, he had the technical ability, the vision and the belief to do that. He was quiet, loved the banter and he would add to it in his own style. He believed in himself, Deano, but he also believed in the team. He was the hardest worker on the pitch, got the goals to back it up and he produced. A quiet icon. The transfer had been talked about for a while and it happened quite late on, the middle of July.

That probably left Harry with limited options. Could we have kept him at Sheffield United? It turns out, with things behind the scenes and the finances, that it was a no."

Skipper Brian Gayle had similar views. "At the end of the day, they had to let him go," he said at the time. "Every player nurtures his own dream move and Brian's dream has come true. We wish him all the best. All of us know that it has been on his mind for some time. It is a big blow to the club, losing him, but we have to lump it and get on with the game. We have lost a loveable bloke and a good player – but not the only good player in the club. Somebody could emerge as the new star of Sheffield United, and who knows who it will be. We have lost one star, admitted. But we might find another."

Faced with a groundswell of fan frustration, United's under-fire directors held their next board meeting in a secret location rather than Bramall Lane and one of the items on the agenda was to whether to accept requests for season ticket refunds, with Greenhill resident John Fiddler amongst those to have demanded their money back. The embattled board almost lurched from one crisis to another, too, as Crystal Palace looked to exploit the uncertainty and lure Bassett back down south. With Bramall Lane far from a settled environment, and the club still swimming against the tide financially, Bassett could have been forgiven for calling time on his United reign. However, he resisted the temptation to resign in protest at Deane's departure, saying quite pointedly: "I have a contract at Sheffield United. Provided they keep their side of the bargain, I will keep mine."

Bassett was also given assurances that the board's intention was to raise more cash for players by improving commercial revenue streams, and that they would also invest in much-needed ground improvements. "I did what I have always done in that situation – I believed them," he wrote in his autobiography. "If I had felt that the right decision was to resign then I would have taken it." Had Bassett followed Deane out of Bramall Lane, there would have been uproar from the supporters and the club would have been left in crisis. For the time being, that nightmare scenario had been partly averted and Bassett's focus switched to life after Deane.

"Me and Harry are still good friends now," Deane said, "but when I left the club, he gave me a lot of stick, which I thought wasn't warranted.

But it's life. We met up and I talked to him about it and he said: 'Deansy, I thought you could have stayed another season.' If he'd said that at the time, it might have been different, but he didn't. I got forced into a situation and if he'd have said: 'Listen Brian, I don't want you to leave.' But it didn't come across that way and I felt I had to leave. That my time was up."

While certain figures at the time disagreed about the exact transfer fee, most independent observers agreed that United could have held out for more from Leeds for their prized asset. Writing in *The Star,* Blades reporter Pritchett described the deal as being "pushed through at indecent and unnecessary haste," adding that Deane was "almost certainly sold cheap." Bassett's loyalty to United, Pritchett wrote, was "stretched almost to breaking point throughout the Deane affair, hence his statement that Deane was sold against his recommendation and that he was trying to build a team, not destroy one."

On his summer holidays, football-mad Bassett regularly asked Pritchett to keep him up to date with the latest transfer news. This time, it was the sale of his star striker that filtered through to Bassett in his Italian hideaway. Whatever the exact figure United received for Deane, Bassett was given just £1m of it to spend on a replacement – and a fortnight before the start of pre-season to find him. "He [Bassett] knows it is not enough," added Pritchett, "and so do the fans. And so, I suspect, does the board of directors."

No other side in the Premier League that summer spent less than United in the transfer market and speaking decades later, Bassett likened Deane's departure to Manchester City losing some of their edge when their own talisman, striker Sergio Aguero, left in 2021. "They didn't find it easy replacing him, when before they were beating teams by six and seven. I knew losing Deano was a major, major problem. He wasn't like one of the other players who I could potentially have covered for. How do you replace your leading goalscorer for the last five seasons? Reg insisted we sold Deano but instead of telling me in May, or when the season ended, it went through in July."

Bassett tried to act quickly and find a replacement, with 6ft West Ham striker Mike Small understood to have rejected a move to Bramall Lane and Liverpool's Ronny Rosenthal also linked. United were credited with interest in John Fashanu, Bassett's former striker at Wimbledon, and spoke to as many as nine other forwards that summer. Bassett tried to bring Danish international Jakob Kjeldberg to Bramall Lane, only for the defender to refuse a trial, while Borussia Mönchengladbach's Togolese striker Bachirou Salou was also targeted. Kjeldberg instead moved to Chelsea, where he spent four years before being forced into early retirement at just 28 years old, while 6ft 3in Salou remained in Germany for most of his playing career and also played for Borussia Dortmund, MSV Duisburg and Eintracht Frankfurt, with a modest scoring record.

Bassett was open at the time about being "suspicious of foreign players coming into our game," with communication a big aspect. "You would never get me signing a Russian or Czech," he wrote in his column for *The Star,* "and have to be looking round for an interpreter all the time." In some ways the approach made sense, at a time when English football was not as diverse as it is now; funds were not in endless supply at Bramall Lane and he could hardly afford to take gambles on players who may not have settled in England. So Bassett began to exploit contacts he had made in Scandinavia, believing that better value players were available there and spending £50,000 on Swede Jonas Wirmola, before scouting the man he hoped could fill Deane's considerable boots. Bassett believed that the strategy may pay off, citing Roland Nilsson's move to the other side of the city as inspiration, but it didn't signal the end of his domestic transfer business, as he considered rivalling Aston Villa for the £1.2m signing of Guy Whittingham.

Bassett acknowledged that spending big on a single Deane replacement would have been an easier approach but instead he decided to spread his budget a little thinner and bolster his squad as a whole. Defender David Tuttle arrived from Spurs and Scot Willie Falconer came in from Middlesbrough, while Norwegian international Jostein Flo was eventually signed as Deane's de facto replacement right on the eve of the new season – meaning he was effectively learning on the job when it came to English top-flight football.

It was far from an ideal scenario for player or manager, who was trying to replace proven quality with potential and in hindsight, a £400,000 gamble from Sogndal in Norway was always destined to struggle to replicate the impact of one of the best forwards in the country at the time. "I don't want Jostein to take the blame," Bassett said. "It wasn't his fault. He just wasn't Deano."

At 6ft 4in tall, Flo at least fitted the bill as Deane's replacement in terms of physical stature. He also had some pedigree at international level, as part of a Norway side that had climbed to second in the FIFA world rankings, and had stood out with his aerial dominance when Graham Taylor's England were brushed aside in Oslo in June of that summer. Flo would play at the 1994 and 1998 World Cups, starring in the latter as Norway came from a goal down against Brazil to win 2-1, and despite the Deane disappointment, there was plenty of excitement around his signature. Not just on the terraces, but in the dressing room too.

"When Jostein came in it was like we'd signed Georgie Best," Jamie Hoyland joked. "He smoked about 40 a day and drank like a fish. He'd just won Norwegian player of the year and when we went out to Norway in pre-season, it was like going out with God. He was getting mobbed all the time. Jostein loved it at United. It didn't go as well as he would have wanted on the pitch but, then again, he was stepping into the big boots of Brian Deane. To be fair, he was great in the dressing room and really took to it.

"He could give as good as he got in terms of the banter, he was right into it and he wasn't shy when it came to the self-policing dressing room culture as well. Big Jos was a brilliant Sheffield United player in that respect. A great guy. Roger Nilsen came in and Jonas Wirmola arrived from Sweden. We already had the likes of Alan Kelly, who was an international with Ireland, and all of a sudden we were getting a bit of credibility in the dressing room. We still had that team spirit but we also needed to move it on a bit in the way we were playing."

Flo's performances for his country certainly suggested that United had found someone who could compensate for the loss of Deane's physical presence up top. "I wanted someone who would be a threat in the air," Bassett said to explain his move for Flo. "Deano had an ability to dribble that others haven't got but I think Flo will be more intelligent than Deano in the box. I know the fans will compare them but I think Flo will win the fans over." Many of them rushed to add Flo to the back of their replica shirts soon after his arrival, and wasted no time in putting his name to the 2 Unlimited dance track *No Limit*. The catchy chant's pay-off was: "Who needs Deano?"

It quickly transpired that, actually, United did.

Deane was more than just a target man and Flo didn't have the power and pace in behind of his predecessor, nor his eye for goal. His return of nine that season wasn't bad in the Premier League but didn't replicate Deane's contributions of 30, 24, 16, 15 and 19 in his five seasons in a red and white shirt and it was clear United needed more. "There was no comparison, was there, between Flo and Deansy?" said kitman John Greaves. "Jostein tried his bollocks off but trying to replace Deane and Agana was like trying to replace Yorke and Cole at Man U, or Shearer and Ferdinand."

One afternoon in Norway, Greaves and French went for a walk from the hotel and noticed a blond-haired lad, with a can of beer in one hand and a cigarette in the other, sitting with five other blokes in a shop doorway. "It was Flo," Greaves laughed. "He was with his town buddies, with a can of beer. Unbelievable. He was a hero over there in Norway. They loved him. But I remember saying to Frenchy: 'Can you imagine Deano doing that, with his pals back in Leeds?'"

Left-back Nilsen knew Flo already from their time together in Norway, and made contact with his compatriot before agreeing the United move from Viking FK in 1993. "Jostein was enjoying his time and spoke highly of the manager and club overall," Niilsen said. "I desperately wanted to come to England but when I arrived, I didn't feel the warmest welcome, to be honest with you. Some of the players were a little bit distant. Others were warmer. Overall it was okay, but not fantastic in any way.

"There were a few incidents in training but being from Norway I was used to having scraps and fights in training, so that didn't bother me. I could defend myself. I proved myself to many of them quite early. The fact that Jostein was there as well helped. He would have said what they could expect of me, which made it a little easier on me."

Flo was also being deployed differently for his country, playing more of a wider role and attacking a diagonal pass from the full-back to head inside to the forward. The cross-field pass became known in Norwegian football as the "Flo pass," which could well have been a big attraction to Bassett. "He used to win all the headers and head them into the centre-forward areas, that was a big part of their attacking strategy and so Bassett obviously thought he could use that," reckoned Gage. "But we played Flo as a centre-forward and he was just totally unsuited there. He couldn't move and he couldn't do the running that was needed to get on the end of the channel balls."

The reasoning was sound enough, as Nilsen and Flo had worked together effectively at international level before linking up again at Bramall Lane. Norway's style also mirrored Bassett's in some ways. "Under Egil Olsen, it was very effective," Nilsen added. "It was not the prettiest and we got criticised for it, but it was really effective because we played the long ball and had runners through the middle. Jostein was heading down into the runners and we created so many situations during the game by doing that. We scored a lot of goals doing that.

"I know Brian Deane well. He was a fantastic player and has a great personality. I met up with him when he was Sarpsborg manager, and again when I went over to England to watch a game. I played with him when he came back under Nigel Spackman. He had more strength to play on than Jostein had and was a more complete attacker. Jostein had strength in the air, while Brian had more on the ball. It was not fair on Jostein to expect him to play like Brian Deane, because Brian was stronger with his feet. Jostein was massive inside the box and was massive when the ball was lifted up diagonal for him to head down. They were his strengths."

Nilsen's agent at the time was close to Bassett, which also helped facilitate the move. "I understood from him at the time that the economy at the club was very tight and that reflected also in the contract. In the beginning, I was not on a lot of money there. It was a poor contract in the beginning, I have to say. The manager was a nice man, but I found him very stressful. A man that was very stressful to be around.

"He seemed like he always had a lot on his mind. He wasn't calm in any sense of the word, always stressful. He was good with the players and was part of the group. He was respectful to the players and made you laugh. I appreciated him as a big personality and that was why he was the manager. He was either bubbly or stressed! I probably didn't get to see his best side by that stage.

"But I enjoyed Sheffield. I had the chance to leave a couple of times because there was interest in me but I stayed because we settled well. I stayed there for many years. It was nice. I lived with my partner, in a quiet environment. She settled really well and loved it there. My first boy was born while I was playing for United and he was in pre-school in Sheffield. I enjoyed the club. I only left because I fell out with Steve Bruce. That's why I left. I was not desperate to leave but Steve Bruce claimed I was faking injury, and I couldn't stand to hear that. Back then I was lacking sodium and salt in my body, so I cramped up all the time.

"Even in the warm up, I would cramp up. It was really strange. It wasn't found until I came to Tottenham and it should have been discovered sooner. It should have been checked. I really felt bad about leaving United. I have two boys who love football and we still follow Sheffield United. I have really good memories of Sheffield United and I really did enjoy my time there. I stayed for many years and to be honest, I loved it there. I thought it was a great place to be."

But hindsight can often be rose-tinted and at the time Nilsen arrived in England, early in the 1993/94 campaign, the Blades were right up against it. A pre-season special in *The Star* summed up the challenge facing Bassett and Co. with the succinct headline: "A season on a shoestring." Pritchett, a close confidant of Bassett during his time at Bramall Lane, correctly predicted that "the signs at the dawn of a new challenge are not good. United's hope, again, seems to lie in salvation and the desperate wish that the loyalty of manager Dave Bassett, clearly furious at the Deane sale while he was out of the country, is not stretched to breaking point. Starved of support when he needs it most, Bassett must buckle down and get on with the job. It is a situation he cannot relish but one he must accept. The trouble is he has walked on water so often, that it has become expected of him."

Life as Deane's predecessor didn't get off to too bad a start for Flo as he scored three goals in his opening four appearances – including on his home debut. Two more followed on the south coast as United roared back from 3-1 down at Southampton to earn a point, and five in his first seven appearances was more than a good enough return. But the goals soon dried up; not just for Flo, but for the Blades. The Norwegian would not find the net again for over five months and United would score only five times in their next 15 matches – two of which were penalties. They ended the year second bottom and with only Chelsea scoring fewer goals. It was glaringly obvious United were struggling without Deane, and Bassett described United as being "up to our necks in muck and bullets, without the firepower to fight back."

The comparisons between Deane and his direct replacement are inevitable but the blame was not squarely at Flo's door. His five goals scored by October 2 remained the highest return of any player by the time he took his tally to six in March in the 2-2 draw at home to Leeds, United's frustrations compounded by the sight of Deane registering a goal and assist on his return to South Yorkshire. The Blades' former talisman was doing what he had done best, running amok on the Bramall Lane pitch – only this time in the blue and yellow of his hometown club, rather than the red and white in which he had made his name. As he sprinted towards the halfway line in celebration after netting the second, it was an untimely reminder of just how much United missed him. By that point of the season, centre-half Brian Gayle, with two goals, had been just as prolific as Flo's strike partners Andy Scott (one), Alan Cork (two) and Adrian Littlejohn (two).

Bassett was still struggling to accept Deane's sale and the cloud of his departure continued to hover over Bramall Lane. The manager was also angry at the timing, feeling a departure only weeks before the season started had put him behind the eight-ball when it came to finding a suitable replacement. Flo arrived only days before the opener at home to Swindon and the loss of United's star man had taken the shine off the season already.

A number of uninspiring early performances did not help matters, either. "I just don't think Harry knew his best team," midfielder John Gannon said. "No one was really making their place their own. I went out on loan at the start of that season to Middlesbrough and came back and the team was still struggling. I ended up getting back in the team near the end. There were a lot of things just not going in the right direction."

Gage was not happy with how the campaign was going on a personal level. "I didn't have a good season. I fell out with Bassett many times that season. I don't know why or what happened but he always seemed to be on my back a lot and ended up moving Carl Bradshaw to right back. It was maybe a quarter of the way through the season, and I got a couple of games there and then he moved me to left back. I felt out of sight and I really wasn't happy. I wasn't happy at all. We were chopping and changing people … just trying to find something to work."

United had won just four league games when they made the short dash across the city to face arch rivals Sheffield Wednesday in the Steel City derby. Yet to lose a league game to the Owls under Bassett, a win would have been just the tonic to help arrest the slide but United were soundly beaten despite a goalless first half. Three Wednesday goals in the space of

12 second half minutes meant Dane Whitehouse's late penalty, his least favourite of his derby collection, was irrelevant as they crashed to a 3–1 defeat. Bassett was fuming afterwards and the alarm bells were beginning to ring. "I knew the end was in sight for me after that match," Hoyland said. "Harry and Wally Downes destroyed us. There was a trip away the following week and they took me off the list. I knew the writing was on the wall then and I thought: 'I'm copping for this [the Wednesday defeat].' In the players' lounge after, Nigel Pearson asked me if I was alright. It wasn't a good feeling. Pearson said to me: 'You played well today,' and I just thought: 'We'll see.' I just had that gut feeling. I was definitely one of those who copped for that defeat."

Bassett knew something had to change and, in particular, more goals were needed if United were going to extend their stay in the top division once more. Summer signing Willie Falconer came and went without making much of an impression, although United were able to recoup the majority of his £400,000 fee when he joined Celtic in February, and the money was put towards a deal to bring in Cardiff's Nathan Blake, who had netted 17 times already that season in the third tier.

Joining two weeks later for £500,000, with reports that half of that fee was only due if the Blades avoided relegation, Bassett described him at the time as a player with a reputation for "being a bit of a rascal" but was not too concerned, believing his power, pace and goal threat was exactly what United needed. Bassett used him sparingly to start with, introducing him from the bench in a bid to ease the pressure on his shoulders before Blake established himself as a star striker in his own right.

Pritchett wrote in *The Star* that Blake "can look a finisher of the highest class with the body strength of a boxer and the quiet assassin's touch essential in the crowded and ruthless penalty box. But undeniably he has those days when the appetite is missing and the commitment is questioned." Later in his career Blake would criticise Blades fans in a newspaper article, describing them as "fickle" and accusing them of turning on him when he was sold to Bolton the following year. But it was a good start at Bramall Lane for the new man, scoring what looked like the winner at Tottenham only for another 90th-minute equaliser to deny United all three points.

Whether sparked by Blake's arrival, or the trip abroad, results certainly picked up and United lost just two of their final 13 matches. Included in that sequence was a famous 2-1 win against Liverpool at Anfield, with Flo bagging a brace after an early Ian Rush goal. Blake scored five goals in 12 appearances, including two in a 2-0 victory over Newcastle which left commentator Clive Tyldesley declaring that "the survival specialists are at it again, and there's a new man at the head of the escape committee," and he certainly gave United more of an edge up front.

Bassett was left to regret that tight finances had not allowed him to bring in Blake earlier but at the time, the lift he brought led to renewed optimism. "The players knew they were in a relegation battle," Bassett said. "I think it dawned on them later rather than earlier but I think they felt if they could show the same spirit and commitment and playing performance, they were capable of getting out of the relegation zone. I also felt we were capable of doing that. The spirit was good and we were hopeful one or two of the teams around us would be struggling for form, which proved to be the case."

Four wins between March and April gave United more than a fighting chance of survival and a point away at fellow strugglers Oldham in the penultimate match of the season – which was creditable in the circumstances, with Simon Tracey sent off 20 minutes from time – meant United headed to Chelsea on the final day in a good position. They were two places above the drop zone with two from themselves, Everton, Ipswich, Oldham and Southampton set to join Swindon in the second tier, and United rightly travelled to the capital with confidence.

Journalist Alan Biggs remembers Bassett giving the regular writers on the United beat a bottle of Champagne on the Friday before the Leicester game, telling them: "Have a drink with us all tomorrow night." United had become masters in the art of escapism and given their recent run of form, few would have backed them not to pull off another one. A win would guarantee survival; anything less and it would be a nervous look at *Ceefax* or the vidiprinter to see how those teams below them were getting on. Fans were glued to portable radios in the away end but any tension they may have travelled with had eased when Flo hooked home the opener on 29 minutes. Everton had also got off to a nightmare start and were 2-0 down to Wimbledon after just 20 minutes; Ipswich were drawing at Blackburn and United, up to 16th in the in-play table, were cruising. A 58th-minute equaliser by Chelsea's Jakob Kjeldbjerg was soon followed by Glyn Hodges' finish with his left thigh on the hour mark to restore United's lead and with Everton still trailing and Ipswich drawing, United were comfortable in 18th position with 30 minutes remaining.

That last half-hour proved a nightmare. Everton were suddenly 3-2 ahead over Wimbledon and Mark Stein's equaliser for Chelsea saw United go into the final 14 minutes in 19th place, and hovering dangerously above the drop zone. It was tense, in the stands and on the pitch, but as it stood, United would be safe. With 30 seconds to go, Hodges jokingly offered to buy the referee a pint if he blew early for full-time. But play continued and Unitedites could only watch on in horror. A Dennis Wise cross, a rare Glenn Hoddle flick-on, a Stein volley at the back post. Three-two Chelsea. The Blades were down.

It was the first time all afternoon that they had been in the bottom three.

Even as they dragged themselves off the Stamford Bridge pitch some United players were unsure of their fate and it was only on their way to the dressing room that reality really hit. Alan Kelly relayed news of results elsewhere to a disconsolate dressing room that Jamie Hoyland described as one of "absolute devastation." In his report for *The Independent*, Geoff Brown described United as "hitherto unflappable escapologists," but this proved to be one incredible act too many. "People say you get what you deserve over the course of a season," Hoyland added. "But I don't think we did, actually."

The silence in the away changing room lasted up to an hour, only being broken by a cameraman being kicked out and coach Wally Downes damaging his hand by punching a wall in frustration. Bassett, who had often travelled to Stamford Bridge to watch games as a youngster, tried to put on a brave face as he discussed relegation with reporters in a corridor. "When you play Russian roulette," he said, "sometimes you get the bullet." That bottle of Champagne from Bassett sat unopened on Biggs' shelf for months.

Defeat was already hard to take but the sense of injustice grew when United's players watched the highlights of Everton's comeback against Wimbledon at Goodison Park. The manner of the winning goal in particular didn't sit right with some, Graeme Stuart's effort squirming through Wimbledon goalkeeper Hans Segers' grasp when he could have thrown his cap on it. Segers, along with fellow teammate John Fashanu, was later accused of being involved in match-fixing, but the first trial

collapsed when the jury were unable to come to a verdict before Segers
– who, ironically, had spent time on loan at United earlier in his career,
returning to Nottingham Forest after Bassett's Bramall Lane arrival –
and Fashanu were cleared at a retrial.

United may have found, and still find, that Everton match a difficult
watch but there were also reasons closer to home for their relegation by
just a single point. Their eight wins that season was the lowest return
of their four-season spell in the top flight, and they registered a stagger-
ing 18 draws – eight more than the previous season's number. Nine of
these were goalless, and seven came in the final 13 matches. Nine of their
16 defeats were also by just one goal. In the end, one more goal in any
of those drawn games would have been enough for survival as Bassett's
pre-season prediction to Brealey, about the sale of striker Deane, proved
devastatingly accurate.

"The biggest thing was not replacing him," Kelly said. "No disrespect
to big Jostein or anybody else but when you're losing a striker who contributed the amount of goals Deano did … they cost money to replace,
don't they? You know then you're going to struggle and, unfortunately,
we did. Everybody will look back on that day of losing Deano and even
the players go: "*Urgh.*" What if? We knew we would have to defend for
our lives, but there were so many draws. Win one of those, and we stay
up. There's your difference."

The heartbreak was still raw on the coach back to Bramall Lane that
evening but, as they pulled into the Cherry Street car park, the players
were surprised to see it packed with supporters in scenes usually associated with promotion rather than relegation. United fans were proud of
their team and the memories they had brought them on the journey from
Division Three to the Premier League, and were intelligent enough to
understand that their club simply lacked the resources to compete in the
top division.

Most were simply in awe of the job Bassett, his staff and players had
done in the circumstances. Kelly has never forgotten that reception. "It
was packed, absolutely packed with fans. The bus pulled into that car
park and had to stop because we couldn't go past any more people. It
was just amazing. I thought: 'Wow, this is incredible.' How can you get
relegated and have that sort of response?"

Fans draped scarves around their heroes and Hoyland still has his to this day. "I thought: 'Oh no, this is where we are going to get lynched,'" the midfielder said. "But to be fair it was just really emotional with fans hugging us." To this day, he cannot bring himself to watch any footage of the Chelsea defeat. "It's still heartbreaking. It's still painful."

Hindsight is a wonderful thing and, in the decades since, Bassett has often wondered if he should have introduced Alan Cork off the bench instead of Hoyland, 14 minutes from time. Cork knew Wise from their time together at Wimbledon, where both had worked under Bassett, and Chelsea had nothing to play for in the league. Had Wise known that United needed the point to survive, Bassett believes that he would have passed the ball backwards, rather than cross into the box for Stein to break United hearts. But it wasn't to be. United were going down. And then, a few painful days later, they were going Down Under.

*"Have I fought pain for the last
20 years? Yes, I have. Do I live in
pain every day? Yes, I do. Do I take
medication? Yes, I do. Do I take
some bad stuff sometimes? Yes, I do.
I know what beats me down and
hurts me every day. I've never had
my kids on my shoulders. I've never
thrown them into a swimming pool.
People don't realise the little things
I've missed. You see dads walking
around with kids on their shoulders,
and my kids can't do it. It's the
simple things."*

– Dougie Hodgson

18

THE MAN FROM DOWN UNDER

Every year, when November turns to December and the build-up to Christmas intensifies, Dougie Hodgson puts his head back at his home in Melbourne and allows his mind to wander back. It was December 1, 1985, when a serious car accident looked like derailing his dreams of playing professional football. Then, once he had overcome the odds to forge himself a career in the game, it came to an official and premature end with the results of a 1998 MRI scan that followed a freak training-ground accident. The date, when he opened the envelope to read the news he was fearing, was familiar. It was December 1.

"Here we go again," Hodgson thought to himself. He cried all the way back home down the motorway. By that point he was at Northampton Town, on loan from Oldham having moved over the Pennines from Sheffield United, and went up for a routine header in training. A disc in his back "exploded," he remembered, and hit his spinal cord. He never played professional football again. "My surgeon said: 'You guys are like boxers. When you head the ball, your brain is smashing around in your head.' The balls were a bit heavier back then and when players kicked the ball as hard as we were, and it was coming out of the clouds, then that's a fair impact."

Hodgson didn't immediately understand the severity of the injury and continued the session, thinking he had just pulled a muscle in his back. Even now he can remember another ball coming his way in the air but instead of heading it, he took a step back and took it down on his chest. No one, least of all Hodgson, knows how devastating the impact of one final header could have been but what followed was 20 years in and out of hospital, wearing neck braces and undergoing remarkably-extensive surgeries costing hundreds of thousands of Aussie dollars.

His hands are different colours because of the spinal damage; to add insult to injury, he is allergic to anti-inflammatory medicine. Hodgson's chirpy demeanour has helped him cope. "It was a great last header, mind," he said. "Went fucking miles."

Hodgson was 29 when his football career came to a premature end but in some ways he considers himself fortunate to have had one at all, having nearly been killed in a car crash caused by a drunk driver when he was a teenager. He instead began working life as a labourer – which put early strain on his back – before combining kickboxing with work as a nightclub bouncer, inadvertently setting into motion the chain of events that would eventually take him to the other side of the world. "One night, at the nightclub I worked at, a bloke tried to give me a slap, so I gave him one first. The police wanted to talk to me about it, and I thought it might be a good time to leave the state."

Hodgson moved to Western Australia and caught the eye playing for semi-professional side Dianella Serbia, earning a call-up to a representative side who just happened to be up against the touring United side who had just been relegated from the Premier League. Almost 13,000 fans were at the world-famous WACA cricket ground in Perth to see goals from Glyn Hodges and Nathan Blake give United a 2-1 victory, but the performance of the chirpy centre-half for the home side had caught visiting manager Dave Bassett's eye.

"I had a great game," Hodgson recalled. "Hodgey and Blakey were up front and I remember Blakey saying: 'This kid doesn't know about playing in friendlies.'" Hodges also got some rough treatment from the defender, albeit of a different kind; feeling a thumb up his backside when he bent over to tie his boots. "I asked him: 'How do you like that?' Hodgson said. "He must have, because we're still mates to this day."

Hodgson linked up with United for their final two games of that dreaded Australia tour, draws with a New South Wales side in Newcastle and an Australian Olympic XI at the now-closed Seagulls rugby league stadium on the Gold Coast, Queensland. "In the first game me and Paul Rogers were at the back and I said to him: 'I've never played in a flat back four before, can you look after me?' Dodge looked at me with a funny look on his face and said: 'I was hoping that you were going to help me, I've never played centre-half before!'

"But I had a great game there and another against the Australia side.

Near the end of the game the skipper, Brian Gayle, said to us: 'Boys, three minutes to go and we are officially on it.' I remember shouting to Carl Bradshaw to tuck in, and he said: 'I can't. There's nothing left in the tank. My pint of lager is empty!'"

It wasn't for long as United – still licking their wounds from that cruel and painful relegation – sampled the generous hospitality that Australia had to offer their tourists before returning to the UK with two new additions in Hodgson – handed a two-year deal by Bassett – and fellow Australian Carl Veart.

Melbourne's *The Age* newspaper reported Hodgson "joining the money trail to Sheffield" but moving to England actually cost him – with $775 in fines to be paid before he was allowed to leave the country. "As a bouncer in pubs, I was thinking I had a great life. I wasn't drinking, I was getting paid, there were beautiful women everywhere. And then Harry came and fucked it all up for me!"

Hodgson's tongue was firmly in cheek there. He had the time of his life in England, meeting his wife and making friends that remain close to this day. The front of the bar in his home features a giant Blades badge and when United were battling Leeds for promotion to the Premier League in 2019, he was following the scores on the internet in the middle of the night because of the time difference.

"In my first pre-season, we went to Switzerland and the Slapshots – Bradshaw, Dane Whitehouse and Mitch Ward – asked if I'd been in trouble with the police before. I asked what had given them that impression, but the smile on my face must have given it away. They said: 'We thought so. No wonder Harry signed you!' One night on that tour, before one of the games, the boys were going out. Harry said I'd played a few games and could have a rest the following day. I didn't go out and drink before matches – I was disciplined and dedicated, and picked my times for it – but five minutes before kick-off, he told me I was playing. Johnny Greaves, the kitman, told me after that he'd set me up. He'd done it to see if I had gone out.

"We lost a game against Viking Stavenger in Norway, and Harry ripped into us. He went around us all and then he got to me. He said: 'You … I don't know. You could go left or you could go right. You could go down the right road or the wrong one. It's up to you.' That stuck in my mind.

"When we got back home, I was walking down the corridor outside

Harry's office at Bramall Lane and heard Paul Beesley's impression of Harry behind me. 'Doogs, you've gone down the wrong path...'"

Hodgson's eventful time at Bramall Lane came to an end in 1997, with 38 appearances and one goal in United colours not quite doing justice to the impact he had at the club. Still fondly remembered by supporters of the time, Hodgson also left his mark on teammates. When striker Petr Katchouro arrived from Dinamo Minsk in his homeland, he couldn't speak English and roomed with Hodgson on away trips. The first word of English that anyone heard the new man say was: "G'day, mate!"

"It was like a family at United," Hodgson said. "I was an Australian boy and all I knew about English football, realistically, was Liverpool and Man United. They called it a family club, which can be a bit cliché, but I really felt that. The likes of Rogers and Sid Whitehouse and John Gannon really took me under their wing. Derek French, the physio and Greavesy. Harry was a character in himself. There were a lot of great people who I still keep in contact with now. Towards the end there was turmoil at the club and when Harry went, it was the end of an era.

"The boys had seen a lot and I can remember Ganns, who was close to Harry, getting us together and saying: 'We've got to get on with the job and do what we need to do. Harry has done what he's done for whatever reason, but we're contracted and we've just got to get on with the job.' And we all followed suit. I was a young, inexperienced kid and I was like a sheep following the leader. That's football. That's the job. Don't get me wrong, it's great when you're doing it, because you get paid to do something you enjoy. But there are so many ups and downs, it's frightening. One minute you're brilliant, the next you're not. Harry had his time, and what a brilliant time it was."

Hodgson initially survived under Bassett's replacement, Howard Kendall, but it was a transitional period and at the end of 1995/96, Bassett's skipper Gayle moved on to Exeter after 135 games of service in a United shirt. United finished ninth that season and come the final game, at home to Port Vale, couldn't go up and weren't at risk of relegation either. "I was told that Gayley was going to play as a farewell and that my season was over, so I went on a 10-day bender," Hodgson said. "Then on the Friday, Harry told me Gayley would be on the bench and I was playing.

"Charlie Hartfield told me that my face was redder than my shirt when I found out. I was blowing out of my arse but did okay, and Gayley came on for his farewell. So I still never knowingly drank before a game! I'm an extrovert. I love people and I love friendships. I love a beer. I'm Australian; I don't mind having a sherbet or six. Or 10. But England taught me how to drink properly, because it was pints. There was a time and a place and we picked our times. We had some fun. I'll rest when I'm dead, and I won't die wondering."

There have been good times, but life has not been all plain sailing and the bravery and determination that defined Hodgson's playing career have been required in spades away from the pitch. In his first season at United he spent a month in hospital after a broken nose kept haemorrhaging and required three operations. No Australian surgeon would touch him after his spinal injury, meaning Hodgson had to regularly fly back to England to have the ends of his nerves burnt off.

He would get nine months of life at a manageable level, but never pain-free, before the ends grew back and the pain returned. By 2020, he had had enough and underwent his biggest operation thus far but it wasn't the end of the matter, going back under the surgeon's knife in 2024 to remove a rib which was putting pressure on one of his key veins.

"Some of the best players have continued playing past when I had to retire. Tony Adams played his best football when he was 30, and a lot of people say that Paul McGrath got better when he got older. I was 29, and a late developer because of my car accident. The man upstairs keeps putting brick walls in front of me and I'll just try and keep knocking them down. That's what we've got to do. If you only get one life, you've got to make the best of it. But it's been a very hilly road.

"Have I fought pain for the last 20 years? Yes, I have. Do I live in pain every day? Yes, I do. Do I take medication? Yes, I do. Do I take some bad stuff sometimes? Yes, I do. It's been a big, hilly road but there have been some positives in there as well. I've got a beautiful wife and two beautiful kids and if I didn't, I probably wouldn't be here. I've seen a psychologist and there have been low parts of my life. Everyone has a journey and everyone has a story. Mine has some ups and downs and some battles I'm still battling now. There's an old saying in football: 'Play now, pay later.' I've gone to bed every night for the last 20-odd years, wondering if I'm going to be better in the morning or worse. You've got to grit your teeth and not let it beat you."

Hodgson has owned a string of businesses since his enforced retirement, including a chemical recycling operation and two juice bar franchises that were affected by the Covid-19 pandemic. He returned to Bramall Lane for a spell of reserve-team coaching, and can still remember first-team boss Neil Warnock telling Hodgson he would be the next manager of United.

He loved coaching, and was good at it. But his dad fell ill and, already struggling with the mental toil of losing his playing career, he returned Down Under. "I can be a pain in the arse, like anyone who's in pain," he admitted. His wife was concerned about him spiralling again after the last big operation, so Hodgson bought himself a child's dummy. "Whenever I'm being a pain, I tell her to give it to me and it'd be the red light for me to pull my head in."

Hodgson's trade-off for living his football dream was all the subsequent pain, the anguish, both physical and mental, and the family effect. Countless hours in operating theatres and rehab centres, big money spent and many years lost. It's impossible not to wonder aloud whether, when he looks back, the destination was worth the journey that followed?

"It's a hard one," he admitted, after a long pause. "I got goosebumps at the question. People ask me all the time if I'd change anything. I'd change the outcome of how I'm feeling, and I would have liked to have done it better. But would I change it, with the experiences I had and the people I met? No, I wouldn't. I'll never forget my career because I wake up every day and am reminded of it, but in the wrong way. I wake up in pain.

"Some days in more pain than when I went to bed. I think: 'Fuck, why am I here?' It's because of football. I still struggle with the game now, mentally. They say losing your career is like losing someone. How do you grieve? Now mental illness is a lot more understood. You couldn't talk about this shit years ago. If you started showing true emotions and how you felt, it was like: 'Suck it up, princess, and get on with it.' Now you're encouraged to talk about it and it helps me. If I bottled it up, I'd be a walking timebomb.

"But everyone is different and I am who I am. I wore my heart on my sleeve and put my body on the line. And I'm paying for it now. It is what it is. I've got to accept it, roll my sleeves up and keep throwing the punches. You think what could have been. I think Neil would have brought me back to United as a player, before I got injured, and you wonder what could have been there. But I also got an opportunity to do something that others dream of doing, even if it's sometimes hard to see it like that.

"There's always someone worse off than you and if you can get that in your head, then you've got a chance to be positive. I'm lucky because I know what causes my problems but a lot of people don't know what gives them theirs. I know what beats me down and hurts me every day. I've never had my kids on my shoulders. I've never thrown them into a swimming pool. People don't realise the little things I've missed. You see dads walking around with kids on their shoulders, and my kids can't do it. It's the simple things.

"I'm not feeling sorry for myself. I've got two beautiful boys and if that's the worst thing that happens, it's not so bad. My life goes medical, work, soccer and if there's a beer at home in there somewhere as well, it keeps me sane. That's the reflection you need to keep positive. Because that tunnel is a fucking dark tunnel, mate. I'm sure a lot of people like me have been in there as well. You've just gotta make sure there's some light at the end of it."

"Eric Cantona tried to knee me in the nuts, so I just took a step back and thumped him. We had a little go again in the tunnel at half-time. I was waiting for him, but Harry ushered me into the changing room and gave me a right coating. In hindsight I should have done to Cantona what he did to me, which was to roll over and get him sent off. But that was not who I was. My natural reaction back then was to just give him one back. That's the way we played. That Sheffield United team didn't roll over for anyone, and we were never going to do that here."

– Charlie Hartfield

19

THE BEGINNING OF THE END

D ave Bassett has always possessed a remarkable turn of phrase and it was in his autobiography, *Settling the Score,* that he perhaps summed up best the behind-the-scenes turmoil that he faced during his time at Bramall Lane. "If you have ever been a passenger on a jumbo jet and heard the chief pilot and his co-pilot arguing how to fly the plane," he wrote, "then you will have some idea of what it was like to be manager of Sheffield United. You never knew from one day to the next if you were going to get a comfortable flight and a safe landing, or if you were going to put your head around the door of the cockpit to find that both pilots had bailed out."

Throughout Bassett's time in South Yorkshire there were no shortage of boardroom dramas but he was far from the only boss in United's history to have to deal with them, either. There have been enough behind-the-scenes shenanigans at Bramall Lane to fill an entire book, the excellent *Fit and Proper* by Matthew Bell and Gary Armstrong which was first published in 2010 and probably has enough material for a second edition in the years since. Its dedication described United, considering their support, as the most underperforming club in the United Kingdom. "We would venture to suggest that few readers would speak well of the way the club they support has been run over the past 30 years," the authors wrote. "The fans of Sheffield United have many tales to tell on the table of woe …"

As do the managers. Balancing out the on-field highlights of Bassett's United reign were numerous off-pitch frustrations; the sale of star striker Brian Deane against his wishes, which essentially signed United's Premier League death warrant and set them back years as a club, and having to lend the club money from his personal wealth to sign a player. Right up there for Bassett was the Sam Hashimi takeover episode, which the manager later described as a pantomime better than Ali Baba. That saga not only highlighted the issues behind the scenes at the time at Bramall Lane but also one of Bassett's big personality traits. He was the eternal optimist, absolutely convinced that United were perennially on the cusp of a new dawn. But as the years rolled on, and the chairs in the boardroom above him were reshuffled like the deckchairs on the Titanic, it slowly began to dawn on him that if he was to keep dragging United forward, kicking and screaming, then he would have to continue doing so on his own.

There were opportunities to leave; some that he turned down comfortably and others that, with the benefit of hindsight, he knows he should have probably taken. One was from Sunderland, in 1995 and just before the Black Cats appointed Peter Reid as their new manager. Bassett had met with Sunderland's chairman, Sir Bob Murray, and was impressed with the club's ambition, despite their battle against relegation at the time. His wife Christine also encouraged him to accept the job, but he remained loyal to United. Reid kept Sunderland up that season and then led them to the Division One title the following campaign; Bassett did leave United nine months later, but without a job to go into elsewhere.

Another of Bassett's self-confessed faults, if it could be described as such, was his loyalty. He openly admits now that if he had experienced such difficulties at any other club he would have wilfully walked away, but something about United was different. He had been touched by the support of the Blades fanbase at some of his lowest moments and the idea of returning that loyalty by jumping ship left him deeply uncomfortable. He also wouldn't be able to forgive himself if someone did take control of the drifting ship and steer it towards more successful and lucrative waters. Promotions, cup finals, maybe even a first experience of European competition. The optimist was forever dreaming.

One of the constants in the boardroom during Bassett's time at Bramall Lane was Reg Brealey, the man who brought him to South Yorkshire back in 1988. Brealey was in many ways an accidental chairman, having no real prior affinity to United before he joined the board and then becoming chairman quickly as the Blades slid into the Fourth Division.

He was instrumental in the appointment of Bassett and had grand plans for United off the field, too, including the construction of a huge new stand in place of the existing Kop and upgrades to Bramall Lane that would include a shopping complex, a hotel and facilities to host multiple other sports, including athletics. The scheme, Brealey felt, would create hundreds of local jobs and help re-establish the city that invented football on the world map. The only obstacle was support from Sheffield City Council, or the lack of it – fuelling decades of suspicion amongst some Blades fans that those in charge of the city were somehow biased against its red and white half.

The rejection of the idea, with the council keen to avoid taking away footfall from Sheffield city centre with the Meadowhall shopping centre still some years away, hit Brealey hard and he even had a second go, upgrading the scheme to a £20m masterplan which was again turned down. Brealey was also suspicious that his own Tory political leanings had impacted the decision by a Labour-led council and he offered to resign if his position as chairman was having a detrimental impact on United moving forward.

A few years later Sheffield was awarded the 1991 World Student Games and the council commissioned a series of venues to act as hosts – including, in what was seen as an ironic twist for United, an athletics stadium. Don Valley cost £29m to build and was demolished in 2013 to save costs. The games cost Sheffield – and Sheffielders – £100m in construction and running costs, with the total bill of £658m – including interest and refinancing, due to finally be paid off in 2023/24's financial year. Long after it had been knocked down.

Brealey was seen by those he worked with as something of a visionary, a man who would come up with ideas by the bucketload – many of which were ahead of their time. He was keen to make football grounds more welcoming places to visit, championing facilities for females and United's image as a "family club." He was also a big advocate for the removal of pitch side fencing well before it was made compulsory, after a fan got his wedding ring caught and ended up losing his finger. But Brealey later described the hobby of owning a football club as amongst the most expensive one could pursue and as the years went on, his cash or his patience – or both – began to run out. He had first publicly stated his wish to sell his shares even before Bassett's whirlwind arrival. But no one reputable had come forward to successfully buy them, and so his ownership continued.

Brealey's problems only intensified when he became the first Brit to be charged under new insider trading laws during his chairmanship of an Indian-based jute company and although he was acquitted when the case against him collapsed in 1991, fellow director Paul Woolhouse said at the time that the episode brought "further bad publicity and embarrassment to the club." It was during a board meeting, filmed by the *BBC* cameras for their iconic *United!* documentary during the 1989/90 season, that Brealey revealed that a concrete offer had been received for his shares. "Blades Shocker: Brealey Sell-out" was the front-page headline in *The Star.*

The new prospective man at the helm of United was Hashimi, unveiled at a Bramall Lane press conference on March 5 in front of nervous-looking existing members of the United board and manager Bassett. Sporting a bushy moustache and huge glasses, Hashimi spoke with a heavy accent for the first time in public about his bid to take over the Blades. "I love the football," his speech ended, "and I love the city."

Reported to have been born into the House of Hashim royal family in Iraq, Hashimi arrived in London as a student in 1976 and came to Bramall Lane promising the backing of four Arab sheiks and a prince, with his backers potentially including the mayor of Jeddah in Saudi Arabia.

At the time it would have been a groundbreaking deal but Woolhouse's self–trumpeted "intuition" told him that something wasn't right about Hashimi, telling the *BBC* cameras: "He isn't a Unitedite, he isn't a Sheffield person, he isn't British." If, as some suspect, the Hashimi episode was orchestrated by Brealey to provoke Woolhouse, it was an elaborate ploy.

But it worked, with Woolhouse later launching a rival bid himself to buy the chairman's shares, alongside another consortium led by the son of former Blades boss Harry Haslam. Hashimi and his entourage were later discovered taking measurements of the Bramall Lane Kop and kicked out by managing director Derek Dooley. In typical United fashion, things turned out to be not quite what they first seemed.

The promises of £1million to spend on players certainly suckered in fans, who were heard chanting at home games about their new-found wealth, but had turned out to be built on sand. They were too good to be true – but that didn't stop the eternal optimist wanting to believe it. Bassett later admitted his regret and embarrassment at the celebratory photographs that appeared in *The Star* with Brealey and Hashimi, the would-be owner wearing a United scarf tightly around his neck. It was as close as he would get to representing the club; just weeks after being hailed as the saviour of United, Hashimi's bid was up in smoke and the Blades – and Brealey – were back to square one. Journalist Tony Pritchett described the Hashimi saga in *The Star* as "an issue that almost wrecked the club."

It was not the last Unitedites heard of Hashimi, as he bizarrely claimed his £6m bid for the Blades was back on again towards the end of May 1990. That came as a surprise to many at Bramall Lane – not least Brealey, who knew nothing about it – and a few years later Hashimi resurfaced again as glamorous business tycoon Samantha Kane. Hashimi had undergone gender reassignment surgery in 1997 and spent £100,000 on breast implants, dental work and other cosmetic enhancements, including a nose job and an operation to remove his Adam's apple.

But life as a woman didn't fulfil the divorced father-of-two, who then underwent another operation in 2004 to revert back to being a man again. Kane, now going by the name of Charles, had her breast implants removed and testosterone replaced oestrogen. The surgeons attempted to fashion a new male appendage, which was non-functioning and left Kane feeling like an "approximation" of the man he once was.

Now Hashimi – thought to be the first person in the world to have changed gender three times – is a woman again, a barrister and property tycoon with the title of Lady Samantha Kane after buying a 64-room Scottish castle. It has been a remarkable journey, even for the standards of the United boardroom, and almost didn't end there. Samantha Kane was considered for the role of United's chief executive in 1998, with a bold plan to attract one million football supporters in Asia and the Middle East to become Blades in an era before such worldwide fandom was commonplace for top clubs in the game.

"I'm happier now than I have ever been," Kane said in an interview with the *Scottish Daily Mail* after buying Carbisdale Castle in 2022. "There are no issues in my head about who I am or my gender. I am a woman. Now I just want a peaceful, dignified existence. I don't want to be remembered solely for my transgender life, because I'm so much more than that."

***

The Sam Hashimi experience had been a chastening one for Sheffield United owner Reg Brealey and despite the episode forcing him to back-track and take his Blades shares off the market, he remained keen to cash in and get out. Brealey was described by some colleagues at the time as someone whose default position was to err on the side of caution and to run United as an ordinary business, as he would any of his other interests across different sectors. It was a sensible approach, but wasn't sexy enough for fellow director Paul Woolhouse. Manager Dave Bassett was not the only one growing a little tired of the constant politicking in the Bramall Lane boardroom.

One of the most vociferous opponents of Hashimi's takeover attempt, Woolhouse – unlike Brealey – was a Sheffield-born businessman and was red and white through and through. A United fan since he was seven years old, Woolhouse began his working life dealing in scrap metal be-fore moving into specialist materials and became a Blades shareholder in the mid-1980s, paying just over £100,000 for a one-eighth stake of the club and a subsequent place on the board.

Described by Bassett as an immaculately-dressed "ladies' man" – but disliked by at least one player, who remembered proudly once throw-ing a roast potato at his head during a dinner to celebrate promotion at Leicester – the balding, well-spoken Woolhouse grew up in an affluent part of Sheffield and long had designs of being the owner of his boyhood club. The ambition moved a step closer in December 1990 – around the same time United ended their long winless run on the field that season – when a deal was struck with Brealey, with a fee of £2.75m reported. United went on to pull off their great escape act, spending relatively big money of £650,000 on Vinnie Jones to help them do so. Things, for a time, were looking rosy.

Then came the Brian Gayle cash saga, which saw Bassett lend the Blades the money to sign the defender, and fan unrest that forced the manager to borrow a police microphone and reassure supporters that star striker Brian Deane had not been sold – yet – and that he was not re-signing in protest. Slowly, signs were showing that, under Woolhouse's ownership, all was still not well at Bramall Lane.

Not for the first time, events on the pitch were overshadowed by those in the boardroom and as Unitedites basked in a winning start to life in the new Premier League era, Brian Deane's historic double downing Manchester United at Bramall Lane in August 1992, what *The Star* described as a "shares riddle" cast more doubt over Woolhouse's ownership. Essentially Woolhouse had failed to honour the agreement he had made with Brealey over control of United, which reverted to the latter after a High Court hearing – not for the last time in the club's history – decided who would own the Blades.

For his money Bassett believes Woolhouse simply overstretched himself financially but the effect was chaotic, with Reg Brealey's brother Len calling for Woolhouse's resignation, alongside fellow directors Stephen Hinchliffe and Michael Wragg. Woolhouse vowed to appeal the decision and to carry on as normal in the interim and against the backdrop of yet more instability upstairs, United hammered Tottenham Hotspur 6-0 on the evening the verdict was returned.

Woolhouse's appeal was heard, and rejected, in May 1993 and he was removed at a United extraordinary general meeting later that month. By December that year he had been declared bankrupt and then, a few months later and amid police queries into his business dealings, he disappeared. After South Yorkshire Police issued a warrant for his arrest, Woolhouse proclaimed his innocence in a letter to *The Star*, sent from overseas. The local Sheffield newspaper later traced him to Miami and then Australia, where his small, rented house had a broken window and graffiti on the walls. It was a far cry from his life of luxury in Sheffield and to this day, he has never been pinned down by law enforcement, despite a fresh appeal on the *BBC's Crimewatch* show. There are even wild rumours that he continues to attend United games, in a clandestine disguise.

One of Woolhouse's first acts as United chairman had been to bring Stephen Hinchliffe onto the Bramall Lane board, effectively sidelining managing director Dooley in the process. Dooley, a trusted confidant of manager Bassett, regularly travelled on the United team coach but was banned from doing so by Woolhouse, who strongly encouraged him to take early retirement and effectively took on Dooley's duties himself in a newly-created chief executive role, paying himself a significant salary in the process.

Hinchliffe was larger than life, almost literally at 6ft 5in tall, and was a qualified accountant, as well as a boyhood Blades fan. He had stand-out blond hair and a solid handshake, smartly-dressed with the number plate SH1 on his Mercedes and a swimming pool that played underwater music at the height of his success.

After a couple of failed early business ventures he made almost £3m as part of a consortium who revived the fortunes of a local furniture company and eventually started buying ailing companies – at an average rate of one per month – with the aim of turning them around. At its peak, his Facia group – headquartered in Sheffield – had 850 British high street shops and employed more than 6,000 people, turning over more than £250m. Hinchliffe also owned a 15 per cent share in his boyhood football club but was forced to resign from the United board as Facia's finances began to unravel. The group collapsed in 1996, with debts of £70m, and Hinchliffe was later twice sent to prison for bribery and fraud.

Brealey's return saw Hinchliffe and fellow director Wragg forced out of the boardroom and also led to the most seismic event in Bassett's Bramall Lane career, and one of the biggest in their recent history; the 1993 sale of Deane, pushed through by the chairman's casting vote. Brealey would later tell Deane privately that the transfer fee United received effectively "saved" the club but from a football perspective it was disastrous and all but sealed the Blades' fate that season. Bassett's relationship with Brealey didn't ever fully recover.

There was *some* welcome news for Bassett, with the end of Woolhouse's short-term stint in charge signalling the return of Dooley in a chief executive role, and Dooley did his best to keep his manager up to speed with the goings-on above him. There was plenty to digest. The directors were effectively heading towards civil war. The boardroom was split. And again Bassett considered resigning.

His decision to stay was influenced by the number of supporters who had urged him to remain in charge but he had made his feelings clear; that the constant toing and froing in the boardroom had to end and someone had to finally invest in order to take the club forward. Otherwise, as things stood, Bassett had taken them as far as he could. Fans and players both shared his concerns about what was happening upstairs, with some of his squad concerned about whether their next pay cheque would arrive and unsure what to believe about the many stories they were hearing and reading. Bassett often wasn't fully sure himself, but did his best to shield his players and keep them focused on their football. "We were not really party to any of that," said winger Ian Bryson, on the boardroom goings-on. "Dave was very good at keeping that separate and hiding what was going on in the background. That was part of his job … keeping the players happy and motivated while being unaware of what was going on above us."

Bassett had long been the glue that held the club together and relegation at Chelsea would have been the perfect opportunity to walk away with his stock high. There was certainly plenty of time to consider his future as the United party's plane left the tarmac en route to Australia for a pre-arranged end-of-season trip, just three days after the heartbreaking defeat at Stamford Bridge had brought their time in the top-flight to a cruel end. It was a trip that no one present wanted to be on and Bassett did his best to lift spirits but, remembering how his relegation prediction to Brealey over Deane's sale had come true 72 hours earlier, he didn't know whether to laugh or cry.

"Harry was so frustrated," recalled midfielder John Gannon. "He was twisted and angry one minute, and then trying to be alright with us the next. He didn't know how to be with us. It was just difficult for him and was difficult for us, too. We all stuck together for three weeks, on this already-arranged trip, but it was not easy under the circumstances." Teammate Jamie Hoyland remembered the mood being worsened further by the drop in wages that relegation would mean for United's players. "Some of the players might have only lost £200 a week, but back then that was a lot," he said. "You missed out on all kinds of Premier League appearance money and bonuses, such as staying up bonuses. You're talking £20,000 each. Now it's a lot more, but back then that was a lot of money to us. It was a huge amount, and we knew that players would have to leave."

There was even short-lived hope that United could somehow earn a reprieve and win back their Premier League place, with the Football Association investigating "financial irregularities" at Tottenham Hotspur in the previous decade. A similar episode earlier in the decade had seen Swindon Town stripped of their promotion and initially relegated to the Third Division – although on appeal they were allowed to stay in the second – and there were very real fears at White Hart Lane that a similar punishment may come their way, which would reprieve United. There was a feeling of limbo, in both London and Sheffield, before the verdict in mid-June – Spurs were fined £600,000, plus costs, and expelled from the following season's FA Cup, with a 12-point deduction; for the next season, not the one that had just been played. The sporting sanctions were later reduced and then removed entirely on appeal, with the fine increased to £1.5m. At the time it was one of the biggest punishments English football had ever seen. For United, it was another kick in the teeth.

Their four-game trip Down Under was not remembered fondly by anyone who was part of it and only prolonged the painful hangover of relegation. United did return with two new signings, in Australians Dougie Hodgson and Carl Veart, but it was a familiar story for Bassett, with the incomings funded by the departures of Carl Bradshaw, to Norwich for £500,000, and defender Tom Cowan's £200,000 switch to Huddersfield. Brealey remained in charge but there were some promising signs of progress with a proposal to build a new stand on John Street – although, true to form, that development dragged on and on, and left Bramall Lane a three-sided ground. As his frustration grew Bassett, in his own inimitable style, began to refer to the empty space as "Fred West's Garden."

Bassett also faced questions about whether his long-term coaching partnership needed evolving after relegation, with some players feeling that training was running the risk of becoming a little stale. "That summer I went in to speak to Bassett because I wanted to see what my future was," said defender Kevin Gage. "Brads had taken my right-back spot but was going to be sold to Norwich. I said to him: 'The standard of the training and coaching hasn't been very good, and I think we need a fresh face to liven it up a little.'"

Brian Eastick, who would go on to coach England at under-19 and under-20 level, subsequently arrived. He was cut from a different cloth to Bassett and Taylor; a more technical-based coach and likened to a schoolteacher in his approach. Players did enjoy the change of scenery but it's perhaps unsurprising he didn't last. One former colleague remembers Eastick telling United's players on a pre-season tour that they couldn't have a night out. Shocked at the departure from what they had become accustomed to, one of the players contacted Bassett and the coach was quickly overruled. His authority was stripped in an instant and from then on, Eastick's position had been rendered pretty much untenable.

With "Fred West's Garden" now hidden behind a makeshift wooden board, and the Blades 10/1 fourth-favourites at the bookmakers to win the Division One title, United's bid for an immediate Premier League return began with a comfortable 3-0 win over Watford, with Jostein Flo off the mark and a beautiful brace from Mitch Ward. Alan Kelly had kept his place between the posts but it had been a far from settled summer for the goalkeeper, who started the campaign on a week-to-week contract after failing to agree a new deal. Kelly was then dropped an hour before the next league match of the season, against Notts County, and spent time in the reserves before eventually returning for the trip to Reading in September.

"We'd agreed a deal, it took a long time to get to it, and I came in to sign it before the game," Kelly said. "One or three things had changed in it and I said: 'Let's sort this out after the game.' I was told that, unless I signed it, I wasn't playing." Kelly was uncomfortable trying to get his head around the contract changes so close to kick-off, so he "politely declined." The late change meant Simon Tracey was given the nod at the last minute and the 2-1 home loss to County proved to be one of a handful of costly defeats against teams at the lower end of the table.

"I eventually did sign a contract," Kelly added. "But when we are talking about characters, Harry maybe didn't realise that the characters he'd signed might come back one day and say: 'Hang on, Harry … I do understand the ins and outs of things and if I think it's not right then I'm going to say to you it's not right.' It was quite frustrating to be in the reserves, but I had to get on with it, bite the bullet and see what happened."

It looked like the bookies had been very generous with their 10-1 pricing after United brushed aside Watford but Bassett's men would win just two more of their opening 15 matches and kicked off November 18th in the table, just a point above the bottom three. The fans had seen enough. There was a protest against the chairman on November 5 ahead of the home match against Bristol City, as the newly-formed Blades Independent Fans Association distributed 10,000 A5 red cards for supporters to hold up before kick-off with the simple directive "spend or go" aimed at Brealey.

United won the match 3-0 in front of 11,568 fans and an atmosphere Bassett described as "poxy," with the manager insisting he would rather have 15,000 fans getting behind the team than 12,000 protesting against directors. But the message appeared to have resonated and during the following home match against Derby County, Brealey sent a message to the fans – via the Bramall Lane's electronic scoreboard – which said he was putting the club up for sale a week later. Was the takeover Bassett had been desperately waiting for all this time finally here?

The man behind the latest Bramall Lane bid was Mike McDonald, a Manchester-born businessman and City fan who also looked at deals for Leicester City and Stoke City, amongst others, before launching a £3.2m bid to buy 52 per cent of United's shares from Brealey. The process was typically difficult, described by McDonald – the 731st richest man in the country at the time, according to the *Sunday Times* Rich List, as "horrendous" and "bloody difficult." When the deal eventually went through it was the end of Brealey's involvement with United and steadily, the golden era was being broken up. Another to leave was midfielder Jamie Hoyland, the boyhood Blade who joined Burnley in the October of that first season back in the second tier. It was not the end he had anticipated. In fact, it was hard to swallow.

An attempt by club officials to recoup his signing-on fee, which they had failed to stipulate at the time of his arrival, meant the way Hoyland's departure was managed marred his time at the club and left a really bitter taste. "Especially when you consider how much the club meant to me and how much I gave while I was there," Hoyland said. "They had messed up, so to get a letter saying they wanted all my kit and stuff back and that I was banned from coming back to Bramall Lane unless I was on official business with Burnley was a hard one to take. I never tossed anything off when I was there as a player, I gave my all every week. I loved the club and I was never flippant about the club in any way. To do that at the end was ridiculous and it did leave a sour taste for a bit. It's healed over now, but it was a really childish thing to do."

Hoyland duly returned his United kit as requested, by dumping it on the floor of Bramall Lane's reception before heading for Turf Moor. The move was a chance for the midfielder to play regular football once more, and it must have been a bittersweet moment for the then 28-year-old when he found the net in a 4-2 win over United the following month, drilling home beyond good friend and future brother-in-law Kelly.

That defeat was one of just three in the league during a remarkable 24-game sequence between November and March that lifted United to within a point of the play-offs. Strikers Nathan Blake and Flo were proving a handful up top, with the likes of Veart and Dane Whitehouse adding to the threat.

Blake bagged four goals in the space of three days, including a bicycle-kick finish, in the 3-1 win over Portsmouth and 2-2 draw at Wolves which should have resulted in all three points but for a very late comeback. The marauding Gage was back in Bassett's plans following the sale of Bradshaw and was a threat from right-back, with United enjoying far more of the ball than they had done the previous four seasons. Gage was named as the fans' player of the year and it proved a far more enjoyable season personally for the defender than he envisaged at one point, having sought clarity on his future not long before. "All of a sudden, I was back in as first choice and that season was fantastic for me because we were going forward a lot. People could see what I was capable of going forward, getting the ball and creating."

United had climbed as high as third with a win over Charlton in March and also added the scalp of leaders Tranmere to the collection. However, a disastrous April, which failed to yield a win from six matches and saw points dropped against struggling Portsmouth and Swindon, killed off hopes of an immediate Premier League return. The Blades' situation was not helped by injuries to Charlie Hartfield, Brian Gayle and Mitch Ward, which took their toll on the squad's depth, and a three-game suspension for Hodges after getting sent off in the reserves away at Notts County in late February. A final day win over Grimsby was irrelevant in the end, sealing an eighth-place finish for 1994/95.

Even the cup competitions brought little joy, and a foray into the Anglo Italian Cup proved far from the exciting venture into European football that United had hoped. The competition was for second-tier sides in England and Italy, but United's involvement was over almost as quickly as it had begun. The first game of the competition, at home to Udinese, saw three players and Bassett sent off on a night to forget as United became too easily wound up by the antics of their visitors.

After a fairly even start, which saw Adrian Littlejohn cancel out Francesco Marino's opener after latching on to a Hodges through ball, the game descended into chaos. Referee Francesco Arena sent Blake off for throwing the ball in the face of Udinese captain Alessandro Calori, and Bassett followed for protesting against the decision with what was described as "a hand gesture" towards the referee. Hoyland's chest-high challenge on striker Fausto Pizzi led to a 15-man brawl after which Hartfield and Udinese winger Marek Kozminski were sent off – and this was all before half-time. Hodges recalled: "It was ridiculous. The referee was Italian who didn't have a clue and he was just atrocious. He was the problem. You expect some of their antics, because that's how they play the game, but if we'd had an English referee, he would not have fallen for it. The players doing that and the referee falling for everything … I was just thinking: 'This is just nuts, it's crazy.'"

At half-time Gage was fuming at his teammates, believing they would be suspended for key upcoming games, before being told in no uncertain terms by Bassett to sit down and shut up because the suspensions didn't count for league games. To add to the madness Hodges, who was also furious during the interval with Blake and Hartfield before Bassett clarified the rules, also saw red in the second half after the visitors had regained the lead. "They had a free-kick just outside the box and I remember someone shouting: 'Where's the wall?'" Hodges said. "It was pointed out that we were in the stands. It was me, Charlie and Blakey."

The Udinese players made their way up to the players' bar after the game and after a few seconds of uncomfortable silence, Hodges handed over a crate of lager for their journey home and informed their guests that they were better off heading for the bus sooner rather than later. "I think the last word he used was 'off,'" Gage laughed. Bassett rather gave up on the competition after that point, leaving coach Wally Downes in charge for the remaining fixtures and not risking too many first team players in a competition he described as being "more aggro than it was worth." Hartfield's red would not be his first that season, either, with another to follow that was perhaps more memorable and costly.

Another FA Cup encounter at home to Manchester United presented the Blades with the chance to repeat their heroics from two years earlier, especially given their impressive league form at the time. The home side were more than proving a match once again for the champions and were unlucky to see a clumsy challenge from Steve Bruce on Blake inside the area go unpunished, with the wind swirling around Bramall Lane thanks to a gaping hole down one side of the ground.

In fairness the conditions probably helped the Blades more than they hindered them, but their task was made that bit harder when Hartfield was dismissed before half-time after clipping Eric Cantona. The midfielder possibly took Bassett's instruction to unsettle the opposition and follow Cantona a bit too literally.

"I don't know if he wanted me to rattle him that much," Hartfield confessed. "Paul Scholes tried to do me in the middle of the park, so I buried him and then they all came running over. Then Eric tried to knee me in the nuts, which is why I did it. I just took a step back and thumped him. We had a little go again in the tunnel at half-time. I was waiting for him, but Harry ushered me into the changing room. He then gave me a right coating.

"I got fined two weeks' wages as well. In hindsight I should have done to him what he did to me, which was to roll over and get him sent off. But that was not who I was. I didn't have that type of reaction in me. My brain didn't work that fast to think like that. My natural reaction back then was to just give him one back. That's the way we played. That Sheffield United team didn't roll over for anyone, and we were never going to do that here."

Any hope United had of staging another upset went with that dismissal, and Bassett was furious with his midfielder. "It was irresponsible and cost us dearly," he fumed. "It did not matter whether Eric Cantona or Mickey Mouse kicked him, he should not have reacted. It cost us the game and it will cost him three matches, a week's money, and maybe his place in the team. He will look back on that mad moment for the rest of his life." To United's credit, the 10 men held out until 10 minutes from time when Mark Hughes broke the deadlock, before Cantona had the last laugh with an iconic chip over Kelly.

Had United been promoted that season – a task made slightly more difficult by the fact only one automatic place was available due to the Premier League reducing in numbers to 20 – it would have helped breathe new life into the club. But it was becoming increasingly clear that Bassett could no longer do it on his own, and it needed a spark from elsewhere to reignite the Blades' fortunes. Bassett had carried United up to this point, covering for the board's shortcomings and their own inability to drive the club forward. His seven-year stint, which included four seasons in the top flight, returned a profit on his transfer business.

Bassett estimates he earned the club a transfer profit in the region of £5m but the only way things would change was with a completely new broom. Instead the boardroom shenanigans continued, with acting chairman Alan Laver demanding repayment of a £300,000 loan he made to Brealey in 1993 – plus the princely sum of £10 he had lent a year later! The matter was settled before it got to court, but rather summed up the toxicity of United at the time.

The 1995/96 season saw United wearing diamonds on their home strip but there was very little sparkle at Bramall Lane, with results mirroring the apathy and lack of direction at the time. McDonald's takeover bid continued to drag on, taking its toll on Bassett and leading to a furious outburst in the media. "I am in limbo, the club is in limbo," he said. "Nobody is in actual authority so I can't even get a decision on purchasing players. There is apathy written all over the club. The situation is ridiculous. I have never been in a position like this. It is the most remarkable situation of my life in football, by far."

Bassett watched on in frustration as transfer targets came and went and he even tried to coax one final playing season out of veteran striker Trevor Francis, after his stint as manager of United's city rivals Wednesday came to an end. It was a move that would have certainly created its fair share of headlines but Bassett was not afraid of left-field signings, even trying to bring veteran striker Keith Edwards back to the Blades for a third spell at one point. Although Francis was the wrong side of 40, Bassett fancied the former England international to still do a job in front of goal if United could provide him with the service. "He was getting on a bit but his touch and all that was great," Bassett said. "We'd been on holiday together with Trevor and his wife Helen and I just thought: 'If we can do his running and get the ball to him, then it could work.'" The plan was scuppered when Birmingham City offered Francis the manager's job, and Bassett went back to the drawing board.

Five straight defeats was a nightmare start to the new campaign and their early-season struggle was perhaps summed up when a header hit the bar twice in defeat at Oldham, before skipper Brian Gayle was sent off for flicking out at a home defender off the ball. United were then booed off by their supporters after conceding two late goals to lose 3-2 at home to Crystal Palace, and Bassett's misery was compounded by speeding and parking tickets in the following days. As weeks went at Bramall Lane, it wasn't one of his finest.

The manager was not alone in his frustration at the deadlock at the top of the club, with columnist Martin Smith writing in *The Star* that "no one – not Dave Bassett, Johan Cruyff or Santa Claus – can achieve anything at United until the absurd boardroom drama is sorted out." The club were leaking cash steadily and at one point owed money to a number of suppliers, including the company who provided their team coach. The powers-that-be even halted the supply of newspapers and stamps to Bramall Lane to save a few quid, while the PFA stepped in with a £50,000 loan to help cash flow.

United were then hit with a transfer embargo and the air of anxiety around the club wasn't helped when the players' wages for September were paid late. The broken promises and lack of progress led to Bassett eventually blowing a fuse in a board meeting. "I was used to it but you can only do it for so long without any help," he said. "No Sheffield United board gave me any help. I had to do it all on my own. There's only so many times you can pull rabbits out of hats."

McDonald's takeover was finally completed on December 2, 1995, with United third-bottom of the table after 20 games, and it was hardly a ringing endorsement of Bassett when the new owner said that the manager had his backing "in the short term." A poor run of form in October had seen a section of United's fan base begin to turn on their manager, and Bassett's position was hardly strengthened when McDonald responded to his wish for new players by publicly pointing out the size of the existing United first-team squad. Bassett was furious, and had been in the game long enough to sense that the writing was on the wall for him at Bramall Lane. "McDonald didn't want me," he later admitted. "When a new owner comes in, he wants his own man and as a manager, you know your days are numbered. I knew it was only a matter of time. Adrian Heath was suddenly at all our games, so it didn't take a genius to work out that Howard Kendall was going to come in. I liked Howard as a bloke, it isn't his fault.

"I'd done all that for Reg and he had gone and dumped me for that board. I didn't even get the pay-off I should have done. It just summed up the club at the time. I was too loyal. I had chances to go to Chelsea, Aston Villa, Leicester, Sunderland ... and I turned them all down. But there you are; that's life. You can't have it all ways, can you? I just carried on thinking we'd get it right somewhere along the line. But I think now, that was me being an old romantic rather than reality."

Paul Rogers was one of the first players out of the door when Kendall arrived, and the club he left was not the one he had joined three years earlier. "With that group of players breaking up a little bit after the Premier League, it was always going to be difficult to bounce back straight away," he said. "Deano had gone, John Pemberton had gone, Paul Beesley had gone, and I got that vibe that Harry wasn't happy with different things regarding the ownership. Harry was trying to run the club, balance the books and get a competitive team on the pitch, and I think we all felt it was coming to an end. We had a run of results as well which didn't really help and underlying that with difficulties in the boardroom as well, it just wasn't the same club any more. It didn't feel the same as it had done previously. It didn't feel together."

The curtain came down on Bassett's reign following a 2-0 home defeat to Huddersfield on December 9, with his departure officially confirmed later that week. United were joint-bottom of the Division One table, with five wins from their 21 games and above basement club Luton Town only on goal difference. The match report in *The Star* described United as "in sad and perhaps terminal disarray" and just 12,126 fans were at Bramall Lane for the final curtain of Bassett's reign, with many of them booing the Blades off at the final whistle. Soon after, the club and manager agreed to part company on amicable terms before Bassett invited the press in his office for a farewell chat, insisting he was leaving in "good spirits."

"I don't think it was a surprise, just because of our position," Gage said. "We weren't a very good team and it just wasn't going right. To be fair, I can't remember him losing any enthusiasm. It wasn't a case of him throwing in the towel … it was just a victim of circumstances. We weren't a particularly brilliant side, we weren't playing well and perhaps there was a lack of enthusiasm from his point of view, because there was a lot of boardroom upheaval at the time. Maybe he was a bit pissed off with it all but, to his credit, I don't remember it filtering down to the dressing room."

The news may not have been a huge shock, but that didn't make it much easier to process. One fan openly wept outside Bramall Lane when the news was announced, while another insisted that: "Without Bassett, this club's finished." Another to shed a tear at Bassett's departure was Simon Tracey, the goalkeeper who had been at loggerheads with United over a new contract and felt somewhat let down by the offer on the table after his many years of loyal service. A bad injury at the time could well have influenced the terms of the new deal and he could have been one of a few players left behind who would benefit from the change of manager, but described himself as "absolutely gutted" at the news.

"I was in tears," he added. "I had a fantastic relationship with him and I was indebted to Harry for bringing me up here, for playing me, for showing faith in me. But towards that last year when he left, I wasn't getting along with him. I never expected it to happen but I knew that him leaving in the end was better for me. I was offered a contract which was fantastic, nearly double my money. So all of a sudden, I felt that I had something to prove when Howard came in and it probably reactivated me."

Bassett can see now, in hindsight, that he was "going through the motions" in the final throes of his United career, gradually worn down by the tide he had been swimming against for so long. It was, he felt, only a matter of time before McDonald came in and he would be out. The Huddersfield defeat was just the final straw. "I was gutted. It was a shame. But we'd reached the point. The players knew we'd reached the end."

There was still time for some last boardroom drama, Bassett claiming he hadn't received the pay-off he was entitled to and inviting McDonald's right-hand man Charles Green into the car park to settle the matter. Many Unitedites from that era would have loved the same opportunity with Green, who perhaps sensibly declined the invitation. Bassett's simple but devastating opinion of Green as a person isn't printable, at least without a couple of asterisks in the very strong four-letter word.

In perhaps the ultimate irony, Bassett won a £2,000 holiday voucher in the half-time raffle against Huddersfield. Having called for financial help all throughout his United tenure, his numbers eventually came in on his final matchday. He used the holiday as a chance to recharge, flying out to America on Concorde ready for the change of scenery that lay ahead. It was the end of an era at Bramall Lane; one never to be forgotten by anyone fortunate enough to have witnessed it.

"I used to think: 'Throw me the No.9 shirt and I'd run through a brick wall for Dave, with one leg.'"

– Derek Dooley

20

A LEGEND AT THE LANE

They were 18th in the second tier when he swept into Bramall Lane in 1988; when he left Sheffield United almost eight years later, they were 23rd in the same division. But to measure Dave Bassett's impact in such rudimentary terms would be plainly ridiculous. This was, by any other measure, one of the most remarkable rides in this historic club's long and proud history. Back-to-back promotions. Leicester. Remarkable great escape acts. Iconic players, games, moments. The first Premier League goal.

Characters and memories that endear to this day, and should never be forgotten.

Bassett, a Wimbledon legend, holds the rare accolade of being named the greatest-ever manager in the history of two different clubs, receiving the honour at United's 125th anniversary celebrations at a glittering Ponds Forge gala dinner back in October 2014. Bassett, despite his pride, felt it a little "unfair" on the likes of John Harris, in charge between 1969 and 1973, because many of those who had enjoyed watching Harris' side are no longer alive.

"You're relying on the people who were around when you were there," he said. "I think the fans knew we had a shit side when I arrived, and within two years they were in the top-flight. Then they had four seasons in the Premier League, getting to Wembley for a semi-final, beating Manchester United in that time, Chelsea and Tottenham ... they had some glorious days out.

I remember one fan saying to me: 'Harry, that was the best period of my fucking life.' And that stayed with me. That's fantastic. It was great for me, that spell at United. But to hear things like that means a lot. He felt proud of his team again."

Bassett's legacy is one of more than 1,000 games in management, a place in the League Managers Association hall of fame and seven automatic promotions, a feat no manager has so far beaten. "Warnock claims he's got eight promotions, which he has, but three were via the play-offs," Bassett said.

"We have a bit of competition. There aren't many sitting out there who have been the greatest manager of two clubs, so they're nice points. I look back at everything with a lot of pride. The Wimbledon story... I'd like to see someone come up with something that can beat it. Going to sixth in the top-flight, on gates of 3,000 people and the lowest wage bill in the world. Vinnie Jones earning £150 a week and scoring the winner against Manchester United.

"Then at United – nearly eight years, and four in the top league, and I made them £5m profit on transfers. I mean, fuck me. No other club could have done that. Perhaps I just picked the wrong people. I should have left a couple of times, but I didn't. I liked it, I liked the club and Derek Dooley, but I should have been ruthless. I fucked up. But I was loyal. I've had a good career, but I could have done better and earned a fair bit more money. I'm not hard up but I could have earned a lot more and could have got a bit more credit. But I can't complain. I've had a fucking good time."

One regret is that he retired too early. After leaving United he was interviewed for the vacant Republic of Ireland job, and came close before the Irish FA plumped for Mick McCarthy, and went on to manage Crystal Palace, Nottingham Forest, Barnsley and Leicester City, where he reached the magic 1,000-game mark and was presented with a crystal memento by Sir Alex Ferguson and a personalised and signed Manchester United shirt by David Beckham.

When he took over Palace two months after leaving the Lane, they were 16th. In the sort of twist of fate that football loves to throw up, his first game in charge of Palace was a goalless draw with the Blades. Bassett took them to third and that season's play-off final, which ended in defeat to Leicester. A man unfairly castigated for his direct style of play at United won the 1997/98 Division One title at Forest playing excellent football, and came close to another promotion at Oakwell before losing the 2001 play-off final to Ipswich.

The obvious question to Bassett seemed to be whether his long-ball reputation pissed him off, or continues to. "Maybe in a way," he admitted. "I am half-regarded as a legend, and some people still see me as that. People hear me speaking and ask if I'm Dave Bassett.

And a lot of the older ones ask: 'Why are you not on Sky?' It's because the younger kids haven't had a clue who I am. I could have carried on but the young kids growing up now, at 40, are thinking: 'Who is he?' Wimbledon didn't get anywhere enough credit for what they did and achieved. They eulogise about managers but I just don't come into that category.

"I wasn't meant to be a superstar manager. There is a certain amount of credit because they all remember certain teams and achievements, but not the credit it deserved. People talk about success stories, like Claudio Ranieri winning the league with Leicester ... Wimbledon came from non-league to finish sixth in the top-flight in nine years. If it's that fucking easy, why hasn't anyone else done it? If I did that now I'd be able to retire with about £100m in the bank!

"I was talking to some Italians in a conference and they said: 'If you did that in Italy, you'd never have to work again.' And I did it well at United. Then I went to Forest and won the league. But all of a sudden you become a bit older and less fashionable. There's a new era with the modern game. What is the modern game? They talk about this DNA where you pass it out from the back, which is fine. But it's not the only way to play football.

"Long ball isn't the only way to play football. I knew that I couldn't play that way at Forest and Barnsley, so we played differently. Wimbledon were top of the Fourth Division, playing the sweeper, and I got the players to change. They bought into it brilliantly.

"Looking back, I should have carried on a bit. But I just got fed up with directors who tried to tell me they knew more than I fucking did. Chief executives telling you: 'We can get this player or that player.' The advent of agents ... it was just changing. But there you are. If someone told me I'd have had the career I had, I'd have gladly accepted that. Great times with Wimbledon and Sheffield United, having a great laugh. Working with those players and having those times on tours was great fun. Great people and characters. Perhaps people are still having a great time now, but it's very different.

"I couldn't manage now. I'm too confrontational, and I tell people as I see it. And they don't like to be told things now. You see chairmen picking players, and for me the managers have got to have the final say. Managers now have become more like head coaches, and that was never my scene. If I had players who I thought were shit, then they weren't good enough to play.

"As I got older, I started to manage differently. I used to go out for a Chinese with the Sheffield United boys, and at Wimbledon. But I didn't do that at Leicester, or Forest. They weren't the type of players who were into that. They were good lads in their own way, but things had maybe changed. Management is hard, especially the way we did it. I remember people saying: 'You can't manage like that.' Well, we did, and it worked perfectly.

"I wanted to build teams that could think for themselves, as well, and that was the good thing at Wimbledon and United. There were individual characters who all had an opinion and were very strong-willed, all of them. I was looking for people who didn't worry about a bit of criticism. When I became a manager, I didn't sit down and read some book or go and ask someone else how it should be done. I just worked it out myself, from my own personality of what I wanted to do. When I played amateur football, I enjoyed a laugh. And I'd like to think that the players laughed as well."

They certainly did. One of midfielder Mark Todd's best memories to this day is a charity night at Bramall Lane, which raised money for leukaemia research and saw United's players singing on stage, in costumes. Todd donned a blonde wig and his first wife's green cardigan to channel Olivia Newton-John's character Sandy in *Grease,* joining Martin Pike to belt out *Summer Nights* in front of a crowd of teammates and fans. Bassett, physio Derek French and two other staff members imitated Queen, with French performing a very passable Freddie Mercury impression.

"I meet up with some of the lads from that era, and we very, very rarely talk about the game itself," said goalkeeper Alan Kelly. "We talk about the memories, the people that were in that dressing room, and we laugh. To be fair, we probably don't talk enough about beating Spurs 6-0, or beating Man United in the cup or winning on the first day of the Premier League season with Deano's goal. We probably don't talk enough about those types of results. It's more about the stories and the group.

"But looking back now, two things stand out to me: one, we had some really good players. And two, we got some fantastic results. But the memories are there to last a lifetime, the experiences we shared together. I was at United with Jamie Hoyland and then 10 years later he ended up being my brother-in-law. I still speak regularly to a lot of the lads from that era, and we really bought into the attitude and mindset of the time – work hard, first and foremost, and then the talent and ability will shine through. Looking at Harry, people think he assembled a team of misfits. But we were anything but."

Despite working with limited resources, to put it kindly, at United, Bassett's recruitment record speaks for itself. There was some misfortune, with Nathan Peel and Julian Winter failing to make a league start between them after being struck by injury and midfielder Martin Dickinson forced into early retirement after a car accident, later becoming a window cleaner.

But the £35,000 invested in Brian Deane repaid itself many times over, even before his big move to Leeds, while United got more than their money's worth from Tony Agana before he went to Notts County for £750,000. It was the era well before detailed analytics, Wyscout and vast teams of specialist scouts; back then, Bassett relied mostly on the knowledge and gut feeling he and his small staff had accumulated over their years in the game. And when they failed to turn up to a match they were supposed to be scouting, as Billy Whitehurst remembers of Wally Downes, there was always the fall-back option of calling an opposition centre-half for a second opinion.

Bassett's success at Bramall Lane was far from a one-man operation. More than one player from the era has described the Bassett-Geoff Taylor partnership as a 'good cop/bad cop' situation and Tony Pritchett, *The Star's* late Blades correspondent, described Taylor as being able to offer "a soothing and responsible influence on [Bassett] when he can. They form a perfect partnership; brash, impulsive and demanding Bassett and Taylor, quiet, thoughtful and ready with the quiet word of advice when necessary. But Taylor can be just as outspoken when the occasion demands."

Striker Peter Duffield remembered Bassett once steaming into the dressing room to read his players the riot act, but being intercepted by Taylor in the corridor before he could. The players, Taylor reasoned, were running their backsides off and on this occasion, the carrot may have been a more appropriate approach than the stick. Duffield chuckled at the memory of Bassett's team-talks, with the manager often so angry that he would move on to the next player to start berating them before he had even finished shouting at another. "It was like those whack-a-mole games at the seaside," Duffield said. "He'd shout your name so you'd look up and then before he finished, he'd move onto someone else, so you could look at the floor again until he came back round to you."

That's not to say Taylor was a pushover, though, and he could be tough when necessary, too. Duffield and Carl Bradshaw once kept him locked in a coach toilet for half an hour, by keeping their feet on the door, and the United No.2 got his revenge after escaping, pinning Duffield up against the wall while holding Bradshaw by the hair and throwing punches at both. Completing the inner circle for the most part were French, kitman John Greaves and youth coaches Keith Mincher and John Dungworth, while Downes, physio Denis Circuit and coach Brian Eastick were added later in the Bassett era as the demands began to grow.

Bassett also had a special affection for managing director Dooley, and the respect was reciprocated. "I used to think: 'Throw me the No.9 shirt and I'd run through a brick wall for him with one leg,'" Dooley once said of Bassett. Dooley was a proper football man who had an understanding of the pressures of the game, which many of his fellow directors lacked, and was also particularly fond of pre-season fishing trips with the coaching staff, who were often tasked with carrying him down river banks.

On one tour, Dooley took off his wooden leg and left it under a sun lounger to go for a swim in the sea, when a sudden monsoon appeared out of nowhere. A number of workers came scurrying out of the hotel to usher their guests inside, with one moving the lounger to be greeted with the sight of Dooley's leg. "He absolutely shit himself," Greaves laughed.

Midfielder Bob Booker was one who felt that he could always approach Bassett or Taylor with a personal issue; for others, including defender Kevin Gage, the manager-player dynamic was strictly a professional relationship. He was one of many to have played under Bassett at both Wimbledon and United, sandwiched between a spell with Graham Taylor at Aston Villa.

"Harry's management style, I tolerated it," he said. "It was successful. I think of myself as being technically a good footballer. I wasn't 6ft 2in and 14 stone, so I had to rely on technique, skill and pace. I got caught up on the Wimbledon bandwagon because we kept winning and it was effective. I started as a creative No.10 player at Wimbledon and played for England youth there too, but there was no place for me in Harry's side. So in the end, he just shoved me right back and I played there for the rest of my career with Bassett.

"I mean no disrespect to him, because what he did with Wimbledon and United was devastatingly effective and I did my best to fit in with that style of football. I had no problems with Harry. We weren't best of mates; he could be one of the lads when he was having a drink and could take the mickey, but if I had some kind of problem I don't think I could go to Bassett. We were never that close.

"I didn't agree with some of his methods and way he treated people sometimes, and thought he could be extremely harsh with some players if we'd lost a game or drawn one that we should have won. Sometimes it can just be a flip of a coin, but he really tore into certain players and I thought it was harsh at times.

"I think he would agree that he didn't give praise out very well. It was difficult to get a 'well done' out of him. It was very much tough love. He played in non-league in the 1960s and 1970s, when it was tough and you stood up for yourself. It was every man for himself, and you sank or swam. He carried that on into management and the players accepted that. We didn't go whining or moaning. And if you were dropped or he tore into you, we didn't sulk about it. Just accepted that's the way he was, and got on with it."

If a player didn't feel comfortable talking to Bassett, many instead went to Taylor or French. "They were good sounding boards," Booker said. "You'd have the craic with Geoff and, if Harry had the hump after a game and went off, Geoff would be in the bar with us and having a beer. He was a good social mixer. All the lads had total respect for Geoff as much as Harry. He was a funny guy, Geoff. When he had his 90th birthday, Vinnie was there, I was there, Harry and a few of the lads came down, like Simon Tracey and John Gannon. He's very highly thought of, that's for sure.

"Frenchy was the comedian. He was the funny bollocks, always the jester and the joker. A very funny man. He could have good banter with the lads. He was class with me, because of my knee; he gave me one-to-one treatment and had it not been for him, then I wouldn't have got through it. For me, having known Frenchy from our Bedmond days, it was like home from home coming up here and Frenchy being there. The lads loved Derek French. He was class in that role that he played. A really good staff member."

Not just for the players, but for Bassett himself. One of the challenges of being the man at the top is sometimes shielding your emotions from the players and giving the illusion – and it sometimes is an act – of being in total control. There were plenty of testing times for Bassett at Bramall Lane; the boardroom shenanigans, players going unpaid and cheques bouncing, shocking starts to seasons that necessitated remarkable escape acts reminiscent more of Harry Houdini than Harry Bassett. It is testament to Bassett's self-confidence – and probably his acting skills – that not many of his players could recall any great moments of self-doubt being projected outwardly, even in the toughest of moments.

One who did was Booker. "There was a vulnerability about him then. But I have been an assistant manager for 11 years, under seven or eight managers, and what you have to remember is that, if the manager is down, he cannot show that. Who is picking him up? It would have been Geoff Taylor or Derek French. He's going to need lifting up.

"You can imagine how the players were feeling back in that great escape season, getting beat every week ... he was exactly the same. Geoff was a very good sounding board for him. They used to row like cat and dog, but he totally respected Geoff and Geoff totally respected Harry. That's the balance as an assistant. You can't just say: 'Yes, yes, yes.' Geoff was not a yes man. He would tell Harry what he thought and respect him that he then had a decision to make.

"Sometimes he would not go with what Geoff was saying, and on plenty of occasions he would. It would often be discussed in team meetings and they would have a disagreement in front of us, where Geoff would say: 'No Harry, you're wrong there.' A bit like the Leicester half-time when they were rowing about the zone man and we were 4-1 up, thinking: 'What the fuck are they rowing about?'

"That's how it worked and that's how that partnership worked. Geoff was the sounding board that Harry bounced off. They were perfect. Frenchy played his part in that as well. They were really good mates, and Harry would ask Frenchy what he thought too. The three of those, with the kitman John Greaves ... it was a really tight four members of staff. They were different characters, but it all came together when it needed to."

One of Greaves' best memories at United came on a trip away, with the Blades waiting in a hotel to come back home to England. French asked captain Brian Gayle for his watch, before wrapping it in a white table napkin and doing his best Tommy Cooper magician impression. "All of a sudden he smashed it three times on the table ... bang, bang, bang," said Greaves. "The lads were pissing themselves. He turned his hand and the pieces of the watch fell out of the napkin.

"Gayley was fuming. I couldn't stop laughing, and he threw me across the room before chasing Frenchy out of it. I don't know what happened, or why it didn't fall out or whatever was supposed to happen. Another time Glyn Hodges arranged a race in the hotel lifts from the 18th floor. As soon as I pressed go, they would all race down and whoever came down first won the bet. They're the moments I look back at fondly."

French describes his old pal and long-time boss as "a very changeable guy," adding: "His thing was his gut feeling. We'd all sit down the night before a game, have a meal on the Friday night if we were away from home, and he'd say: 'This is what we'll go with.' Then we'd wake up in the morning and he would've had a gut feeling and changed it. 'He won't be playing now; we're doing this instead.'

"He'd have his contract head. If you tried to get more money out of him, he'd usually go and have a crap and you'd have to talk to him through the door while he was on the toilet. He did that to me twice. He had his annoying head as well, and he just changed from one to the other with a click of the fingers.

"If we'd lost away from home, we'd get on the coach and he might come on an hour later. Everyone would be sulking and he'd come on and crack a joke to lighten the mood. It might be: 'Ron Atkinson thinks you're shit, and that's why I've kept you waiting.' It'd break the ice, and then he'd get beaten up. They'd bundle him up the coach. He got done a few times, but it was how he kept everyone together.

"Everyone was in it together. We had everything there. I remember one exercise for team bonding, when the players got in a circle and linked arms. There were one or two on the outside and they had to get in the circle, through the others. Some of the fights it resulted in were incredible, but that was how they used to get everyone together. They'd try and jump over the top or steam through, and Harry used to love all that.

"I knew exactly what made him tick in the end. I knew what to tell him and what he'd think was important, and also what to keep from him. You had to be that judge, because they're busy men. Harry was a workaholic, a proper workaholic. He'd be out every night, watching games somewhere. But that was him, that was how he worked, and he'd expect everyone else to do the same. He's a very, very clever man as well. He never changes, he is what he is, and whoever you are, he can talk to you.

"He's a legend to Sheffield United, and a legend to me as well. He's been hard work at times, and we were never paid what we should've been paid, or deserved to be paid, but I don't think money comes into it when it's football. I would have done it for free. But I would never tell them that.

"We used to do the kit back then as well and even now, I still wake up at night wondering if I've put my running-on bag on the coach. I remember forgetting it for a game, and I had to go and get some bits and pieces off the other club we were playing. And to this day, I still wake up worrying about putting it on the coach. And then I think: 'You idiot, what are you doing?' But that just shows you. Because it's so intense, and it's every day, it becomes a part of your life."

Bassett's methods have been described, and decried, as old school but as the game began to change in the 1990s, he was not so much keeping pace with it as leading it. "Harry had a real intelligence in terms of where the game was going," said midfielder Mark Todd. "That wraparound care, mental and physical coaching. Electrolytes and zinc tablets and individual plans, based on physical profile and strength and conditioning programme.

"We'd be in the little gym at the top of the Bramall Lane car park, running with little five-pound ankle weights. Then you'd take them off and feel like you're running at 150 mph. Hurdles and individual weight programmes. There's Harry's intelligence for you, looking at what a future player would need and getting ahead of the game.

"In the third and second divisions, he was very detailed in his set plays and things like that. Then we got to the first and he asked himself: 'Where does it go from here?' And he looked at that wraparound care. Some of the exercises, we had to buddy up with a teammate and review and give feedback to their group on their traits and strengths and whatever, as a player. It was very football based. I suppose your personality emanates in your playing style. My buddy was Trace and quite bluntly, he said: 'It's always obvious when Toddy isn't playing. Because he isn't the same person.' And he was right. It was Harry's way of throwing another little bomb in there.

"Harry always tells me I should have done much better in the game, because I was two-footed and could get about. When we catch up, he always chucks it at me and says that I let things get to me too much. When you're in the team, the whole thing flows. But the psychological side of the game is where I was lacking; being able to rationalise why I wasn't not playing or whatever. Looking back, I guess I was just immature. I was a mardy bastard. With huge self-doubt.

"I probably didn't do myself too many favours in and around the group and had the odd argument with Geoff and Harry. Particularly Geoff. I remember playing in the reserves at Forest and getting whipped off at half-time after arguing with Geoff. I went in on the Thursday and had it out with Harry. 'What the fuck was that about?' I explained my reasoning and he said: 'Fair enough, you little fucker. By the way, you're starting Saturday.' He used to flip the psychology.

"He was so clever, and made you so accountable, within the first 10 seconds after a game. Even if you'd won. 'This was your job, why didn't you do it?' Take responsibility. 'You tell me why you're not in the team. Don't look at me or pass the buck elsewhere.' His whole philosophy was based on honesty. Look at the personalities he brought in, like Billy Whitehurst and Vinnie Jones. Big personalities, but good players and good men."

It could be brutal but as Bassett's Blades revolution began to gather pace, it was a journey that not many wanted to miss out on. Midfielder Mark Dempsey was one who bowed out of his own accord, after deciding that Bassett's style of play was not aligned to his upbringing at

Manchester United. After observing the Blades' remarkable rise to the top-flight soon after, Dempsey has since privately admitted it was the wrong decision.

Todd, who also had been schooled in the Red Devils' style at The Cliff, had similar initial reservations. "Everyone knew how Harry played, because he'd had a lot of exposure at Wimbledon with how they infiltrated the top leagues and did magic things. I had a choice to make. I asked myself: 'What are you in the game for?' Was I there to be a Man United-type player, or was I there to win games and get promotions and enjoy a good time?

"But looking back, selfishly, my challenge was one of the greatest. I had to flip what I'd learned for three years at Man United. I was renowned for playing around corners, because I'd been hot-wired to do that. Scanning. Passing the ball properly, to feet or into space, not just blindly lumping it or playing the percentages. So my whole passing range and ability just had to change.

"It was hard work, playing that way as a midfielder. We did everything, all over the pitch. I remember Tommy Docherty at Rotherham saying: 'Fuck me, Toddy, how many miles do you cover?' It would be great to have the GPS data that players have now. I reckon it would have been about nine or 10 miles per game! Being in a winning team was important. I'd been there when we were shit and got relegated. All of a sudden, the mood changed. The crowds went from about 9,000 to 20,000, and you wanted to be out there. It was all you wanted to do."

Jock Bryson remembers Bassett as "one of the best managers I have ever worked with by a country mile. He took me from playing part-time in Scotland to playing in the English Premier League. I was a part-time footballer in Scotland – working on a farm, milking cows, training twice a week, with a game on the Saturday, and then having to work the Sunday. Going from that to playing in the English First Division, within three years, was bonkers, really, when you think about it.

"Nowadays, it just wouldn't happen. But it did happen and I was fortunate to join a group of lads who were ambitious and a manager who knew how to get the best out of players. We had two promotions and the next minute our first game of the season was against Liverpool. It was just remarkable. Something I cannot put into words.

"We were very close as a team and a lot of the lads are still friends for life. We had very good players. The lads who scored the goals obviously get all the credit, and that's fine. We have no problem with that. But the rest of us were part of their development. Like Brian Deane's development in becoming an England player. We all stuck together, and many of us are still close."

Bryson still cringes at the memory of a charity night at Bramall Lane, with Joe Elliott – the Def Leppard lead singer and Blades fan – in attendance. "I got stitched up and had to go up and sing *Mull of Kintyre*," Bryson said. "It lasts six and a half minutes. I am no singer and I have never been so embarrassed in all my life. It was the worst six and half minutes of my United career. To be fair, Joe didn't say anything. But the look on his face when he heard my voice was enough."

After a short spell at Barnsley following his United departure, Bryson found another home at Deepdale. "When I became captain at Preston, there was a lot of stuff I brought in there that was part of what Dave did, in terms of team building and getting the team together," he said. "To me, and I have always said this, the team is everything. We got promoted at Preston and Gary Peters was the manager. Gary played under Dave at Wimbledon, so he understood that side of it as well. He was well into that side of it.

"When I left United, Bassett came to me and said: 'Look, you're not going to feature as much next season, so what do you want to do?' I was shocked. I had played a couple of games and did quite well. I was reasonably confident that moving on wouldn't happen. I was disappointed, but that's football."

"All I will say is they got relegated the next season," Bryson joked. "And I have told Bassett that."

Alongside his ruthless streak Bassett could also be fiercely protective of his players and after goalkeeper Graham Benstead attracted some criticism for rolling the ball out of his area and kicking it long to United's forwards early in the manager's reign, he made it clear to supporters that his No.1 was only following his orders. "There was a lot of pressure on each individual," Benstead recalled. We overloaded teams. It was new then and quite an innovative, effective way to play football. Everyone knew their jobs and it was a system of moving parts.

"I remember before we played Huddersfield once and Harry said to me: 'Right, Benno ... you're gonna roll the ball out.' I used to dribble it out 15 yards or so, and plant it down the right-hand side of the box. And if it went out for a throw, I used to get a thumbs-up from the bench because we'd build from there. I'm not saying I was the first to do it, but we were the first to use that way of thinking and get the advantage.

"We weren't just long ball, 'kick it long' players. If we had to play, we could play, but we did what we had to do to get results. Get it in their half as quickly as we could. Results justified it over the years and there are 'keepers still dribbling it out and playing long now. A lot of things have changed in football but the basics are still quite old fashioned.

"I still believe that they can't score if the ball's in their half and the closer the ball is to their goal, the more likely you are to score. It got us success at the time and it's harsh how Harry has that reputation of being direct. People tend to forget that we didn't have the immaculate pitches that teams have now. So I think it is unfair that he was perceived like that. But Harry would laugh it off, and just say: 'Look at the results.'"

United weren't one-trick ponies, either. After studying Bury's defensive set-up ahead of one game, Bassett correctly predicted that they would try to play Deane and Tony Agana offside from Benstead's long kicks out of his area. So the two strikers came back with Bury's back four to stay onside, with Todd and Peter Duffield tasked with running from deep. They both stayed onside and Duffield squared to Todd for a tap-in for 1-0. "It was like a double bluff," Todd said. "The detail and the preparation, game by game, was so good." Deane scored his customary goal and United sealed three more vital points on their way to promotion.

***

As football becomes increasingly corporate and elitist, and more and more out of touch with the average man, woman and child who used to be the game's lifeblood, it is more important than ever for clubs to retain a sense of their identity and history – who and what makes them unique. Some scoff at the idea of a football "DNA" and although it has admittedly become something of a buzzword in the modern era, it also remains the case that, in Sheffield United's recent history, the few periods of relative success have come under managers who subscribed to similar styles and non-negotiables.

Dave Bassett's Blades were perfect embodiments of what United, as a club, represents; humble, hard-working, spirited, determined, and all number of similar words that could also represent the average Sheffielder, with a sprinkling of talent and "fuck you" attitude mixed in for good measure. They never took a backward step and were afraid of no one, seeing challenges of bigger teams and more established names as something to embrace and take on, rather than fear and be intimidated by.

United's crowd responded in kind, and one of the prevailing themes from supporters of that era is a sense that their side, on their day, could beat *anyone* they crossed paths with. They sometimes did, they sometimes fell short. But each man in those red and white stripes, whether they were born a stone's throw from Bramall Lane or 200 miles away, gave their all. And on the rare occasions they didn't, they had an angry Bassett to contend with in the dressing room.

Looking back, it is fascinating to contemplate how different United's recent history could have been had the winds of change blown in a slightly different direction over Bramall Lane. If luck had been on their side in the FA Cup semi-final against Wednesday, with a first final appearance since 1936, at the time of writing, continuing to elude them. If fortune had favoured them on that fateful final day in 1994 at Chelsea, when it felt like the whole world conspired against them to seal what, for most of the afternoon, appeared to be an impossible relegation. If someone – anyone – had seized the initiative in the Bramall Lane boardroom and provided what was desperately needed to kick this great football club on to the level it deserves to be at. United, again at the time of writing, remain the biggest club in English football to have never played in a recognised European competition.

Bassett worked miracles on a shoestring budget for years – to the extent that he was being relied on to pull rabbits out of hats, rather than revered for it – and it's more than reasonable to assume that, with a few more quid in his transfer kitty and a better calibre of player achievable, he could have evolved the club even further. Instead United, as they so often manage to do, grabbed defeat from the jaws of victory and were left floundering in the second tier for 12 years before finally returning to a much-changed top-flight in 2006/07, for a single season, and another cruel and painful relegation. By that point 14 years of television money had flowed into the pockets of clubs at the top table while United were left picking at the crumbs they left behind in the second tier, and their previous contemporaries like Manchester United, Liverpool and Chelsea were now operating not just on another planet, but in another stratosphere.

After relegation in 2007 it was another dozen years before United were back in the Premier League and this time it was under the management of one of Bassett's boys, homegrown right-back and boyhood Blade Chris Wilder. Bassett had actually recommended Wilder for the United job a year before he was eventually offered it, and watched on proudly as his protege took the Blades from the third tier to the First Division in double-quick time – built on many of the same foundations Wilder had experienced first-hand during Bassett's era all those years before. Their styles of football may differ dramatically, but their fundamental demands and non-negotiables are noticeably similar.

Wilder, whose second reign as United boss began in late 2023, readily admits that Bassett is a "mentor" figure but is also very much his own man and by no means a Bassett clone. The two still remain good friends, as well as being United's two greatest managers of the modern era, while a number of other former Bassett players also moved into coaching after hanging up their boots. They include Glyn Hodges, Paul Stancliffe and Bob Booker, with Booker convinced that their former manager's influence played a big part. "One hundred per cent, without a shadow of a doubt," he said. "I know Chrissy is a big advocate of Harry and if he wanted to chat about something, the first phone call he would make would be to Dave Bassett. I am sure that anyone who has been in a coaching role would have had a phone call to Dave Bassett. I did that many a time. He was the first one I would ring up."

Bassett's association with Bramall Lane continued decades after he left, after being sounded out by Kevin McCabe to advise on the identity of United's next manager following the resignation of Gary Speed just before Christmas in 2010. After a caretaker spell from John Carver, Unitedite Micky Adams accepted the job offer – against Bassett's advice. Adams brought Bassett back in a consultancy role and in his 2024 book *Mucky Boots,* McCabe claimed that Bassett has since told him that he should have taken the job himself ... and that United would not have been relegated to League One that season if he had. When United did drop out of the Championship, and Adams was sacked, Bassett thought McCabe would offer him a sensational chance to return – at 66 years of age and 16 years after he first left. "I thought Kevin was going to offer me the job," Bassett said in *Mucky Boots.* "When, years later, I asked him about it, he said: 'Well, I was waiting for you to ask.' I told him I wouldn't have come back. I'd moved away, and the team was poor. Part of me fancied it, but I didn't want the aggro of living in a flat by myself."

Another of the biggest legacies of Bassett's era is the number of players from outside the Steel City, and mostly London, who have remained in and around Sheffield, decades after hanging up their boots. Kevin Gage now owns a 15th century, Grade II-listed hotel and pub just over the border in Dronfield, while Simon Tracey is a Sheffield-based scout for Brentford. Skipper Brian Gayle's son, Josh, went on to work for United while Todd and fellow midfielder John Gannon both took up scouting roles with Manchester City from their Sheffield bases.

Even Bassett and his family stayed living in Dore well after his United departure, before eventually returning to London. "That was a great part of the story, a Cockney coming up north," said Todd. "Reg Brealey was a clever guy and Harry wanted that type of challenge, but also had the personality to pull it off.

"I think he genuinely thought he was going to be successful, although maybe not as quick as he was. It was a cheap group. He was polishing these pieces of coal into diamonds, with Deano being the ultimate diamond. The timings and the type of signings he brought in were superb, even people like Johnny Francis. A great guy. Was there anyone I didn't really take to? I don't think so. That's quite rare in football.

"I class myself as a citizen of Sheffield now. I've been here since 1987 and I say I've got two passports! I have so many friends and brilliant family here and it's home now. It's a massive city, the fourth biggest in England, but so underrated. Sheffield is not brash, and doesn't shout about itself. Probably to its detriment at times. But you fall in love with it. Because of this game, Sheffield and Sheffield United keep giving you these moments. My mate is a joiner, who has done some work at my house, and he gave me 'Notts County discount.' Because he was in the away end when I scored that goal and he still remembers how it made him feel.

"I grew up in Belfast in the 1970s, which had its own challenges, and the kids used to say to me: 'Everywhere you go in Sheffield, people say hello to you.' It keeps my ego ticking over a wee bit. People just come up to me at Bramall Lane and pat me on the back, asking: 'How you doing, Toddy?' and it means a lot. Legacy is the biggest thing in life. All the adulation, the moments, just being involved in a successful squad … it's what you're in it for.

"People have said that those couple of years, and that renaissance, was the happiest period of their lives. To have been in it, and be quite a big cog in the wheel, and see the joy we gave people, is quite humbling. To have had a positive effect. All we did was run about and create a bit of chaos and score a lot of goals. You don't feel the immense pride the fans have in their team at the time, because it's our job.

"I would have loved to have been a top, top player, but I didn't have that amount of talent. So you make the best of what you've got. It could have been different, but I'd never have met Caroline in the Unit nightclub on that night and had the kids and the life I do. It's amazing but also a bit scary too. Football, and life, can turn on a knife edge in a split second. The journey is so fluid.

"Such a tiny percentage of the population get to play professional football, but we were all just so humble – and remained humble, which is why we kicked on again. I lost my place sometimes and then all the time in Division One. It's like winning round after round and you're just about to win the title, and then Harry doesn't pick you. So you go down, and have to get yourself up again. But it's a brilliant life. You've got to make the most of it.

"Looking back, I think Harry's personality defined the culture of the football club. Because of what had gone before, God rest Billy who gave me my break. Harry plotted it out. The success came quickly, so he was making quicker decisions on who could come in and help the group. As we reached that level, what now? Who's going to make us better? How do we kick on? Even the bit-part players always played their part. All of a sudden, we were six months or 12 months ahead of where he thought we'd be. Plotting and planning. 'I'll have to buy him six months earlier than planned, because we're ahead of the curve.' To keep the group competitive. Never once did I, or any of the players, think we'd be sat in the top division, two years after going down into the third.

"It wasn't even like we were average. We'd been relegated. We were shit. The group was shit. No disrespect to anyone who was in there but, as a group, we were shit. We went down. How do you turn it around that quickly, and then go back-to-back promotions after relegation? It's never been done here.

"Once we got some momentum, his personality was able to handle that. There were no big-time Charlies. Harry made sure of that. Even if you'd played well, he'd drag you back down to earth. It was about the group, not you, and no one was allowed to get ahead of themselves egotistically. I remember coming back from away games to Bramall Lane and then straight into town. *Boom.* I was once lifted on the shoulders of some fans, at the back of Sinatra's nightclub on Carver Street.

"That's what you're in it for. We're just ordinary people. Yes, there's a God-given talent but it's a tough gig. Suddenly the expectation rises and you go from the previous season's mindset of bang average to a winning mentality. 'I have to win because we can get promoted here.' Us and Wolves were top dogs, and we wanted this. Us and Leeds the season after. We had to up our game every week. And it's tough, really tough. But because we were so joyous, young and bouncy and together, we just said: 'Bollocks to it. Let's go for it.'

"We just went *whoosh.* It wasn't like we were cruising at 10,000 feet ... we were supersonic at 30,000 or 40,000. It wasn't a massively intelligent way of playing because it wasn't intricate or sophisticated but in its execution it was beautiful. Beautiful. We just took off, didn't we?

"Up and up and up, vertically almost. Off the tarmac and up into the air for two seasons. If there'd been a moon landing, we could have gone for it. We were that fucking good."

ACKNOWLEDGEMENTS

The idea to write this book first came to me a long time ago now, after I had finished *We're Not Going to Wembley* – the story of Sheffield United's promotion to the Premier League in 2018/19. We were all riding the euphoria of an incredible period for the club, going from mid-table in League One to the top-flight in what seemed like no time at all. After reading it, one veteran of Dave Bassett's Bramall Line spell wondered aloud why nothing similar had been written about another iconic Blades era.

I quickly realised that telling the on-field story of the remarkable Bassett era would not do it justice. Football was the thread that bound it together, of course, but it was about so much more; the characters, the stories and the legacy that endures to this day. I must thank my pal Nathan Hemmingham – good man, very lucky pool player – for coming on board and helping get the project over the line when I had countless hours of interviews gathering dust, and every former player, staff member or fan who gave up their time to chat. Spending a few fascinating hours with Bassett in London, finishing off an interview with one of my early heroes in Alan Kelly in a supermarket car park and trudging through a field of mud to speak to Billy Whitehurst stand out, but every single person added something unique and colourful to the project and for that, I am very grateful.

As ever my utmost gratitude goes to my wonderful fiancée Natalie and daughter Charlotte for their patience while I spend countless late-night hours on my laptop or days in the Sheffield library, and to everyone else who helped make this project a reality. Thank you to the authors of the books that have been referenced in this one, and those who contributed photographs, statistics or just general interest in the book. I just hope it does some justice to a wonderful era. Up the Blades.

Danny Hall, 2024

I must start by thanking dear friend Danny Hall, of Vertical Editions, for his offer to join him on this book. We have a mutual love of this great football club and shared countless journeys on trains, planes and automobiles during our time together as Sheffield United reporters. I also enjoyed plenty of convincing pool victories, but that's another story. To be part of a project like this is something I have always wanted to do. Dave Bassett's era defined me as a Blade.

Danny's offer to come on board with his latest book has allowed me once again to be the 11-year-old who was sat on the top tier at Filbert Street on May 5, 1990; the obsessed teen who would make his way across Graves Park and down Warminster Road to watch the team train; buy the *Flashing Blade* and get a quarter of Vinnie's mix from Bri and Irene's on a matchday. The 15-year-old heartbroken after Chelsea and the Norton College student reading on *Ceefax* in December 1995 that Bassett's time was all over. I often wondered why I wore a "Brealey Out" sticker as a kid. Too young to understand the workings of a football club, I went with the crowd but this book explains just why fans were calling for change.

Listening to the players recall their memories of that era brought it all back and told me so much more than I thought I knew about that era. They say never meet your heroes, but thanks to this book and my job I have met and spoken to all of mine from that time and this group is exactly what you hoped they would be. Courteous, respectful and full of memories. I cannot thank them enough for their help and time. They all loved talking about this era and ended every conversation the same way: "If you need anything else, just give me a call." It turns out this is an era they cherish just as much as we do.

Thanks to the Sheffield United media team for their help and support over the years and to my wife Caroline. As a football writer you spend more time out of the house than you do in it, but she knows how much this club means to me and how reporting on it and writing about it in this book has been a labour of love. And to my two children Georgie and Alfred, who I hope one day will have the same Blades bug that I do!

Nathan Hemmingham, 2024

SUBSCRIBERS' ROLL OF HONOUR

Both the publisher and author would like to thank fans who pre-ordered Bassett's Blades *via Vertical Editions, sealing their name in Bramall Lane history forever more.*

Tom Ackroyd
Dr. Peter Ackroyd
Chaz Adams
Mark Allsebrook
Darren Angell
Phil Ashton
Steve Ashton
Anthony Ashton
Mark J Ashton
Gary Atkinson
Dean Bagshaw
Gary Balding
Kevin Barber
David Bartles
Jade Barton
Les Baxby
Mark Beattie
Wesley Beer
John Arthur Bell
Simon Binns
Gemma Binns
Trevor David Bishop

Andrew Black
Michael Blades
Andy Blagden
Lee Blagden
Andy Bond
Ian Booker
Kevin Booth
Michael Bower
Steve Bows
Adrian Boyer
Paul Boyer
David Boyer
Wendy Bradford
Darren Briggs
Shaun Briggs
Thomas Brossler
Paul Broughton
Nick Brown
Stewart Bruck
Gary Brunt
Mark Buck
Sam Buckley

Lucas Burgoyne
Simon Burgoyne
John Burkinshaw
Neil Burrows
Andy Butler
David Capewell
Andrew Carson
John Chappell
John Charlesworth
David Cheetham
Christopher Clark
David Clarkson
Victor Claydon
Sean Coates
Paul Collins
Mark Colton
Allan Cooper
Tony Cosentino
Dave Crooks
Steve Cryan
Jacqui Cryan
Richard Cryer

Nick Cryer
Scott Currie
Molly Damms
Paul Laister Daniels
Steven Davies
Paul Davis
Ben Dawber
Paul Deakin
Phil Deakin
Chris Dennison
Andrew Denny
Kevin Dickinson
Richard Dickson
David Dooks
Charlotte Downes
Steve Draper
Stewart Ducker
Steve Dye
Ken Elliott
Mark Ellison
Luke Elmore
Steve Faulkner
Alan James Fidler
Freddie Fletcher
Beverley Flower
Arthur Foreman
Martin Fox
Wayne Francis
Dave Fratson
Oliver Furmanski
Carl James Garnham
Kev Gascoigne
Paul George

Philip Gibson
Carly Louise Gill
Richard Gilson
Kevin Globe
Brendan Godbehere
Stuart Goddard
David Gormley
Matt Grayson
Ricky James Greaves
Andy Guest
Chris Hall
Richard Hall
Brendan Hall
Martin Hambling
Gary Hammonds
Joshua Liam Hancock
Mark Hardy
Mark Hargate
Kev Harland
Peter J Harvey
Pete Havenhand
Terry Hemmingham
Glyn Heppenstall
Richard Higginbotham
Steve Higgins
Martin Higgins
Linda Hill, nee Blake
Wendy Hill
Richard Hill
Philip Hill
Eric Hilton
David Hinsley
Dan Hirst

Michael Hobson
Timothy Holloway
Christopher Hood
Steve Hoole
Lee Hopkins
Keith Houghton
Mark Hughes
Russell Hunt
Bob Ibbertson
Alan Ibbotson
Suzanne Ibbotson
Paul Jenkinson
Peter Jennings
Brian Jessop
Christopher Jones
Mick Jones
David Kaye
David King
Stuart J. Lancaster
Robert Layhe
Ian Ledger
Paul Ledger
Steve Lee
Cheryl Lee
Chris Lewis
Andrew Loveday
Craig Mallender
Chris Mann
Ewan Mapplebeck
Ian Markham
Russell Markham
John Marsh
Roger McKenna

Kevin Megson
Tom Moore
Paul Morley
Steve Moxon
Ron Moxon
Barrie Mullins
Rob Myers
Simon Newbold
Mick Norton
Martin O'Leary
Pete O'Leary
Patrick O'Mara
Kevin Oliver
David Oxley
George Ozols
Tony O'Brien
Alan Palfreyman
Carol Palfreyman
Malcolm Parker
Ian Parkin
Neil Parsons
Max Payne
Robert Pemberton
Eddie Penistone
Mark Phelan
John Phelan
Jamie Pigott
Jonathan Pinchin
Andrew Pogmore
George Proctor
Roger Purdy
Aswad Qadeer
Paul Reynolds
Steven Rhodes

Dean Rhodes
Simon Rich
Tony Robinson
Andy Robinson
Chris Rogers
Steve Rogerson
Stephen Rogerson
Brent Rudd
Frank Rushby
Kevin Ryan
Mick Scanlan
Alan Scholey
Jonathan Scott
Craig Shaw
Stephen Shaw
Gary Simmons
Gary Sinclair
Robin Skinner
Julian Skirrow
Damon Slack
Martyn Slater
Justin Thomas Smith
Darren Smith
Terence Smith
Michael Smith
Christian Spooner
Jane Stacey
Ryan Staniland
John Stannard
Jonathan Starbrook
John Starbrook
Dave Stoker
Steve Stubbs
Andy Styan

Daniel Talbot
Gary Taylor
Matthew Taylor
Russ Taylor
Howard Thomas
Ken Thompson
Richard Thorpe
Sebastian Tingle
John Tingle
Kevin Tosh
Andy Treherne
Paul Tully
Lee Tuplin
Russ Turner
Amy Blade Turner
Curt Unwin
Chris Varney
Hugh Walton
Dennis Ward
Nicholas Waymouth
Paul Wentworth
Phil Whitaker
Mark Ashley White
Chris Wills
Jeff Wilson
Richard Windle
Jonathan Winfield
David Womack
Paul Wood
Arthur Woolley
Sarah Woolley
Richard Wragg
David Wright
David Youle

UP THE BLADES!

Inside tonight:
United's 12-page promotion special

BLADES GLORY
— OWLS DOWN

Goal—happy United go up in style Wednesday relegated in horror show

THAT sinking feeling: Ron Atkinson pictured at Hillsborough this afternoon as the Owls went out of Division One

GLORY, GLORY FOR UNITED . . . GLOOM AND DOOM FOR WEDNESDAY.

United made story of promotion to the First Division with a champagne-style 5-2 victory at Leicester. Wednesday crashed 3-0 at home to Forest and were relegated as Luton pulled off an incredible 3-2 victory at Derby.

A goal down at Leicester in nine minutes United put on an unstoppable first half show as Leicester Mills put the home team in front but then Paul Wood, Bruce Deane, Tony Agana and Wilf Rostron smashed four goals past the former Wednesday keeper Martin Hodge to put the team at the gates of the First Division.

In injury-time of the first half Leicester pulled one back but United, hanging on to what they had got, defied Leicester in a tight second half to romp through to promotion in front of 8,800 fantastic followers. Leicester played the whole of the second half without Martin Hodge, playing defender Marc North in goal.

Leeds pipped United for the championship with a 1-0 success at Bournemouth while Newcastle were down 4-1 at their North-East derby at Middlesbrough. Bournemouth were relegated to Division Three.

Wednesday's defeat was their biggest at home this season and their fifth in their last six games, in a match of tension and drama watched by a crowd of more than 29,000.

Behind to an early goal by England left back Stuart Pearce, they were always chasing the game.

Forest, always dangerous on the break, scored a second goal through Pagrin in the second half. Nigel Jemson and Tommy Gaynor might have had four goals between them, and finally substitute Franz Carr, who had a spell on loan at Wrexham, set up a third goal from Jemson.

The scoreboard at Hillsborough at one stage wrongly showed that Derby had made it 3-3 against Luton, a result that would have saved the Owls from relegation.

Saltergate crowd drama

CHESTERFIELD's arsenal home match with Grimsby was overshadowed by a crowd incident which forced a 12 minute hold-up when Grimsby supporters were carried away on stretchers.

A crowd of 1,500 had seen Chesterfield take a third minute lead through John Ryan but a serious incident at the nineteenth forced the referee to take the players off the pitch while the injured were treated for head wounds.

Score! for £200

THIS is the last listed contest of the season and your last chance to win £200 in our goal time contest. Last week's winner was Marilyn Baggaley, of Prince Wish, Darnall, Sheffield, who matched three of the four times on her card against the times for goals scored in last week's selected matches.

Check your card with our square of the list listing matches you could win £200.
SHEFF WED V NOTT'M FOR
LEICESTER V SHEFF UTD
PORTSMOUTH V BARNSLEY
ROTHERHAM V NORTHAMPTON
SCUNTHORPE V DONCASTER